"Late have I loved you, Beauty so ancient and so new, late have I loved you!" (See reading no. 214) Augustine of Hippo (354–430) as he was imagined by an anonymous eighteenth-century artist.

AWAKENING FAITH

Daily Devotions from the Early Church

JAMES STUART BELL

WITH PATRICK J. KELLY

ZONDERVAN

Awakening Faith
Copyright © 2013 by James Stuart Bell

This title is also available as a Zondervan ebook.
Visit www.zondervan.com/ebooks.

Requests for information should be addressed to:

Zondervan, *Grand Rapids, Michigan 49530*

Library of Congress Cataloging-in-Publication Data

    Awakening faith : daily devotions from the early church / [compiled by]
James Stuart Bell with Patrick J. Kelly.
      pages cm
    ISBN 978-0-310-51487-9 (hardcover)
    1. Fathers of the church. 2. Meditations. 3. Christian literature, Early I.
Bell, James S. II. Kelly, Partick J., 1980-
    BR63.A68 2013
    242'.2—dc23   2013015622

Cover design: Ron Huizinga
Interior design: David Conn
Editorial: Madison Trammel, Bob Hudson

Printed in the United States of America

13 14 15 16 17 18 19 20 21 22 23 /DCI/ 20 19 18 17 16 15 14 13 12 11 10 9 8 7 6 5 4 3 2 1

To Andy Blaski, follower of the Fathers

Also by James Stuart Bell

The Spiritual World of the Hobbit (with Sam O'Neal)
From the Library of C. S. Lewis (with Anthony B. Dawson)
From the Library of A. W. Tozer (with Lyle Dorsett)
From the Library of Charles Spurgeon
Angels, Miracles, and Heavenly Encounters

INTRODUCTION

The Fathers of the Church, generally understood to be the key teachers and leaders of Christianity's first eight centuries, deserve their title of *Fathers* for a few reasons. One is the filial respect that we give to our own fathers. Our earthly fathers came before us. They are older and wiser, and they are at least partially responsible for our existence. Thus it is right to respect them as our elders. So too the church Fathers.

Furthermore, since the Church Fathers are among the first Christians, we tend to think of them as our forebears, not unlike how Israel thought of its patriarchs Abraham, Isaac, and Jacob. For all of the Fathers' virtues and flaws, we are of the same stock and possess the heritage they passed on. Most significantly, they were the propagators and caretakers of our early faith, nurturing it when it was young, correcting it in its adolescence, providing it wisdom in its young adulthood, and serving as an enduring model of faithfulness as it progressed to maturity. Whether we are familiar with them or not, they are truly the Fathers of our faith, and we owe them a great debt.

But aren't such ancient teachers just for scholars and theologians or for pastors who like to occasionally embellish their preaching with history? We do not believe so. Unlike some in the West today, these earliest Christian leaders did not, for the most part, have the luxury of being just scholars or theologians — they were by and large also shepherds with flocks to care for, and their writings were grounded in their everyday concerns for believers. In their preaching and teaching, they worked out questions like: Who was Jesus Christ? How did he save us? What do I do now that I am saved? What do I have to look forward to? How does my faith help me endure the hardships of this world? Their writing and preaching agendas were parallel to those of modern pastors; that is, they wanted to better understand Scripture and the Gospel, and to proclaim both to believers and unbelievers alike.

So the Church Fathers are not just for the historically or academically inclined. Why should any other Christian, particularly any evangelical Christian, read the Fathers today when he or she could read contemporary answers to these questions? There are good reasons besides historical curiosity. Each Father's strengths and emphases vary, some affirming much of what we do today, others serving as a corrective against some of the imbalances in our current preaching, teaching, and Christian living. Overall, though, they shared a great commitment to Christian doctrine. In a time when followers of Christ were killed for their beliefs, and later, when doctrinal controversies threatened to split the church (which at the time was generally united), theology mattered. It undergirded the lives of Christians in a way that deserves our consideration, since contemporary evangelicals can be tentative about or unaware of doctrine. You will find that the objectivity and certainty of Christian truths, particularly truths about Jesus Christ, are a unifying feature in this volume.

Another strength of the Church Fathers is their commitment to Scripture. They readily made the words of Scripture their own words, comfortably seeing all of life through a biblical worldview. Their minds were so steeped in Scripture that some Fathers found it difficult to write a single paragraph without multiple references to the Bible. They established a pattern of unselfconsciously interpreting Scripture both theologically and applicationally at once. This is all the more impressive when we consider that many of them had limited access to the Bible and were often quoting from memory and not from the text itself. This explains some of the unique syntax or paraphrasing (or, in some cases, misquoting) that you will find in their Scripture references. By and large, however, their command of the biblical text and their familiarity with both Old and New Testaments were remarkable and will be quite obvious as you spend a year reading through the Fathers. Don't be alarmed by the occasional reference to the Apocrypha; some of the early Fathers considered it canonical, or part of Scripture.

A third strength, perhaps the most valuable for this volume, was the Church Fathers' commitment to personal virtue and Christlikeness. The best Christians in every age take sanctification seriously, without diminishing the work of the Spirit and his grace in transforming us. The Fathers exemplified this understanding. They discussed and exhorted every possible virtue, especially love, humility, mercy, purity, and generosity. Their blessing to us is the seriousness with which they treated virtue, and their refusal to deconstruct or reduce the teachings of Jesus to make them more palatable or easier to achieve. They were clearly not interested in softening the edges of their exhortation for the sake of complacent believers — pursuing a holy life was difficult in their view, but nonetheless imperative.

Perceptive readers will notice the Fathers' almost exclusive focus on personal virtue rather than broader societal changes, which may be frustrating at first blush to Christians whose understanding gives primacy to social justice. Yet the Fathers uphold a rather accurate presupposition that since sin and evil are so ubiquitous, the most effective battle against them is fought in the hearts of individuals. Their care for the treatment of the poor and responsible stewardship of money speaks to their concern for systemic injustice; nevertheless, they emphasized personal responsibility over any kind of utopianism.

If there are strengths in their writings, there must be weaknesses, right? Perhaps, but for the purposes of devotional reading the selections in this book showcase those things they emphasize that today's evangelicals do not, generally to our detriment. For instance, one prevalent theme of the Fathers is seeing life as a race or trial, with the hoped-for reward of glory at the finish. They unabashedly hoped for heaven and the consummated work of Christ. They yearned to see God's face. Sharing in Christ's glory is a very common feature of the Fathers' writing. A corollary is their recognition of the fallenness of this present life and the suffering that many believers have to endure. Experiencing persecution firsthand, the early Fathers demonstrate that one fruit of suffering is more passionately believing and hoping in the promises of the Gospel.

A particularly interesting feature of their writing is their concern for pastors. The Fathers tended to be critical of themselves in their role as shepherds, and they took seriously the Scriptural injunctions of caring for their flocks. We see in them a holy fear of the coming judgment, where each would be rewarded or punished according to his deeds, and pastors with special gravity. The Christian church today has a thriving subculture of pastor-directed ministries, and pastors can profit from studying the Fathers' zealous care for their flocks and the burden of responsibility they felt.

The Fathers are a rich source of Christian nourishment, impossible to adequately plumb in 366 short readings over the course of a year. Some of you may discover a new love for a period of Christian history that you have long ignored; others will simply be encouraged by the ancient Christian wisdom. Either way, we present this collection with the prayer that your faith will be reawakened as you read writings from the early church's own awakening faith. May you discover new (or are they old?) ways of thinking, praying, and obeying our Lord. And may these readings spur you to delve into the rich treasury of the church's history, discovering your own favorite Fathers that you can return to again and again.

AWAKENING FAITH

✛ 1 ✛

LOVE UNITES US

Finally, all of you, be like-minded, be sympathetic, love one another,
be compassionate and humble. (1 Peter 3:8)

If Christ is with me, what should I fear? The waves and the sea and the anger of powerful people might be rising against me, but they are no scarier than a spider's web. Had you not detained me here, I would have left today to face those things at home. For I always say, "Lord, your will be done," not what this or that person wants me to do, but what God wants me to do. That is my strong tower, my immovable rock, my staff that never breaks. If God wants something, let it be done! If he wants me to stay here, I am grateful. But wherever he wants me to be, I am no less grateful.

Yet where I am, there you are too, and where you are, I am. For we are a single body, and the body cannot be separated from the head nor the head from the body. Distance separates us, but love unites us, and death itself cannot divide us. For my body may die, but my soul will live on and be mindful of my people.

You are my fellow citizens, my fathers, my mothers, my brothers, my sisters, my sons, my daughters, my limbs, my body. You are my light, sweeter to me than the visible light. What the rays of the sun give me does not compare to what I get from your love. The sun's light is useful in my earthly life, but your love is fashioning a crown for me in the life to come.

John Chrysostom

✢ 2 ✢

THE TRANSFIGURATION IS OUR VICTORY

There he was transfigured before them. His face shone like the sun, and his clothes became as white as the light. (Matthew 17:2)

The great reason for this transfiguration was to remove the scandal of the cross from the hearts of his disciples and to prevent the humiliation of his passion from disrupting the faith of those who witnessed it — even though it was a hidden glory.

A second reason is to allow the whole body of Christ to understand the kind of transformation that it would receive as his gift. The members of the church look forward to a share in that glory that first blazed out in Christ their head.

The Lord himself had spoken of this when he foretold the splendor of his coming: "Then the just will shine like the sun in the kingdom of their Father" (Matt. 13:43). Saint Paul the Apostle bore witness to this same truth when he said, "I consider that the sufferings of the present time are not to be compared to the future glory that is to be revealed in us" (Rom. 8:18). In another place he says, "You are dead, and your life is hidden with Christ in God. When Christ, your life, is revealed, then you also will be revealed with him in glory" (Col. 3:3–4).

No one should fear to suffer for the sake of justice; no one should lose confidence in the reward that has been promised. The way to rest is through toil, the way to life is through death. Christ has taken on himself the whole weakness of our lowly human nature. If then we are steadfast in our faith in him and in our love for him, we win the victory that he has won, we receive what he has promised.

Leo the Great

✦ 3 ✦

JOY IN YOUR BLESSINGS

Those who belong to Christ Jesus have crucified the flesh with its passions and desires. Since we live by the Spirit, let us keep in step with the Spirit. (Galatians 5:24–25)

Lord, shed the brilliant light of your wisdom upon our darkened souls, so that we may be enlightened and serve you with renewed purity. Sunrise marks the hour for men and women to begin their toil, but prepare a dwelling in our souls for the day that will never end. Help us to know the resurrection life and let nothing distract us from the delights you offer.

Teach us to find our joy in your blessings! Lord, we have your memorial inside of us, received at your spiritual table; let us have its full reality, when all things will be made new.

You give us a hint of the goodness you have prepared for us when we observe your Spirit working inside of us to make our souls beautiful.

Savior, your crucifixion marked the end of your mortal life; teach us to crucify ourselves and make way for our life in the Spirit. Use your resurrection to make our spirits great, and show us our new selves in the mirror of the sacraments.

Lord, bless our souls with the spiritual vision of you, and our bodies with your warmth and sweetness. The mortality lurking in our bodies spreads corruption through us; cleanse this corruption with the healing waters of your love. Help us come to our true city and see it now in a vision, like Moses on the mountaintop.

Ephrem the Syrian

✢ 4 ✢

LET US NOT OFFEND GOD

*The human spirit is the lamp of the LORD that sheds light
on one's inmost being. (Proverbs 20:27)*

We must remember how near God is and that no thought of ours nor any conversation we hold is hidden from him. It is therefore right not to turn our backs and flee from God's will. We should prefer to offend stupid and foolish people, puffed up and taking pride in their boastful speech, than offend God.

Let us revere the Lord Jesus, whose blood was shed for us. Let us respect those in authority and honor the elders. Let us train the young in the fear of God. Let us lead our wives toward all that is good. Let them show that they are lovers of chastity by their conduct; let them reveal a pure and sincere disposition by their gentleness; let them manifest the control they have over their tongues by their silence; let them love all who have a holy fear of God equally, without prejudice.

Your children must also become disciples of Christ. They must learn how effective humility is before God, what chaste love can accomplish with God, and how good and noble is the fear of God, for it brings salvation to all who live holy lives with a pure heart. The Spirit in us is the searcher of our thoughts and the counselor of our hearts.

The Father is merciful in all he does and full of generosity; he is loving to those who fear him. He gives his graces with gentleness to those who approach him with undivided hearts. We should remove all our duplicity and distrustfulness in response to his excellent and honoring gifts.

Clement of Rome

✦ 5 ✦

PRAY AS HE TAUGHT US

I pray also for those who will believe in me through their message,
that all of them may be one, Father, just as you are in me and I am
in you. May they also be in us so that the world may believe
that you have sent me. (John 17:20–21)

Christ has already foretold that the hour was coming when "true worshipers would worship the Father in spirit and in truth" (John 4:23). And he has fulfilled this promise, in that we have received the Spirit, and the truth given to us by his own holiness, so that we may worship in spirit and truth using the prayer he has taught us.

What prayer could be more in the spirit than the one given to us by Christ, who sent the Holy Spirit upon us? What prayer could be more in the truth than the one spoken by the lips of Christ, who is truth himself? To pray contrary to the way the Son has taught us is ignorant and sinful. He spoke of this command when he said, "You reject the command of God, to set up your own tradition" (Mark 7:9).

So let us pray as God our master has taught us. When we approach the Father with the words his Son has given us, and let him hear the prayer of Christ repeated with our own voices, we recite a family prayer. Let the Father recognize the words of his Son. Let the Son, who lives in our hearts, be spoken from our lips. He is our advocate before the Father; when we ask for forgiveness for our sins, why not use the words given to us by our advocate? He tells us: "Whatever you ask the Father in my name, he will give you" (John 16:23). What could be a more effective prayer than the words of Christ's own prayer?

Cyprian of Carthage

✣ 6 ✣

DO NOT DELAY
YOUR MERCY

Blessed are the merciful, for they will be shown mercy. (Matthew 5:7)

Not even sleep should interrupt you in your duty of mercy. Do not say, "Come back and I will give you something tomorrow" (Prov. 3:28). There should be no delay between your intention and your good deed. Generosity is the one thing that cannot be delayed.

"Share your bread with the hungry, and bring the needy and the homeless into your house" (Isa. 58:7) with a joyful and eager heart. "He who does acts of mercy should do so with cheerfulness" (Rom. 12:8). The grace of a good deed is doubled when it is done with promptness and speed. Giving spitefully or against one's will is distasteful and far from praiseworthy. When we perform an act of kindness we should rejoice and not be sad about it.

If you think that I am right, then let us visit Christ whenever we can; let us care for him, feed him, clothe him, welcome him, and honor him; not only at a meal, as some have done; or by anointing him, as Mary did; or only by lending him a tomb, like Joseph of Arimathea; or by arranging for his burial, like Nicodemus, who loved Christ halfheartedly; or by giving him gold, frankincense, and myrrh, like the Magi did before all these others. The Lord of all asks for mercy, not sacrifice (Matt. 9:13), and mercy is greater than myriads of fattened lambs. So let us show him mercy in the persons of the poor and those who today are lying on the ground, so that when we leave this world they might receive us into everlasting dwelling places, into Christ our Lord himself, to whom be glory forever and ever. Amen.

Gregory of Nazianzus

✢ 7 ✢

FORGIVENESS AND HOLINESS

We were therefore buried with him through baptism into death in order that, just as Christ was raised from the dead through the glory of the Father, we too may live a new life. (Romans 6:4)

Dear friends, at every moment "the earth is full of the mercy of God" (Ps. 119:64), and nature itself is a lesson for all the faithful in the worship of God. The heavens and the sea and all that is in them bear witness to the goodness and omnipotence of their Creator, and the marvelous beauty of the elements' obedience to him warrants an expression of gratitude from the intelligent creation.

But with the return of that season marked out in a special way by the mystery of our redemption, and of the days that lead up to the Easter feast, we are summoned more urgently to prepare ourselves by a purification of spirit.

The special note of the Easter feast is this: the whole church rejoices in the forgiveness of sins. It rejoices in the forgiveness not only of those who believe for the first time and are baptized, but also of those who are already numbered among God's adopted children.

Initially, men and women are made new by the rebirth of baptism. Yet we still require a daily renewal to repair the shortcomings of our mortal nature, and despite whatever progress has been made everyone must continue to grow in holiness. All must therefore strive to ensure that on the day of redemption none may be found in the sins of their former lives.

Leo the Great

⌖ 8 ⌖

HIS GLORY WITHIN US

He will be great and will be called the Son of the Most High. The Lord
God will give him the throne of his father David. (Luke 1:32)

The Creator still works to design things that can add to your glory. He has made you in his image so that you might make the invisible Creator present on earth, in your person; he has made you his ambassador, so that the vast empire of the world might have the Lord's representative. Then in his mercy God assumed the body that he made for you, because he wanted to be truly visible in a man, where before he was only seen in humans as an image. Now he would truly become human, whereas before men and women were only his symbol.

And so Christ is born, so that through his birth he might restore our nature. He became a child, was fed, and grew so that he might inaugurate the age that would remain perfect forever, as he created and intended it to be. He supports humanity so that humanity might no longer fall. And the creature he had formed from the earth he now makes heavenly; and what he had given a human soul he now enlivens with a heavenly spirit. In this way he fully raised humanity to God, and took out of him all sin, all death, all suffering, all pain, and everything earthly, through the grace of our Lord Jesus Christ, who lives and reigns with the Father in the unity of the Holy Spirit, now and forever, for all the ages of eternity. Amen.

Peter Chrysologus

✢ 9 ✢

ENLARGE YOUR DESIRES

*One thing I ask from the LORD, this only do I seek: that I may dwell in
the house of the LORD all the days of my life, to gaze on the beauty of
the LORD and to seek him in his temple. (Psalm 27:4)*

It might perplex us that God asks us to pray, when he knows
what we need before we ask him, if we do not realize that our
Lord does not want to know what we want—for he cannot fail to
know it—but wants us rather to exercise our desire through our
prayers, so that we can receive what he is preparing to give us. His
gift is very great indeed, but our capacity is too small and limited
to receive it. That is why we are told, "Enlarge your desires, do not
bear the yoke with unbelievers" (2 Cor. 6:13–14).

The deeper our faith, the stronger our hope, the greater our
desire, the larger our capacity will be to receive that gift, which is
very great indeed. "No eye has seen it"; it has no color. "No ear has
heard it"; it has no sound. "It has not entered the human heart"; the
human heart must enter into it (1 Cor. 2:9).

With our faith, hope, and love we are always praying with tireless desire. However, at set times and seasons we also pray to God
in words, so that through prayer we may instruct ourselves and
mark the progress we have made in our desires and spur ourselves
on to deepen them. The more fervent the desire, the more satisfying
its fruit will be. When the Apostle tells us, "Pray without ceasing"
(1 Thess. 5:17), he means this: be constantly in a state of desire for
the life of eternal happiness, and ask for it from him who alone is
capable of giving it.

Augustine

✣ 10 ✣

THE MANY BENEFITS OF THE PSALMS

Praise the LORD. How good it is to sing praises to our God, how pleasant and fitting to praise him! . . . He heals the brokenhearted and binds up their wounds. (Psalm 147:1, 3)

A psalm imparts serenity to the soul; it is the author of peace, which calms confused and frantic thoughts. It softens the wrath of the soul, and reigns in what is uncontrolled. A psalm forms friendships, unites those separated, and pacifies those in dispute. What two people can be enemies who have together uttered the same prayer to God? Psalmody and choral singing, therefore, establish a bond toward unity, joining the people into a harmonious union of one choir, and produce the greatest of blessings, charity.

A psalm is a city of refuge from the demons, a means of getting help from the angels, a weapon against fears by night, a rest from toils by day, a safeguard for infants, an adornment for those at the peak of health, a consolation for the elderly, a most beautiful ornament for women. It comforts the lonely. It takes command of the passions.

It is the elementary textbook of beginners, the improvement of those advancing, the solid support of the perfect, and the voice of the church. It brightens the feast days; it validates the sorrow that is in accordance with God. For a psalm calls forth a tear even from a heart of stone. A psalm is the work of angels, a heavenly institution, a spiritual incense.

Basil the Great

⊹ 11 ⊹

ONLY GOD DESERVES WORSHIP

The God who made the world and everything in it is the Lord of heaven and earth and does not live in temples built by human hands. And he is not served by human hands, as if he needed anything. (Acts 17:24–25)

Men of Greece, why do you wish to bring the civil authority into contention with us, as if in a boxing match? And why am I to be hated as a treacherous villain if I do not share some of your beliefs and practices? Does the king order the payment of tribute? Then I am ready to pay it. Does my master command me to act as a slave and to serve him? Then I acknowledge the servitude.

That is to say, it is right for one man to show honor to his fellow man, but only God should be feared — God alone, who is invisible to human eyes and immeasurable by human designs. Only when you command me to deny him will I disobey; I would rather die than show myself false and ungrateful.

Our God did not begin to exist in time: he alone is without beginning, and he himself is the beginning of all things. God is a spirit, not in or a part of the world, but the Maker of material things and their various forms. He is invisible and untouchable, being Creator of both sensible and invisible things. We know him from his creation and perceive his invisible power through his works.

I refuse to worship the things of this world, which he has made for our sakes. The sun and moon were made for us: how can I adore my own servants? How can I think that trees and stones are gods? Nor should we behave as if God needed our gifts and offerings, as you do with your gods, since the one indescribable God is in need of nothing and is misrepresented if we treat him as a needy God.

Tatian

✦ 12 ✦

PURITY OF HEART (I)

God, the blessed and only Ruler, the King of kings and Lord of lords,
who alone is immortal and who lives in unapproachable light,
whom no one has seen or can see. (1 Timothy 6:15–16)

The happiness God promises us is limitless. Once you have gained this blessing, what is left to desire? By seeing God you possess all things. In the language of Scripture, to see is to have. "May you see the good things of Jerusalem" (Ps. 128:5) is the same as "May you possess the good things of Jerusalem." When the prophet says, "May the wicked man be carried off and not see the glory of the LORD" (Isa. 26:10), he means, "May he not share in the glory of the Lord."

One who has seen God has, in the act of seeing, gained all that is good: life without end, everlasting freedom from decay, undying happiness, a kingdom with no end, lasting joy, true light, unapproachable glory, perpetual rejoicing—in a word, the complete blessedness.

This is the wonderful hope held out by the beatitudes. But the condition for seeing God is purity of heart, which causes me to wonder if purity of heart is something impossible, something beyond the power of our nature. If seeing God is dependent on purity of heart, and if Moses and Paul did not attain this vision—they say that neither they nor anyone else can see God (Ex. 33:20; 1 Tim. 6:16)—then this promise of Christ's seems to be something impossible to realize.

What benefit is there to knowing how we can see God if we do not have the power to do it? As long as the way to heaven is impassible what do we gain by knowing about the happiness of heaven? It saddens and annoys us when we realize it is impossible to attain the good things we are deprived of! [Continued in next entry . . .]

Gregory of Nyssa

✦ 13 ✦

PURITY OF HEART (II)

My heart says of you, "Seek his face!" Your face, LORD, I will seek.
(Psalm 27:8)

Surely the Lord does not encourage us to do something impossible for humans? The truth is different. He does not command wingless creatures to become birds, nor land animals to live in the water. So if in the case of other creatures the command is according to the creature's capacity, and he does not ask them to do something beyond their nature, we should maintain hope of gaining what is promised by the beatitude.

John, Paul, Moses, and many other believers did achieve that sublime happiness that comes from the vision of God; Paul, who said, "There is stored up for me a crown of righteousness, which the judge who judges justly will give me" (2 Tim. 4:8), and John, who leaned on the breast of Jesus (John 13:23), and Moses, who heard God saying to him, "I know you above all others" (Ex. 33:17).

If these men are blessed, and if blessedness means the vision of God is granted to the pure in heart, then purity of heart — which brings blessedness — is not impossible.

So we can say that Paul and others truthfully teach that seeing God is beyond our power — yet what the Lord promises us is true too, that those with pure hearts will see God.

Gregory of Nyssa

✢ 14 ✢

THE LIKENESS OF GOD

Whoever serves me must follow me; and where I am, my servant also will be. My Father will honor the one who serves me. (John 12:26)

We first ask why it was that Christ is the first teacher in Christian history to teach on virginity? This doctrine was reserved for the Lord alone to teach, since it was him alone who taught us how to draw near to God after coming down from heaven. Also, it is fitting that he who was the first and most holy of priests, of prophets, and of angels, should also be esteemed as the first and chief of virgins.

In the past, men and women were not yet perfect and therefore were unable to receive perfection, which is virginity. For though they were made in the image of God, they had yet to receive God's likeness. But the Word was sent down into the world with the purpose of perfecting humanity, and so he took upon himself our form, disfigured by many sins, in order that we might receive the divine form.

We show that we are truly fashioned in the likeness of God when we represent his features in a human life—when we, like skillful painters, stamp them upon ourselves as though we were canvases and learn the path he showed us. God was pleased to put on human flesh for this reason: that if we looked on Christ's life in the flesh, we could see the divine pattern for our own lives as if it were drawn on a canvas, and be able to imitate the one who painted it. For Christ was not someone who thought one thing and did another; nor did he believe one thing and teach another. No—whatever was truly useful and right, he both did and taught.

Methodius

⊹ 15 ⊹

CHRIST SHARES OUR SUFFERINGS

To this end I strenuously contend with all the energy
Christ so powerfully works in me. (Colossians 1:29)

Jesus Christ is one man with a head and body, both the Savior of the body and the body itself, two in one flesh, in one voice, in one suffering.

If when you say "Christ" you mean his head and body, then his sufferings are in him alone. But if by "Christ" you mean just the head, then you must say his sufferings are not in himself alone. For if the sufferings of Christ are in Christ alone, how can Paul, a member of Christ, say this: "That I may fill up in my flesh what is lacking of the sufferings of Christ" (Col. 1:24)?

Your sufferings are added because they were lacking in the body. Yours do not overflow the cup, but fill up a portion. You suffer your allotted measure to contribute to the total suffering of Christ, who suffered as our head and suffers in his members, that is, ourselves.

Each one of us pays their debt to what may be called our Christian commonwealth. According to our store of strength we contribute a tax of suffering. The final reckoning of all suffering will not take place until the end times.

But do not think that the righteous who were sent to foretell the coming of the Lord did not belong to the body of Christ. In the blood of Abel, the whole city speaks, and so on until the blood of Zechariah. The same city goes on speaking in the blood of John, in the blood of the apostles, in the blood of the martyrs, in the blood of Christ's faithful people.

Augustine

✢ 16 ✢

THE THIRD DAY

Remember how he told you, while he was still with you in Galilee:
"The Son of Man must be delivered over to the hands of sinners,
be crucified and on the third day be raised again." (Luke 24:6–7)

Even on the cross he did not hide himself from sight; rather, he made all creation witness to the presence of its Maker. Then, having let his body be seen as truly dead, he did not allow that temple of his body to linger long, but immediately on the third day raised it up, impenetrable and incorruptible, the reward and token of his victory.

It was, of course, within his power to have raised his body and displayed it as alive directly after death. But the all-wise Savior did not do this, so that no one would deny that it had really or completely died. Besides this, had the interval between his death and resurrection been less than two days, the glory of his incorruption might not have been as glorious. He waited one whole day to show that his body was really dead, and then on the third day showed it as incorruptible to all. The interval was no longer, so that people would not have forgotten about it and grown doubtful about whether it were actually the same body. No — while the affair was still ringing in their ears, and their eyes were still straining, and their minds in turmoil, and while those who had put him to death were still close by and could witness to the fact of it — the Son of God after three days showed his once-dead body immortal and incorruptible. It was evident to all that the Savior did not die a normal death, but an extraordinary death that destroyed the power of death.

Athanasius

❖ 17 ❖

DEATH IS OUR KEY TO FREEDOM

Once you were alienated from God and were enemies in your minds because of your evil behavior. But now he has reconciled you by Christ's physical body through death to present you holy in his sight, without blemish and free from accusation. (Colossians 1:21–22)

It was by the death of one man that the world was redeemed. Christ did not need to die if he did not want to, but he did not see it as we do. He did not look on death as something to be despised, something to be avoided, and his dying was the best way to save us. His death is life for all. We are sealed with the sign of his death; when we pray we preach his death; when we celebrate the supper we proclaim his death. His death is victory; his death is a sacred sign; each year his death is celebrated with solemnity by the whole world.

What more should we say about his death? What more, when this divine example proves that it was death alone that won freedom from death, and death itself was its own redeemer? Death is then no cause for mourning, for it is the cause of humankind's salvation. Death is not something to be avoided, for the Son of God did not think it beneath his dignity, nor did he seek to escape it.

Death was not part of nature; it became part of nature. God did not decree death from the beginning; he prescribed it as a remedy. Because of sin human life was condemned to torturous labor and unbearable sorrow and was burdened with wretchedness. There had to be a limit to its evils; death had to restore what life had forfeited. Without the assistance of grace, immortality is more of a burden than a blessing.

Ambrose

✛ 18 ✛

BEHEADING OF
JOHN THE BAPTIST

*When Elizabeth heard Mary's greeting, the baby leaped in her womb,
and Elizabeth was filled with the Holy Spirit. (Luke 1:41)*

Blessed John, the forerunner to Christ, suffered imprisonment and chains as a witness to our Redeemer, and gave his life for him. His persecutor demanded not that he should deny Christ, but only that he should keep silent about the truth. Nevertheless, he died for Christ. Does Christ not say, "I am the truth" (John 14:6)? Therefore, since John shed his blood for the truth, he died for Christ.

Through his birth, preaching, and baptizing, he bore witness to the coming birth, preaching, and baptism of Christ, and by his own suffering he showed that Christ would also suffer.

He was strong enough to accept the end of his earthly life by shedding his blood after a long imprisonment. He preached the freedom of heavenly peace, but was thrown into irons by ungodly men; he was locked away in the darkness of prison, even though he was a bright and shining lamp, and came bearing witness to the light of life, who is Christ. John was baptized in his own blood, though he had the honor of baptizing the Redeemer of the world, to hear the voice of the Father above him, and to see the grace of the Holy Spirit descending upon him.

For John, enduring temporal suffering for the sake of the truth was not a heavy burden; in fact, it was easily faced and even desirable, for he knew eternal joy would be his reward.

Bede the Venerable

✤ 19 ✤

A GREATER DELIVERANCE (I)

And when the Israelites saw the mighty hand of the LORD displayed against the Egyptians, the people feared the LORD and put their trust in him and in Moses his servant. (Exodus 14:31)

The Israelites witnessed marvels, but you also will witness marvels, greater and more splendid than the ones they saw on their departure from Egypt. You did not see Pharaoh and his armies drowned, but you have seen the devil and his weapons overcome by the waters of baptism. The Israelites passed through the sea, but you have passed from death to life. They were delivered from the Egyptians, but you have been delivered from the powers of darkness. The Israelites were freed from slavery to pagans, but you have been freed from slavery to sin.

Do you need another argument to convince you that the gifts you have received are greater than theirs? The Israelites could not look on Moses' glorified face, even though he was their fellow servant and brother. But you have seen the face of Christ in his glory, as Paul cried out: "We see the glory of the Lord with faces unveiled" (2 Cor. 3:18).

In those days, Christ was present to and followed after the Israelites, but he is present to us in a much deeper sense. The Lord was with them because of the favor he showed to Moses; now he is with us not because of anyone's obedience, but out of love. After Egypt the Israelites roamed the desert, but after our departure we will live in heaven. Their great leader and commander was Moses; we have a new Moses, God himself, as our leader and commander. [Continued in next entry ...]

John Chrysostom

✢ 20 ✢

A GREATER DELIVERANCE (II)

Jesus has been found worthy of greater honor than Moses, just as the builder of a house has greater honor than the house itself. (Hebrews 3:3)

What distinguished the first Moses? Scripture tells us that Moses "was more gentle than anyone upon the earth" (Num. 12:3). We can say the same of the new Moses, for Christ has the Spirit of gentleness united to his inmost being. In those days Moses raised his hands to heaven and brought down manna, the bread of angels; the new Moses raises his hands to heaven and gives us the food of eternal life. Moses struck the rock and brought forth streams of water; Christ touches his table, strikes the spiritual rock of the new covenant, and draws forth the living water of the Spirit. The covenant is like a fountain in the middle of Christ's table, so that the flocks may draw near to this living spring and refresh themselves in the waters of salvation.

This fountain, this source of life, this table surrounds us with countless blessings and fills us with the gifts of the Spirit, therefore approach it with a sincere heart and a pure conscience, so that you receive grace and mercy in your time of need. Grace and mercy be yours from the only begotten Son, our Lord and Savior Jesus Christ; through him and with him be glory, honor, and power to the Father and the life-giving Spirit, now and always and forever. Amen.

John Chrysostom

✢ 21 ✢

PRAY WITH MODESTY AND DISCIPLINE

Then all the churches will know that I am he who searches hearts and minds, and I will repay each of you according to your deeds.
(Revelation 2:23)

Our speech and petitions should be disciplined when we pray and done with quietness and modesty, for we are standing in God's sight. We must please God's eyes with the movements of our body, and his ears with the way we use our voices. For just as a shameless person will be noisy with his or her cries, it is fitting for the modest to pray in a moderate way. Furthermore, the Lord has taught us to pray in secret, in hidden and remote places, in our own bedrooms; this is most proper for the faithful since it shows us that God is everywhere and hears and sees everything, and the fullness of his majesty is present even in hidden and secret places, as it is written: "I am a God close at hand and not a God far off. If a man hides himself in secret places, will I not see him? Do I not fill the whole of heaven and earth?" (Jer. 23:23–24).

When we meet together for worship and celebrate with God's priest, we should remember our modesty and discipline; we should not broadcast our prayers at the top of our lungs, nor blab a petition with undisciplined long-windedness. After all, God does not listen to the voice but to the heart and should not be pestered by our voices if he sees our thoughts, which the Lord proves when he says, "Why do you think evil in your hearts?" (Matt. 9:4).

Cyprian of Carthage

✣ 22 ✣

CAPTAINS OF THE SHIP (I)

Epaphras, who is one of you and a servant of Christ Jesus, sends greetings. He is always wrestling in prayer for you, that you may stand firm in all the will of God, mature and fully assured. (Colossians 4:12)

In her voyage across the ocean of this world, the church is like a great ship being pounded by the waves of life's different stresses. Our duty is not to abandon ship, but to keep her on her course.

The ancient fathers showed us how to carry out this duty: Clement, Cornelius, and many others in the city of Rome; Cyprian at Carthage; Athanasius at Alexandria. They all lived under pagan emperors, and they all steered Christ's ship — his precious bride, the church. They did this by teaching her and defending her, by their labors and sufferings, even to the point of shedding their blood.

I am terrified when I think of this responsibility. "Fear and trembling came upon me and the darkness" of my sins "almost covered me" (Ps. 55:5). I have freely accepted the task of guiding the church but would gladly abandon my post if I could justify it by the example of the fathers or by Holy Scripture.

Since this is not the case, and since the truth can be assaulted but never defeated or falsified, let us find encouragement in the words of Solomon: "Trust in the LORD with all your heart and do not rely on your own understanding. Think of him in all your ways, and he will guide your steps" (Prov. 3:5 – 6). In another place he says, "The name of the LORD is an impregnable tower. The just man seeks refuge in it and he will be saved" (Prov. 18:10). [Continued in next entry ...]

Boniface

✝ 23 ✝

CAPTAINS OF THE SHIP (II)

*Timothy, my son, I am giving you this command in keeping with the
prophecies once made about you, so that by recalling them you may
fight the battle well, holding on to faith and a good conscience.*
(1 Timothy 1:18–19)

Let us hold on to what is right and prepare our souls for trial. Let us wait upon God's strengthening aid and say to him, "LORD, you have been our refuge in all generations" (Ps. 90:1).

Let us trust in God, who has placed this burden upon us. What we cannot bear ourselves we can bear with Christ's help. For he is all-powerful and he tells us, "My yoke is easy and my burden is light" (Matt. 11:30).

Let us continue to fight until the day of the Lord. The days of anguish and of tribulation have overtaken us; if God wills it, let us die for the holy laws of our fathers, to be worthy of obtaining the eternal inheritance with them.

Let us be neither dogs that refuse to bark, nor silent bystanders, nor unfaithful servants who run away from the wolf. Instead let us be careful shepherds watching over Christ's flock. Let us preach God's entire plan of redemption to the powerful and to the humble, to the rich and to the poor, to people of every class and age, as long as our strength will carry us, in season and out of season, as Saint Gregory writes in his book of Pastoral Instruction.

Boniface

✤ 24 ✤

FIVE PATHS OF REPENTANCE

Repent, then, and turn to God, so that your sins may be wiped out,
that times of refreshing may come from the Lord, and that he may
send the Messiah, who has been appointed for you—even Jesus.
(Acts 3:19–20)

One path of repentance is the condemnation of your own sins: "Be the first to admit your sins and you will be justified" (Isa. 43:26). For this reason the prophet wrote, "I said: I will confess my sins to the LORD, and you forgave the wickedness of my heart" (Ps. 32:5). The Lord will forgive you if you condemn your own sins, and you will be slower to commit them again. Allow your conscience to accuse you here and now so that it does not accuse you before the Lord's judgment seat.

That is one very good path of repentance. Another but no less valuable one is to forget the harm our enemies have done to us, control our anger, and forgive our brothers' and sisters' sins against us. Then our own sins against the Lord will be forgiven. In this way you have another way to atone for sin: "For if you forgive your debtors, your heavenly Father will forgive you" (Matt. 6:14).

Do you want to know of a third path? It consists of prayer that is fervent, careful, and heartfelt.

Almsgiving is the fourth, whose power is great and diverse.

Finally, living a modest and humble life takes sin away. Proof of this is the tax-collector who had no good deeds but offered his humility instead and was relieved of a heavy burden of sins (Luke 18:9–14).

John Chrysostom

✦ 25 ✦

OBEYING HIS SOVEREIGN WILL

Do I take any pleasure in the death of the wicked? declares the
Sovereign LORD. Rather, am I not pleased when they turn
from their ways and live? (Ezekiel 18:23)

Let us turn our attention to the blood of Christ and recognize
how precious it is to God his Father, since it was shed for our
salvation and brought the grace of repentance to the entire world.

If we review the various ages of history, we see that in every
generation the Lord has offered the opportunity of repentance to
whomever was willing to turn to him. When Noah preached God's
message of repentance, all who listened to him were saved. Jonah
told the Ninevites they were going to be destroyed, but when they
repented, their prayers gained God's forgiveness for their sins and
they were saved, even though they were not God's people.

Under the inspiration of the Holy Spirit, the ministers of God's
grace have spoken of repentance; even more, the Master of the
universe himself spoke of repentance with an oath: "As I live, I do
not wish for the death of the sinner but for his repentance" (Ezek.
33:11).

In other words, God wants all his beloved ones to have the
opportunity to repent and he confirms this desire by his own
almighty will. That is why we should obey his sovereign and glorious will and prayerfully beg for his mercy and kindness. We should
be humble before him and seek his compassion, as we also reject
vanity, quarreling, and jealousy, which only lead to death.

Clement of Rome

✢ 26 ✢

BOAST IN THE LORD

It is because of him that you are in Christ Jesus, who has become for us
wisdom from God—that is, our righteousness, holiness and redemption.
Therefore, as it is written: "Let the one who boasts boast in the Lord."
(1 Corinthians 1:30–31)

What is the right kind of boasting? What is the source of human greatness? Scripture says, "The man who boasts must boast of this, that he knows and understands that I am the LORD" (Jer. 9:24). So our greatness, our glory and majesty, is to know in truth what is great, to hold fast to it, and to seek glory from the Lord of glory.

Boasting in God is perfect and complete when we take no pride in our own righteousness but acknowledge that we are utterly lacking in true righteousness and have been made righteous only by faith in Christ.

Paul boasts of the fact that he holds his own righteousness in contempt and seeks the righteousness of faith that comes through Christ and is from God. He wants only to know Christ and the power of his resurrection and to participate in his sufferings by dying with Christ in the hope that he may arrive at the resurrection of the dead.

In Paul we see all arrogant pride laid low. There is nothing left for us to boast of in our humanity, for our boasting and hope lie in putting to death all that is our own and seeking the future life that is in Christ. Since we have its firstfruits in the person of Christ, we now live entirely in the grace and gift of God.

Basil the Great

✦ 27 ✦

A THREEFOLD FORM OF DEVOTION (I)

When I heard these things, I sat down and wept. For some days
I mourned and fasted and prayed before the God of heaven.
(Nehemiah 1:4)

There are three things that make faith stand firm, devotion remain constant, and virtue endure: prayer, fasting, and mercy. Prayer knocks at the door, fasting gathers, mercy receives. Prayer, fasting, and mercy: these three are united, and they give life to each other.

Fasting is the soul of prayer, and mercy the lifeblood of fasting. Do not try to separate them; they cannot be separated. If you only have one or two of them, you have nothing. So if you pray, fast; if you fast, show mercy; if you want your petition to be heard, listen to the petitions of others. If you do not close your ear to others, God's ear is open to you.

When you fast, you see the hunger of others. If you want God to know that you are hungry, recognize that another is hungry. If you hope for mercy, show mercy. If you want kindness done to you, do kindness to others. If you want to receive, give. If you deny others what you ask for yourself, your request is a mockery.

Adopt this pattern when you practice mercy: show mercy to others in the same way, with the same generosity, with the same willingness, as you want others to show mercy to you.

Use prayer, mercy, and fasting as a single plea to God on your behalf, one speech in your defense, a threefold united prayer in your favor. [Continued in next entry ...]

Peter Chrysologus

✢ 28 ✢

A THREEFOLD FORM
OF DEVOTION (II)

This is what the LORD Almighty said: "Administer true justice;
show mercy and compassion to one another. Do not oppress
the widow or the fatherless, the foreigner or the poor. Do not
plot evil against each other." (Zechariah 7:9–10)

We should use fasting to make up for what we have lost by hating others. Through fasting we offer our souls in sacrifice to God, and there is nothing more pleasing to him, as the Psalmist says, "A sacrifice to God is a broken spirit; God does not despise a bruised and humbled heart" (Ps. 51:17).

Offer your soul to God, and give him the gift of your fasting, so that your soul may be a pure offering and a living sacrifice, remaining your own but in God's full possession. There is no excuse for not doing this, since we are supposed to give him ourselves, so we are never without the means to give.

To make these offerings complete, mercy must be added. Fasting bears no fruit unless it is watered by mercy. Fasting dries up when mercy dries up. Mercy is like rain on the soil of fasting. However much you cultivate your heart, clear the dirt of your nature, root out vices, sow virtues, if you do not release the waters of mercy, your fasting will bear no fruit.

When you fast, if your mercy is little your harvest will be small; what you pour out in mercy flows back into your barn. Therefore, you actually lose by saving it up, but gain abundantly by scattering it widely. Give to the poor, and you give to yourself. You will not be allowed to keep what you have refused to give to others.

Peter Chrysologus

✤ 29 ✤

EARTHLY GOODS AND HEAVENLY HOPE

In his great mercy he has given us new birth into a living hope through the resurrection of Jesus Christ from the dead. (1 Peter 1:3)

Our Lord Jesus Christ, born true man without ever ceasing to be true God, began in his person a new creation, and by the manner of his birth gave humanity a spiritual origin. What mind can grasp this mystery, what tongue can fittingly recount this gift of love? Guilt becomes innocence, old becomes new, strangers are adopted and outsiders are made heirs. Rouse yourselves, men and women, and recognize the dignity of your nature. Remember that you were made in God's image; though corrupted in Adam, that image has been restored in Christ.

Use creatures as they should be used: the earth, the sea, the sky, the air, the springs and rivers. Give praise and glory to their Creator for all that you find beautiful and wonderful in them. See with your bodily eyes the light that shines on earth, but embrace with your whole soul and all your affections "the true light which enlightens every man who comes into this world" (John 1:9). Speaking of this light the prophet said, "Draw close to him and let his light shine upon you and your face will not blush with shame" (Ps. 34:5). If we are indeed the temple of God and if the Spirit of God lives in us, then what all believers have within themselves is greater than what they admire in the skies.

For we are born in the present only to be reborn in the future. Our attachment, therefore, should not be to the transitory; instead, we must be intent upon the eternal. Let us think of how divine grace has transformed our earthly natures so that we may contemplate more closely our heavenly hope.

Leo the Great

✦ 30 ✦

GIVE, AND THEN TAKE WITH YOU

Jesus looked at him and loved him. "One thing you lack," he said. "Go, sell everything you have and give to the poor, and you will have treasure in heaven. Then come, follow me." (Mark 10:21)

You are going to leave your money behind you here whether you want to or not. But whatever share of glory you have received through your good works, that you can take with you to the Lord. Everyone will stand round you in the presence of the heavenly judge, and they will acclaim you as one who feeds the hungry and gives to the poor, and they will call you a merciful benefactor.

Remember the future hopes you store up for yourself by casting off the material cares of this life. Come, spread your wealth around, be generous, give extravagantly to those who are in need. Then it will be said of you as it is in the Psalms: "He gave alms and helped the poor: his righteousness will endure forever" (Ps. 112:9).

How grateful you should be to your own divine benefactor; how cheerful you should be at the honor he has bestowed on you, that you do not have to make a nuisance of yourself at other people's doors, but other people come and bother you at your own! But right now you are grumpy and no one can get to you. You avoid meeting people in case you feel obliged to give even a small amount. You say only one thing: "I have nothing to give you. I am only a poor man." Indeed you are poor and utterly bankrupt! Poor in love, poor in humanity, poor in faith in God, and without any hope of eternal happiness.

Basil the Great

❖ 31 ❖

FEED HIM WHO WILL FEED YOU

Remember this: Whoever sows sparingly will also reap sparingly, and whoever sows generously will also reap generously. (2 Corinthians 9:6)

Brothers and sisters, I know that I am not righteous, having been lifted up out of filth by Christ, and I do not exalt myself. But I am saddened when I look at you because it seems none of you, out of so great and well-equipped a group of people, fights for the poor. Not only that, but none of you is an encouragement to others who are in the fight. You speak against worldly evils, yet you stuff yourselves with luxuries. Your needy brothers and sisters fight against a world opposed to them—but do you, stuffed with wealth, fight with them or even support them in their fight?

You fools! Do you not see that even one member's fight is the fight of the whole? The whole church stands or falls on the victory of one member. You want peace in your camp, yet you see your brother just outside showing you that there is no peace for him. Have pity that you may first and foremost be saved.

Clearly you have no fear of the Lord, who cries aloud with your brother and commands that we give food even to our enemies. Consider good Tobias, who will share with you again, and who everyday shared his table with the poor man. You fools—seek to feed him who will in the future feed you!

Do you expect the poor man to prepare a meal for you when he is busy preparing his own burial? The brother oppressed with poverty, wasting away, cries out at the overstuffed bellies of the rich when his belly is distended. If a poor man has not placed himself in front of you, find one in the crowds and take him home to dinner. Refresh Christ by feeding this man.

Commodianus

✤ 32 ✤

THE POWER BEHIND
THE UNIVERSE

In his hand is the life of every creature and the breath of all mankind.
(Job 12:10)

The divine Word of the Father governs and presides over all. Simply through a nod, by his power, the heavens revolve, the stars move, the sun shines, the moon goes through her circuit, the air receives the sun's light and heat, and the winds blow — the highest mountains are established, the sea is rough with waves, and living things grow — the earth abides on its course and bears fruit, and man is formed and lives and dies again, and all manner of things have their life and movement — fire burns, water cools, fountains spring forth, rivers flow, seasons and hours come round, rains descend, clouds are filled, hail is formed, snow and ice congeal, birds fly, creeping things go along, sea creatures swim, the sea is navigated—the earth is sown and grows crops in due season, plants grow, and some are young, some ripening, others become old and decay, and while some things are vanishing others are being born and are coming to light.

All these things and more, whose number and variety is impossible to know, God moves and orders by his own nod. He is the worker of wonders and marvels, the Word of God, giving light and life, establishing and upholding the universe as one.

And although he is himself over all things, both Governor and King and organizing power, he does all things for the glory of his Father, so that by the works he accomplishes he gives us knowledge of the Father's glory.

Athanasius

❖ 33 ❖

HOPE, JUSTICE, AND LOVE

*For through the Spirit we eagerly await by faith the righteousness
for which we hope. (Galatians 5:5)*

I have been thinking that if my concern for you inspires me to pass on to you some of the teaching I have received, then perhaps I will be rewarded for ministering to your souls. Consequently, I am writing you, so that you may have perfect knowledge along with your faith.

The Lord has given us these three basic doctrines: hope for eternal life, the beginning and end of our faith; justice, the beginning and end of righteousness; and love, which bears cheerful and joyous witness to the works of righteousness. Now, the Lord has made the past and present known to us through his prophets, and he has given us the ability to taste the fruits of the future beforehand. Thus, when we see prophecies fulfilled in their appointed order, we ought to grow more fully and deeply in awe of him. Let me suggest a few things—not as a teacher, but as one of you—which should bring you joy in the present situation.

When evil days are upon us and sinister people gain power, we must attend to our own souls and seek the ways of the Lord. In those times obedient fear and perseverance will sustain our faith, and we will need courage and self-restraint as well. Provided that we hold fast to these virtues and look to the Lord, then wisdom, understanding, knowledge, and insight will enter our minds and make joyous company with our faith and love.

Barnabas

⊰ 34 ⊱

ANOINTED BY THE HOLY SPIRIT (I)

What shall we say, then? Shall we go on sinning so that grace may increase? By no means! We are those who have died to sin; how can we live in it any longer? Or don't you know that all of us who were baptized into Christ Jesus were baptized into his death?
(Romans 6:1–3)

This is something amazing and unheard of! We did not actually die, get buried, and rise again — we only did these things symbolically, but we have been saved in actual fact. It is Christ who was crucified, who was buried, and who rose again, and all this has been attributed to us. We share in his sufferings symbolically and gain salvation in reality. What boundless love for humankind! Christ's undefiled hands were pierced by the nails; he suffered the pain. I experience no pain, and no anguish, yet because I share in his sufferings he freely grants me salvation.

We became like anointed ones when we received the sign of the Holy Spirit. In fact, everything took place in us through images, because we ourselves are images of Christ. Christ bathed in the river Jordan, giving to its waters the fragrance of his divinity, and when he came up from them the Holy Spirit descended upon him, divinity resting upon divinity. Likewise, we were anointed with oil after we came up from the sacred waters of baptism. The oil is an image of the Holy Spirit, by whom Christ was anointed and of whom Isaiah prophesied in the name of the Lord: "The Spirit of the LORD is upon me, because he has anointed me. He has sent me to preach good news to the poor" (Isa. 61:1). [Continued in next entry ...]

Cyril of Jerusalem

✤ 35 ✤

ANOINTED BY
THE HOLY SPIRIT (II)

But you have an anointing from the Holy One,
and all of you know the truth. (1 John 2:20)

When we were baptized into Christ and clothed with him, we were transformed into the likeness of the Son of God. Having predestined us to adoption as sons and daughters, God gave us the likeness of Christ in his glory; living as we do in communion with God's anointed Son, we are rightly called "the anointed ones." God was speaking of us when he said, "Do not touch my anointed ones" (Ps. 105:15).

Christ's anointing was not by human hands, nor was it with ordinary oil. On the contrary, the Father himself elected him to be the Savior of the whole world, and the Father himself anointed him with the Holy Spirit. The words of Peter bear witness to this: "Jesus of Nazareth, whom God anointed with the Holy Spirit" (Acts 10:38).

The oil with which Christ was anointed was a spiritual oil; it was, in fact, the Holy Spirit himself who is called "the oil of gladness" because he is the source of spiritual joy (Ps. 45:7; Heb. 1:9). And we have also been anointed with oil and through it have entered into fellowship with Christ and received a share in his life. Do not think that it is only ordinary oil; it becomes the gift of Christ and is the instrument through which we receive the Holy Spirit. Symbolically our foreheads and bodies are anointed with this visible oil, but our souls are sanctified by the holy and life-giving Spirit.

Cyril of Jerusalem

✤ 36 ✤

WE REJOICE AND SUFFER AS ONE

If one part suffers, every part suffers with it; if one part is honored,
every part rejoices with it. (1 Corinthians 12:26)

My very dear brother Cornelius [a priest in Rome], we have heard of the glorious witness that your courageous faith has given. When we learned of the honor your witness had won, we were filled with such joy that we felt we were sharing in your praiseworthy achievements. After all, we have the same church, the same mind, and the same unbroken harmony. Should a priest not take pride in the praise given to a fellow priest, as if it were given to him also? What kind of brotherhood fails to rejoice when its brothers rejoice, wherever they are?

Dear brother, the faith of your community is bright and shining, and even the blessed Apostle praised it. He foresaw in the Spirit the praise deserved by your courage and unbreakable strength; his praise of your fathers also testified to the challenge overcome by the sons. Your unity and strength are shining examples of these virtues to the rest of us.

Divine providence has now prepared us. God's merciful design has warned us that the day of our own struggle, our own contest, is at hand. With the shared love that binds us together, we are doing all we can to exhort our congregation and giving ourselves unceasingly to fasting, vigils, and praying together. Using these heavenly weapons gives us the strength to stand firm and endure; they are spiritual defenses and God-given armaments that protect us.

Let us then remember one another and be united in mind and heart. Let us pray without ceasing, you for us, we for you. Our shared love will relieve the strain of these great trials.

Cyprian of Carthage

✣ 37 ✣

MARY AND THE CHURCH

As Jesus was saying these things, a woman in the crowd called out,
"Blessed is the mother who gave you birth and nursed you." He replied,
"Blessed rather are those who hear the word of God and obey it."
(Luke 11:27−28)

Indeed the blessed Mary did the Father's will, but it was a greater thing for her to have been Christ's disciple than to have been his mother, and she was more blessed in her discipleship than in her motherhood. Her happiness was first bearing in her womb the one she would later obey as her master.

The Virgin Mary is both holy and blessed, and yet the church is greater than she is. Mary is a part of the church, a member of the church, a holy and most eminent member, but still only a member of the entire body. The body undoubtedly is greater than she is, as only one of its members. This body has the Lord for its head, and head and body together make up the whole Christ. In other words, our head is divine—our head is God.

Now, brothers and sisters, give me your whole attention, for you also are members of Christ; you also are the body of Christ. Consider how you yourselves can be those of whom the Lord said, "Here are my mother and my brothers" (Matt. 12:49). Do you wonder how you can be the mother of Christ? He himself said, "Whoever hears and fulfills the will of my Father in heaven is my brother and my sister and my mother" (Matt. 12:50). How is this so? Because although there is only one inheritance and Christ is the only Son, in his mercy he chose not to remain alone. It was his wish that we should also be heirs of the Father, and coheirs with himself.

Augustine

⊹ 38 ⊹

VIRTUE'S SECRET REWARD

But store up for yourselves treasures in heaven, where moths and vermin
do not destroy, and where thieves do not break in and steal.
(Matthew 6:20)

A virtuous life brings great splendor; a peaceful conscience and a calm innocence make for a happy life. As the risen sun hides the globe of the moon and the light of the stars, so the brightness of a virtuous life, glittering in pure glory, casts all other things into the shade.

A life is clearly blessed when it is not valued by the estimation of outsiders, but is a judge of itself and known by its own inner feelings. It does not need popular opinion as its reward, nor does it fear punishment. The less it strives for earthly glory, the more it rises above it. The rewards of present things are only shadows by comparison to future ones and are a hindrance to eternal life, as it is written in the Scriptures: "Truly, I say to you, they have received their reward" (Matt. 6:2). This is said of people who want to boast to the whole world of their generosity to the poor. It is the same in the case of fasting done only for outward show. "They have their reward," he says.

Therefore a virtuous life consists in showing mercy and fasting in secret, to train you to seek a reward from your God alone and not from people. For if you seek it from others you have your reward, but if you seek it from God you have eternal life, which no one can give but the Lord of Eternity.

Ambrose

✤ 39 ✤

NO TEMPTATION BEYOND OUR STRENGTH

But when you are tempted, he will also provide a way out so that you can endure it. (1 Corinthians 10:13)

Scripture says, "God chastises every son whom he acknowledges" (Heb. 12:6). But the bad shepherd says, "Perhaps I will be exempt." If he is exempt from suffering, then he is not numbered among God's sons. You will ask, "Does God indeed punish every son?" Yes, every one, just as he chastised his only Son. His only Son—born of the substance of the Father, equal to the Father and "in the form of God" (Phil. 2:6), the Word through whom all things were made—he could not be chastised. For this reason he was clothed with flesh so that he might know chastisement.

God punishes his only Son who is without sin; does he then leave unpunished an adopted son who is with sin? The Apostle says that we have been called to adoption.

But those who are weak should not be deceived with false hope nor broken by fear. Otherwise they may fail when temptations come. Say to them, "Prepare your soul for temptation" (Sir. 2:1). Perhaps someone is faltering, trembling with fear, and perhaps is unwilling to face suffering. You have another passage of Scripture for the fearful soul: "God is faithful. He does not allow you to be tempted beyond your strength" (1 Cor. 10:13). Make that promise while preaching about the sufferings to come, and you will strengthen the person who is weak. When someone is held back because of excessive fear, promise the person God's mercy. Our comfort is not that temptations will be lacking, but that God will not permit anyone to be tempted beyond what he or she can bear. In this manner you will be hardening the weak one.

Augustine

⊹ 40 ⊹

THE HUMILITY OF GOD

*For my eyes have seen your salvation, which you have prepared
in the sight of all nations: a light for revelation to the Gentiles,
and the glory of your people Israel. (Luke 2:30–32)*

Lowliness is assured by majesty, weakness by power, mortality by eternity. To pay the debt of our sinful state, a nature that was incapable of suffering was joined to one that could suffer. Thus, in keeping with the healing that we needed, one and the same mediator between God and humanity, the man Jesus Christ, was able to die in one nature and unable to die in the other.

He who is true God was therefore born in the complete and perfect nature of a true man, whole in his own nature, whole in ours. By our nature we mean what the Creator had fashioned in us from the beginning, and took to himself in order to restore.

He took the nature of a servant without stain of sin, enlarging our humanity without diminishing his divinity. He emptied himself; though invisible he made himself visible; though Creator and Lord of all things he chose to be one of us mortal humans. Yet this was the condescension of compassion, not the loss of omnipotence. So the one who as God had created humankind, became, as a servant, human himself.

Thus the Son of God enters this lowly world. He comes down from the throne of heaven yet does not separate himself from the Father's glory. He is born in a new condition, by a new birth.

Leo the Great

❖ 41 ❖

WALK WITH THE LORD

For we brought nothing into the world,
and we can take nothing out of it. (1 Timothy 6:7)

Neither I nor anyone like me can equal the wisdom of the blessed and glorious Paul. When he was in your city, he fully and courageously taught the men the word of truth; when he was absent, he wrote you letters. By carefully studying these letters, you can strengthen yourselves in the faith that has been given to you. This faith is the mother of us all, followed by hope, preceded by love — love of God, of Christ, and of our neighbor. For anyone who has love is far from sin.

We must begin by teaching ourselves how to walk in the commandment of the Lord. Then you should teach your wives to walk in the faith that has been handed down to them, in love and in chastity. They must love their husbands with complete fidelity, but they must cherish all others equally, and with self-control; they must raise their children in the discipline that comes from fear of God.

God, as we know, is not mocked. Let us walk in a way that is worthy of his commands and his purposes. Deacons, in the same way, must be blameless in the sight of his goodness, for they are servants of God and of Christ, not of people. They must avoid lies, hypocritical talk, and greed. Merciful and diligent, they must control all their desires, walking according to the truth of the Lord who became the servant of all. If we please him in this life, we shall receive the life to come; for he has promised us that he will raise us from the dead, and if we lead lives worthy of him that we shall reign along with him. This is what our faith tells us.

Polycarp

❖ 42 ❖

WE NEED CHRIST'S DEATH

Nor did he enter heaven to offer himself again and again, the way the high priest enters the Most Holy Place every year with blood that is not his own. Otherwise Christ would have had to suffer many times since the creation of the world. But he has appeared once for all at the culmination of the ages to do away with sin by the sacrifice of himself. (Hebrews 9:25–26)

Holiness could only be given to humans by the humanity assumed by one who was God, so that God might overcome the tyrant by force, and deliver us, and lead us back to himself through the mediation of his Son. The Son arranged this for the honor of the Father, to whom the Son is clearly obedient in all things.

The Good Shepherd, who lays down his life for the sheep, came to the land where you used to offer sacrifice, searching for the straying sheep. When he found it, he took it on his shoulders, which also carried the wood of the cross, and led it back to the life of heaven.

Christ, the light of all lights, follows John, the lamp that goes before him. The Word of God follows the voice in the wilderness; the bridegroom follows the bridegroom's friend, who prepares a worthy people for the Lord by cleansing them with water in preparation for the Spirit.

We need God to take our flesh and die so that we can live. We have died with him so that we can be purified. We have risen again with him because we have died with him. We have been glorified with him because we have risen again with him.

Gregory of Nazianzus

✢ 43 ✢

WE ASCEND WITH CHRIST (I)

For you died, and your life is now hidden with Christ in God.
When Christ, who is your life, appears, then you also will appear
with him in glory. (Colossians 3:3–4)

Today our Lord Jesus Christ ascended into heaven; let our hearts ascend with him. Listen to the words of the Apostle: "If you have risen with Christ, set your hearts on the things that are above where Christ is, seated at the right hand of God; seek the things that are above, not the things that are on earth" (Col. 3:1–2). For just as Christ remained with us even after his ascension, likewise we are already in heaven with him, even though what is promised to us has not yet been fulfilled in our bodies.

Christ is now exalted above the heavens, but he still suffers all the pain that we have to bear here on earth, for we are his body. He showed this when he cried out from above, "Saul, Saul, why do you persecute me?" (Acts 9:4) and when he said, "I was hungry and you gave me food" (Matt. 25:35).

So why do we not strive to find rest with him in heaven even now, through the faith, hope, and love that unite us to him? While in heaven he is here with us; and while on earth we are there with him. He is here with us by his divinity, his power, and his love. And though we cannot be in heaven by divinity, as he is on earth, we can be there by love, since we are in him by love. [Continued in next entry …]

Augustine

✣ 44 ✣

WE ASCEND
WITH CHRIST (II)

*For just as each of us has one body with many members, and these
members do not all have the same function, so in Christ we, though
many, form one body, and each member belongs to all the others.*
(Romans 12:4–5)

He did not leave heaven when he came down to us; nor did he
abandon us when he went up again into heaven. We know
that he was in heaven even while he was on earth, as is shown by
his own statement: "No one has ever ascended into heaven except
the one who descended from heaven, the Son of Man, who is in
heaven" (John 3:13).

These words are explained by our union with Christ, for he is
our head and we are his body. It is true that no one has ascended
into heaven except Christ, because we are in Christ and ascend with
him! He is the Son of Man by his union with us, and we are sons and
daughters of God by our union with him. So the Apostle says, "Just
as the human body, which has many members, is a unity, because
all the different members make one body, so is it also with Christ"
(1 Cor. 12:12). He too has many members, but one body.

Out of compassion for us he descended from heaven, and
although he ascended alone, we also ascend, because we are in him
by grace. Thus, no one but Christ descended and no one but Christ
ascended — not because there is no difference between the head and
the body, but because the head and body are a union that cannot be
separated.

Augustine

✢ 45 ✢

COUNTING IT ALL JOY

*I have fought the good fight, I have finished the race, I have kept the
faith. Now there is in store for me the crown of righteousness, which the
Lord, the righteous Judge, will award to me on that day—and not only
to me, but also to all who have longed for his appearing.*
(2 Timothy 4:7–8)

Even though he was thrown in prison, Paul lived in heaven. He
accepted beatings and wounds with more thankfulness than
others accept gifts. He loved suffering for Christ as much as a prize
and actually thought of them as prizes, calling them "graces."
Think about that! "To depart and be with Christ" was the reward
he had coming (Phil. 1:23), while remaining in the flesh would be a
struggle. But his longing for Christ was such that he chose to defer
his reward and stay in the fight to satisfy Christ.

We can see that being separated from Christ was a painful
struggle for Paul—a greater affliction than actual torture would be.
On the other hand, to be with Christ would be a matchless reward.
Yet, for the sake of Christ, Paul chose the separation.

You may say, "But because of Christ, Paul found all this pleasant." I cannot deny that, for he derived intense pleasure from what
would sadden us. And it was not just the physical danger he was in
all the time, but also the intense sorrow that he counted as a joy in
Christ, as he cried out, "Who is weak that I do not share the weakness? Who is scandalized that I am not consumed with indigna-
tion?" (2 Cor. 11:29).

So I urge you not simply to admire Paul's virtues and affections
for Christ, but also to imitate his example, which is possible since
we share his nature in every respect. And if we do this, we can share
his crown as well.

John Chrysostom

⊷ 46 ⊶

PRAY FOR THE WHOLE CHURCH

But when you pray, go into your room, close the door and pray to your Father, who is unseen. Then your Father, who sees what is done in secret, will reward you. (Matthew 6:6)

Although he tells you that every place is a place of prayer, our Savior says, "Go into your room." But by "room" you must not imagine a place enclosed by walls that hide your body, but the room that is within you, the room where you hide your thoughts, where you keep your affections. This room of prayer is always with you, wherever you are, and it is always a secret room, where only God can see you.

You are told to pray especially for the church, for the whole body, for all its members, your brothers and sisters; the badge of membership in this body is love for each other. If you pray only for yourself, you pray for yourself alone. If each one prays only for him or herself, he or she receives less than the one who prays only for others. But as it is, because each prays for all, all are in fact praying for each one.

To conclude, if you pray only for yourself, you will be praying, as we said, for yourself alone. But if you pray for all, all will pray for you, for you are included in all. In this way there is a great reward; through the prayers of each individual, the whole body intercedes to God for each member. In prayer there is no pride, but an increase of humility and a richer spiritual harvest.

Ambrose

✢ 47 ✢

UNITED WITH CHRIST

*Whoever acknowledges me before others, I will also acknowledge before
my Father in heaven. (Matthew 10:32)*

The business of this life should not preoccupy us with its anxiety and pride, so that we no longer strive with all the love of our heart to be like our Redeemer and to follow his example. Everything that he did or suffered was for our salvation: he wanted his body to share the goodness of its head.

First of all, in taking our human nature while remaining God, so that the Word became man, he left no member of the human race, the unbeliever excepted, without a share in his mercy. Who does not share a common nature with Christ if he or she has welcomed Christ, who took our nature, and is reborn in the Spirit, through whom Christ himself was born?

Again, who cannot recognize in Christ his or her own infirmities? Who would not recognize that Christ's eating and sleeping, his sadness and his shedding tears of love, are marks of the nature of a slave?

It was this nature of a slave that had to be healed of its ancient wounds and cleansed of the defilement of sin. For that reason the only begotten Son of God became also the Son of Man. He was to have both the reality of a human nature and the fullness of the godhead.

The body that lay lifeless in the tomb is ours. The body that rose again on the third day is ours. The body that ascended above all the heights of heaven to the right hand of the Father's glory is ours. If then we walk in the way of his commandments and are not ashamed to acknowledge the price he paid for our salvation in a lowly body, we too will rise and share his glory.

Leo the Great

❖ 48 ❖

POSSESSING ALL THINGS

*Yes, and I will continue to rejoice, for I know that through your prayers
and God's provision of the Spirit of Jesus Christ what has happened to
me will turn out for my deliverance. I eagerly expect and hope that I
will in no way be ashamed, but will have sufficient courage so that now
as always Christ will be exalted in my body, whether by life or by death.
(Philippians 1:18–20)*

The most important thing of all to Paul was knowing that Christ loved him. This love caused him to consider himself happier than anyone else; without it, he would not be satisfied being the friend of principalities and powers. He preferred to have this love and be least among people, even among the damned, than not to have it and be among the rich and powerful and honored.

To be separated from that love was, in his eyes, the worst and most severe torment. The pain of that loss by itself would have been hell, an unbearable torture.

Because of Christ's love for him, he thought of himself as possessing life, the world, the angels, the present and future, the kingdom, the inheritance, and countless blessings. Nothing except the love of Christ moved him to sadness or delight, since he saw nothing on earth as bitter or as sweet in comparison.

The things of this world were as valuable to Paul as withered grass in the field. The tyrants and villains that raged against him were no more than gnats to him. Death, pain, and torments were child's play to him, so long as he could use them to advance the cause of Christ.

John Chrysostom

⊰ 49 ⊱

GOD THE FATHER AND CREATOR

Then they asked him, "Where is your father?" "You do not know me or my Father," Jesus replied. "If you knew me, you would know my Father also." (John 8:19)

The sentence "I believe in one God the Father" is rightly followed by the phrase "Creator of all things visible and invisible," so that we should understand that he is not only the Father of the Son but also the Creator of all the creatures, and should think of the difference that exists between Father and Creator and between Son and creatures. He is the Father of the Son and the Creator of the creatures. The creatures were created later, while the Son was from the beginning with him and from him. This is the difference between Father and Creator. He is called the Father of the one who was born of him, and the Creator of all the natures that are outside him and that were created from nothing by his will.

Two things render it obligatory for us to praise God: because he is Father and because he is Creator. We must, however, understand the difference between the two. It is not because he is Father that he is also Creator, and it is not because he is Creator that he is also Father. Indeed he is not the Creator of the one whose Father he is, nor is he the Father of those whose Creator he is. He is called the Father of the Son because the Son is from him and of the same substance as him, and he is the Maker and the Creator of the creatures because he brought them to existence from nothing.

Theodore of Mopsuestia

✦ 50 ✦

SHORT AND LONG PRAYERS

In the same way, the Spirit helps us in our weakness. We do not know what we ought to pray for, but the Spirit himself intercedes for us through wordless groans. (Romans 8:26)

The monks in Egypt are said to offer frequent prayers, but these are very short and hurled like swift javelins. Otherwise their watchful attention, a necessary quality for anyone at prayer, could be dulled and could disappear through long delays. Through this practice they clearly demonstrate that a person must quickly seize the moment when the Spirit moves him but also must not linger with empty words when he is distracted.

Excessive talking should be kept out of prayer, but that does not mean that one should not spend much time in prayer, as long as a fervent attitude continues to accompany the prayer. To talk at length in prayer is to perform a necessary action with an excess of words. To spend much time in prayer is to knock with a persistent and holy passion at the door of the one upon whom we call. But in our day-to-day life, this task is often accomplished more through sighs than words, more through weeping than speech. He "places our tears in his sight, and our sighs are not hidden from him" (Ps. 38:9), for he has established all things through his Word and does not need human words.

Augustine

✢ 51 ✢

A STRONG AND STABLE CHARACTER

Blessed is the one who perseveres under trial because, having stood the test, that person will receive the crown of life that the Lord has promised to those who love him. (James 1:12)

A strong and stable character is made by meditating on holy things, and his spirit endures. An unshaken spirit, strengthened by a solid faith in the future glory, is energized and protected against all the devil's tactics and the world's threats. During persecution the earth is darkened to us, but heaven opens up; the antichrist waves a sword, but Christ is our shield; death is brought on, but eternal life follows. What an honor, and what a happiness, to depart joyfully from this world, to go toward glory and away from anguish and pain—in one moment we close our eyes that look on the world of humankind, and the next moment we open them and immediately see God and Christ! Think of the speed of this joyous departure! You are suddenly withdrawn from earth to find yourself in the kingdom of heaven.

Grasp these thoughts with your heart and mind and reflect on them day and night. If a soldier of God is faced with persecution, his or her devoted preparation for battle will ensure victory. And if our summons to heaven comes sooner, our faith will be rewarded, as it was prepared beforehand as a witness of martyrdom. In this case we would immediately receive our reward in God's judgment.

In a time of peace our testimony is godly thoughts and actions, but in a time of persecution the battle wins the crown.

Cyprian of Carthage

✦ 52 ✦

THE WORD TOOK A BODY

That which was from the beginning, which we have heard, which we have seen with our eyes, which we have looked at and our hands have touched — this we proclaim concerning the Word of life. (1 John 1:1)

Our faith is not founded upon empty words, nor are we carried away by speculation or tricked by false arguments. On the contrary, we put our faith in words spoken by the power of God, spoken by the Word himself at God's command. God wished to win men and women back from disobedience, not through forced slavery, but by an appeal to human free will for freedom.

The Word spoke first of all through the prophets, but because the language of their message was hard to understand, the Father sent the Word in person, commanding him to show himself openly so that the world could see him and be saved.

We know that by taking a body from the Virgin he refashioned our fallen nature. We know that his manhood was of the same clay as our own; if this were not the case, we could hardly be expected to imitate him. If he were a different substance than I, he would not have ordered me to do as he did, because by my nature I am so weak. A demand like this could not be reconciled with his goodness and justice.

No, he wanted us to know that he was just like us, so he worked, he was hungry and thirsty, and he slept. He endured his passion without protest; he submitted to death and revealed his resurrection. He offered his own manhood as the firstfruits of our race to keep us from losing heart when suffering comes our way, and to make us look forward to receiving the same reward as he did, since we know that we possess the same humanity.

Hippolytus

⁘ 53 ⁘

BEING PREPARED TO SUFFER

Endure hardship as discipline; God is treating you as his children. For what children are not disciplined by their father? (Hebrews 12:7)

What sort of pastors are they who, for fear of offending their congregants, not only fail to prepare their sheep for temptations, but even promise them worldly happiness? God himself made no such promise to this world. On the contrary, God foretold hardship upon hardship in this world until the end of time. And you expect the Christian to be exempt from these troubles? Precisely because of being a Christian, he or she is destined to suffer more in this world.

For the Apostle says, "All who desire to live a holy life in Christ will suffer persecution" (2 Tim. 3:12). But when you, shepherd, speak your own words and not Christ's, you disregard what the Apostle says, saying instead, "If you live a holy life in Christ, all good things on earth will be yours in abundance." Is this the way you build up the believers? Look at what you are doing and where you are putting them! You have built them on sand. The rains will come, the river will overflow and rush in, the winds will blow, and the elements will dash against the house you have built. It will fall, and its ruin will be great (Matt 7:26–27).

Lift them up from the sand and put them on the rock. Let them be in Christ if you wish them to be Christians. Let them reflect on suffering, though their own will never match that of Christ. Let them center their attention on Christ, who was without sin but made restitution for what we had done. Let them consider Scripture, which says to them, "He chastises every son whom he acknowledges" (Heb. 12:6). Let them prepare to be chastised or else prepare to renounce his sonship.

Augustine

✣ 54 ✣

BE SUBJECT TO A MENTOR

*Timothy, my son, I am giving you this command in keeping with the
prophecies once made about you, so that by recalling them you may fight
the battle well, holding on to faith and a good conscience.*
(1 Timothy 1:18–19)

If you are pompous and powerful and rich, it is necessary for you
to have a godly mentor and teacher. Learn reverence, even if it
starts with one person, and learn fear, even if it starts with the same
person. Learn how to listen to at least one individual at first, who
speaks harshly but with healing words. It is good for your eyes to
not always seek pleasure, but to sometimes weep and feel pain for
the sake of spiritual health. There is nothing more harmful to the
soul than uninterrupted pleasure, and your tears will wash away
your blindness, if your mentor's instruction does not cure it.

Fear this man (or woman) when he is angry; feel pain at his dis-
appointment; praise him when his anger abates; and learn when
you are deserving of punishment. Let him lose sleep over you,
interceding to God on your behalf with prayers and supplications,
because the Father does not withhold mercy when his children ask
for it. He will pray purely for you like an angel of God, struggling
on your behalf. This is sincere repentance.

God is not mocked (Gal. 6:7), nor does he listen to superficial
prayers. He searches the marrow and knows the heart of humanity,
hears those who are in the fire, and listens to those who call out to
him from the whale's belly (Jonah 2). He is near to whoever believes
and far from the ungodly if they do not repent.

Clement of Alexandria

❖ 55 ❖

THE INTERNAL WITNESS

But now that you have been set free from sin and have become slaves of
God, the benefit you reap leads to holiness, and the result is eternal life.
(Romans 6:22)

There are many hidden martyrs, bearing witness to Christ each day and acknowledging Jesus as the Lord. The Apostle knew this kind of martyrdom, this faithful witness to Christ. "This is our boast," he said, "the witness of our conscience" (2 Cor. 1:12). How many have borne witness in public but denied it in private! "Do not believe every spirit," he said, "but know from their fruits" whom you should believe (1 John 4:1). Be faithful and courageous when you are persecuted internally, so that you might do the same when you are persecuted in public. Even in those unseen persecutions there are kings and governors and judges with terrible power. You have an example in the temptation endured by the Lord.

In another place we read, "Do not let sin be king in your mortal body" (Rom. 6:12). You know which kings you must stand before, the ones who sit in judgment in your heart, where sin is in control. There are as many kings as there are sins and vices; it is these kings who attempt to rule our souls. These kings have their thrones in many hearts. But if any of you acknowledges Christ, you immediately make a prisoner of this kind of king and throw him down from the throne of your heart. How can the devil maintain his power in someone who builds a throne for Christ in their heart?

Ambrose

✤ 56 ✤

WOUNDS OF LOVE

*"He himself bore our sins" in his body on the cross, so that we might
die to sins and live for righteousness; "by his wounds you have been
healed." (1 Peter 2:24)*

God, you are yourself the fountain to be desired forever and ever, and consumed forever. Lord Christ, always give us this water and be for us the source of the "living water which wells up to eternal life" (John 4:14). I ask you for your great benefits. Who does not know them? You, King of glory, know how to give great gifts, and you have promised to give them; there is nothing greater than you, and you bestowed yourself upon us; you gave yourself for us.

So we ask that we might know you better and more fully, and that you give us nothing but yourself. For you are our all: our life, our light, our salvation, our food and our drink, our God. Inspire our hearts with the breath of your Spirit; wound our souls with your love, so that the soul of each and every one of us may truthfully say, "Show me my soul's desire," for I am wounded by your love.

These are the wounds I wish for, Lord. Blessed is the soul wounded by love. Such a soul seeks the fountain of eternal life and drinks from it, although it continues to thirst and its thirst grows greater as it drinks. Therefore, the more the soul loves, the more it desires to love, and the greater the soul's suffering, the greater its healing. So let us ask Christ, the good and saving physician, to wound the depths of our souls with a healing wound—the same Jesus Christ who reigns in unity with the Father and the Holy Spirit, forever and ever. Amen.

Columbanus

✢ 57 ✢

THE PREFIGURATIONS OF THE CROSS

Each one threw down his staff and it became a snake. But Aaron's staff swallowed up their staffs. (Exodus 7:12)

The wonders accomplished through the tree of Christ's cross were foreshadowed clearly by the types and figures that existed in the past. Meditate on these, if you are eager to learn. Was it not the wood of a tree that enabled Noah, at God's command, to escape the destruction of the flood together with his sons, his wife, his sons' wives, and every kind of animal? And surely the rod of Moses prefigured the cross when it changed water into blood, swallowed up the false serpents of Pharaoh's magicians, divided the sea at one stroke, and then restored the waters to their normal course, drowning the enemy and saving God's own people? Aaron's rod, which blossomed in one day in proof of his true priesthood, was another figure of the cross. And did not Abraham foreshadow the cross when he bound his son Isaac and placed him on the pile of wood?

By the cross death was slain and Adam was restored to life. The cross is the glory of all the apostles, the crown of the martyrs, the sanctification of the saints. By the cross we put on Christ and cast aside our former self. By the cross we, the sheep of Christ, have been gathered into one flock, destined for the sheepfolds of heaven.

Theodore the Studite

❖ 58 ❖

THE WAY OF LIGHT (I)

This is the message we have heard from him and declare to you: God is
light; in him there is no darkness at all. If we claim to have fellowship
with him and yet walk in the darkness, we lie and do not live out the
truth. (1 John 1:5–6)

Consider now the way of light. All who are intent on reaching their appointed goal must be very careful in everything they do. Now these are the directions that have been given to us for this journey: love your Creator; reverence your Maker; give glory to him who redeemed you when you were dead; be committed to this one thing, but have many spiritual treasures; avoid those who travel down death's highway; hate whatever is displeasing to God; detest all hypocritical pretense; do not abandon God's commandments. Do not act falsely, but be modest in whatever you do; claim no credit for yourself. Plot no evil against your neighbor, and do not give pride an entrance into your heart.

Love your neighbor more than your own life. Do not kill an unborn child through abortion, nor destroy it after birth. Do not stop disciplining a son or daughter, but bring them up from childhood in the fear of the Lord. Do not set your heart on what belongs to your neighbor, and do not give in to greed. Do not associate with the arrogant, but cultivate those who are humble and virtuous.

Accept as a blessing whatever comes your way, knowing that nothing ever happens outside of God's sovereignty. Avoid duplicity in thought or in speech, for such deception is a deadly snare. [Continued in next entry ...]

Barnabas

✢ 59 ✢

THE WAY OF LIGHT (II)

But if we walk in the light, as he is in the light, we have fellowship with
one another, and the blood of Jesus, his Son, purifies us from all sin.
(1 John 1:7)

Share whatever you have with your neighbor, and never say, "This is mine." If you both share an imperishable treasure, should you not share what is perishable? Do not be hasty with words; the mouth is a deadly trap. For your soul's good, make every effort to live chastely. Do not hold out your hand for what you can get, only to withdraw it when it comes to giving. Cherish as someone precious anyone who speaks the Word of the Lord to you.

Night and day you will remember the day of judgment; every day you will seek out the company of God's faithful, either by preaching the Word or earnestly exhorting them. And always be thinking about how you can save souls with what you say or through the work of your hands. Make amends for your past sins.

Never hesitate to give, and when you do give, never grumble; does God repay a grumbler? Preserve the traditions you have received, adding nothing and taking nothing away. There will always be evildoers close by. Be fair in your judgments. Never stir up dissension, but act as peacemaker and reconcile the quarrelsome. Confess your sins, and do not begin to pray with a guilty conscience.

Such then is the way of light.

Barnabas

✧ 60 ✧

FINAL WORDS OF SAINT MACRINA

The God of peace will soon crush Satan under your feet.
The grace of our Lord Jesus be with you. (Romans 16:20)

[Macrina was the sister of Gregory of Nyssa and Basil the Great] You, Lord, have freed us from the fear of death. You have made the end of this life the beginning of true life. You rest our bodies in sleep for a season and waken them at the last trumpet. You gave us the earth, which you fashioned with your hands, to keep in safety. One day you will take what you have given and transfigure it with grace and immortality. You have saved us from the curse and sin, having become both for our sake. You have broken the heads of the dragon who had snatched us in his jaws of disobedience. You have shown us the way of resurrection, broken the gates of hell, and eliminated the one who had the power of death, the devil. You have given us a sign of your wrath and love in the holy cross, which destroys the adversary and saves our lives.

God, whom my soul has loved with all its strength, to whom I have dedicated my body and soul from childhood until now — give me an angel of light to lead me to the place of refreshment. You who broke the flaming sword and restored humans to paradise, remember me in your kingdom, because I was crucified with you and have feared your judgments and asked for your mercies. Carry me across the chasm, and do not allow the slanderer to stand in the way. Forgive me my sins, those in word and deed and thought. You who have the power even on earth to forgive sins, forgive me so that I may be made new, and judged righteous when I am before you. Let my soul come into your hands spotless and pure as an offering to you.

Gregory of Nyssa

✦ 61 ✦

EAT AND DRINK
OF THE LORD

On the last and greatest day of the festival, Jesus stood and said in a loud
voice, "Let anyone who is thirsty come to me and drink." (John 7:37)

The Lord Jesus Christ is the fountain of life, and accordingly he invites us to drink him in, as from a fountain. Whoever loves him, drinks him. The one who is filled with the Word of God drinks of Christ, and so does the one who fully loves and desires him. The one burning with the love of wisdom drinks of him.

For the Lord is sweet and pleasing, and it is right to eat and drink of him but remain ever hungry and thirsty, since he can never be consumed entirely. Though he can be eaten, he is never consumed; he is never diminished by what we take, because his bread is eternal and his fountain is everlasting.

The prophet says, "You who thirst, go to the fountain" (Isa. 55:1). He is the fountain for those who are thirsty but are never satisfied by earthly drink. Therefore he called to himself the hungry who were never satisfied with their food and drink, and raised them to a blessed state where their hunger and thirst are satisfied.

If you thirst, drink from the fountain of life; if you are hungry, eat the bread of life. You are blessed if you hunger for this bread and thirst for this fountain, for in so doing you will desire to eat and drink forever. What you will eat and drink is perfectly sweet and your appetite for more will never be quenched. It is tasted forever, but forever more greatly desired. Hence the prophet-king says, "Taste and see how sweet, how agreeable the LORD is" (Ps. 34:8).

Columbanus

✢ 62 ✢

TITLES OF THE HOLY SPIRIT

*He saved us, not because of righteous things we had done, but because
of his mercy. He saved us through the washing of rebirth and renewal
by the Holy Spirit. (Titus 3:5)*

The titles given to the Holy Spirit stir the soul of anyone who hears them and make him realize that they speak of the Supreme Being. We call him the Spirit of God, the Spirit of Truth who proceeds from the Father, the Steadfast Spirit, the Guiding Spirit. But his first and most appropriate title is the Holy Spirit.

All creatures depend on the Spirit for their sanctification. The Spirit is the source of holiness, a spiritual light, and he enlightens every mind to help it search for the truth. The power of the Spirit fills the whole universe but acts in each person according to the measure of their faith.

Though shared by many, he remains unchanged; his self-giving is no loss to himself. The Spirit is like the sunshine, which permeates the whole atmosphere, and spreads over land and sea, and is enjoyed by each person as if it were shining for him alone. Likewise the Spirit pours out his grace with full power, sufficient for everyone at the same time, while each individual is blessed by his fullness.

The Spirit raises our hearts to heaven, guides the steps of the weak, and brings to perfection those who are making progress. He brings knowledge of Christ to the saved and makes them spiritual by communion with himself.

From the Spirit come foreknowledge of the future, understanding of the mysteries of faith, insight into the hidden meaning of Scripture, and other special gifts. Through the Spirit we become citizens of heaven, enter into eternal happiness, and abide in God. Through the Spirit we acquire a likeness to God.

Basil the Great

✢ 63 ✢

THE SECOND TREE

They killed him by hanging him on a cross, but God raised him
from the dead on the third day. (Acts 10:39–40)

How precious the gift of the cross, how splendid to contemplate! In the cross there is no mingling of good and evil, as in the tree of paradise: it is wholly beautiful to behold and good to taste. The fruit of this tree is not death but life, not darkness but light. This tree does not cast us out of paradise, but opens the way for our return.

This was the tree on which Christ, like a king on a chariot, destroyed the devil, the Lord of death, and freed the human race from his tyranny. This was the tree upon which the Lord, like a brave warrior wounded in his hands, feet, and side, healed the wounds of sin that the evil serpent had inflicted on our nature. A tree once caused our death, but now a tree brings life. Once deceived by a tree, we have now repelled the cunning serpent by a tree. What an astonishing transformation! That death should become life, that decay should become immortality, that shame should become glory! Well might the holy Apostle exclaim: "Far be it from me to glory except in the cross of our Lord Jesus Christ, by which the world has been crucified to me, and I to the world!" (Gal. 6:14). The supreme wisdom that flowered on the cross has shown the folly of worldly wisdom's pride. The knowledge of all good, which is the fruit of the cross, has cut away the shoots of wickedness.

Theodore the Studite

✤ 64 ✤

TEMPTATIONS TO SIN

So with you: Now is your time of grief, but I will see you again and you
will rejoice, and no one will take away your joy. In that day you will
no longer ask me anything. (John 16:22–23)

Suppose you are tempted to file a lawsuit for monetary gain. Imagine your father comes to you and says, "I fathered you and raised you. Partner with me in this evil, and forget the law of Christ," and whatever else an unregenerate sinner would say.

At the same time, imagine the Savior comes to you and says, "You were born into sin and were dead, and I regenerated you. I freed you, healed you, and ransomed you. I will show you the face of the Father. Call no one on earth your father. Let the dead bury the dead (Luke 9:60), but follow me. For I will give you a rest of profound and unspeakable blessings, which no eye has seen, nor ear heard, nor the heart of man or woman imagined; a rest into which angels desire to look, to see what good things God has prepared for the saints and the children who love him (1 Cor. 2:9; 1 Pet. 1:12). I am the one who feeds you, giving my body as bread and my blood as the drink of immortality, and the one who eats and drinks of this no longer experiences death. I am the teacher of heavenly lessons. I fought with death for you and paid your death for you, which you owed for your sins and unbelief toward God."

After hearing both sides, decide for yourself and cast your vote for your own salvation! Should your brother or sister likewise tempt you to sin, or your child, or spouse, or anyone, let Christ conquer the tempter. For he fights on your behalf.

Clement of Alexandria

⁂ 65 ⁂

FROM THE RULE
OF SAINT BENEDICT

Come, my children, listen to me; I will teach you the fear of the
LORD. . . . Turn from evil and do good; seek peace and pursue it.
(Psalm 34:11, 14)

Whenever you start a good work you should first fervently ask
Christ our Lord to bring it to perfection, and to forget our
past sins, and continue to honor us as his children. We pray this first
so that Christ might not grow impatient with our sins and throw
us into everlasting punishment, like an angry father disinherits his
sons. For we must always give back to him the good things he has
given to us and not act like wicked servants who refuse to follow
him to glory.

Just as there are evil passions and bitter spirits that separate us
from God and lead us to hell, there are also holy passions that guard
us from sin and lead us toward eternal life. Monks should put these
passions into practice by having an abundant love for each other:
that is, they should "surpass each other in mutual esteem" (Rom.
12:10), accept each other's physical and moral weaknesses with
the utmost patience, and compete with each other in humility. No
one should pursue his own good, but instead what seems good for
another (Phil 2:4). They should display brotherly love in a chaste
manner, fear God in a spirit of love, and look up to their abbot with
a genuine and submissive affection. They should put Christ before
everything else—and may he lead us all to everlasting life.

Benedict of Nursia

⊹ 66 ⊹

INVITING CHRIST IN

As Jesus went on from there, he saw a man named Matthew
sitting at the tax collector's booth. "Follow me," he told him,
and Matthew got up and followed him. (Matthew 9:9)

"As he sat at the table in the house, many tax collectors and sinners came and sat down with Jesus and his disciples" (Matt. 9:10). The conversion of one tax collector gave many other sinners an example of repentance and pardon. Notice also how this anticipates Matthew's future status as apostle and teacher of the nations: as soon as he was converted he drew a whole crowd of sinners to him, to follow the same road to salvation. He took up his appointed duties while taking the first steps in the faith, and from that moment he fulfilled his obligation and grew in honor.

Matthew arranges a dinner celebration for the Lord in his earthly home but also sets a banquet for him in his heart, which he provides through faith and love. Our Savior attests to this: "Behold I stand at the door and knock; if anyone hears my voice and opens the door, I will come in and eat with him, and he with me" (Rev. 3:20).

When we hear Christ's voice, we open the door to receive him, meaning that we freely obey his commands and commit ourselves to doing his will. Christ dwells in the hearts of his chosen ones through the grace of his love; he enters so that he might eat with us and we with him. He is always refreshing us by the light of his presence, increasing our devotion to him and longing for heavenly things. He is delighted by the pleasing banquet in our hearts.

Bede the Venerable

✦ 67 ✦

INDESCRIBABLE LOVE

Blessed is the one whose transgressions are forgiven,
whose sins are covered. (Psalm 32:1)

Let the one who has love in Christ keep the commandments of Christ. Who can describe the blessed bond of God's love? What person can describe how exceedingly beautiful it is, with words to match the reality? Love takes us to unimaginable heights. Love unites us to God. Love covers a multitude of sins. Love bears all things and is long-suffering in all things. There is nothing ugly and nothing arrogant in love. Love allows no separations; love causes no rebellions; love does all things in harmony. God's elect have been made perfect through love; without love nothing is pleasing to God. In love the Lord has taken us to himself. Because of the love he had for us, Jesus Christ gave his blood for us according to God's will; he gave his flesh for our flesh and his soul for our souls.

Love is a thing so great and wonderful that its perfection is indescribable with words. Who has merited a gift like this except those to whom God has graciously given it? Considering this, let us request his mercy and pray that we may live blameless in love, free from partialities that favor one person above another.

All generations since Adam up to now have passed away, but those who have been made perfect in love have a place among the saints, and will be revealed at the coming of Christ's kingdom. For it is written, "Enter into your secret chambers for a little while, until my wrath and fury pass away; and I will remember a good day, and will raise you up out of your graves" (Isa. 26:20; Ezek. 37:12). We are blessed if we keep God's commandments in the harmony of love, so that through love our sins may be forgiven.

Clement of Rome

✢ 68 ✢

HOUSE OF PRAYER

Do you not know that your bodies are temples of the Holy Spirit, who is
in you, whom you have received from God? You are not your own.
(1 Corinthians 6:19)

Prayer is like an honored ambassador standing before God. It gives joy to the spirit and peace to the heart. There is a difference between prayer and naked words. Prayer is the longing for God, a love too deep for words, something not natural to man but a gift of God's grace.

When the Lord gives this kind of prayer to someone, he gives him riches that cannot be taken away and heavenly food that satisfies the spirit. If you taste this food you are set on fire with an eternal longing for the Lord; your spirit burns as if it were the most intense fire.

Practice prayer from the beginning. Paint your house with the colors of modesty and humility. Make it radiant with the light of justice. Decorate it with the finest fabrics of good deeds. Build the walls with stones of faith and generosity. Crown it with the pinnacle of prayer. Do this and you will be a perfect dwelling place for the Lord. You will become a splendid palace for him, and through his grace he will live inside you, with his image enthroned in the temple of your spirit.

John Chrysostom

⊷ 69 ⊷

LET THE WORD GO DEEP

The law of the LORD is perfect, refreshing the soul. The statutes of the LORD are trustworthy, making wise the simple. The precepts of the LORD are right, giving joy to the heart. The commands of the LORD are radiant, giving light to the eyes. The fear of the LORD is pure, enduring forever. The decrees of the LORD are firm, and all of them are righteous.
(Psalm 19:7–9)

No one can understand Holy Scripture without constant reading, according to the words: "Love her and she will exalt you. Embrace her and she will glorify you" (Prov. 4:8).

The more you devote yourself to a study of the sacred utterances, the richer your understanding of them will be, just as the more the soil is tilled, the richer the harvest.

Some people have great mental powers but cannot be bothered with reading; what reading could have taught them is devalued by their neglect. Others have a desire to know but are hampered by their slow mental processes; yet application to reading will teach them things that the clever fail to learn through laziness.

The person who is slow to grasp things but tries hard is rewarded; equally, whoever does not cultivate their God-given intellectual ability is condemned for despising their gifts and sinning by sloth.

Learning unsupported by grace may get into our ears, but it never reaches the heart. It makes a great noise outside but serves no inner purpose. But when God's grace touches our innermost minds to bring understanding, his Word, which has been received by the ear, sinks deep into the heart.

Isidore of Seville

✢ 70 ✢

ACTIONS SHOULD MATCH OUR WORDS

Then I will teach transgressors your ways,
so that sinners will turn back to you. (Psalm 51:13)

Why is the Lord's name blasphemed? Because we say one
thing and do another. When they hear the words of God
on our lips, unbelievers are amazed at their beauty and power, but
when they see that those words have no effect in our lives, their
admiration turns to scorn, and they dismiss such words as myths
and fairy tales.

They listen, for example, when we tell them that God has said,
"It is no credit to you if you love those who love you, but only if you
love your enemies, and those who hate you" (Matt. 5:44, 46). They
are full of admiration at such extraordinary virtue, but when they
observe that we not only fail to love people who hate us, but even
those who love us, they laugh at us, and the Name is blasphemed.

I believe I have given you good advice. None who follow it will
regret doing so but will save both their own souls and mine, since
I have been their counselor. The reward is great for converting an
erring soul and saving it from perishing.

To make sure that none of us is lost, we must repent from the
bottom of our hearts. Since we have been commanded to go out and
rescue idolaters and to instruct them, is it not even more important
to save souls who already know God? For all to be saved, we have
to help one another and support the weak in their struggle to live a
good life. When one of us does wrong, the others should warn and
persuade the wrongdoer of his or her error.

Second-Century Writer

✢ 71 ✢

GOD SUSTAINS FAITH

"Where did this man get these things?" they asked.
"What's this wisdom that has been given him? What are these
remarkable miracles he is performing?" (Mark 6:2)

I give unceasing thanks to my God, who kept me faithful in the day of my testing. Today I can offer him sacrifice with confidence, giving myself as a living victim to Christ, my Lord, who kept me safe through all my trials. I can say now, "Who am I, Lord, and what is my calling, that you worked through me with such divine power? You did all this so that today among the Gentiles I might constantly rejoice and glorify your name wherever I may be, both in prosperity and in adversity. You did it so that, whatever happened to me, I might accept good and evil equally, always giving thanks to God."

God showed me how to have faith in him forever, as one who is never to be doubted. He answered my prayer in such a way that in the last days, ignorant though I am, I might be bold enough to take up so holy and so wonderful a task and imitate in some degree the heralds of his Gospel, whom the Lord had long ago foretold would bear witness to all nations.

How did I get this wisdom, which was not mine before? I did not know the number of my days or have knowledge of God. How did such a great and salutary gift come to me, the gift of knowing and loving God, though at the cost of homeland and family? I came to the Irish peoples to preach the Gospel and endure the taunts of unbelievers, putting up with reproaches about my earthly pilgrimage, suffering many persecutions, even bondage, and losing my birthright of freedom for the benefit of others.

Patrick

⊹ 72 ⊹

HIS YOKE IS EASY

*The LORD, the LORD, the compassionate and gracious God, slow
to anger, abounding in love and faithfulness, maintaining love to
thousands, and forgiving wickedness, rebellion and sin.
(Exodus 34:6–7)*

To give the lesson of God's will to save us, Christ revived
the man who had been left stripped and half-dead from his
wounds after falling into the hands of the brigands; he poured wine
and oil on the wounds, bandaged them, placed the man on his own
mule, and brought him to an inn, where he left sufficient money to
have him cared for, and promised to repay any further expense on
his return.

Again, he told how the Father, who is goodness itself, was
moved with pity for his reckless son who returned and made
amends by repentance; how he embraced him, dressed him once
more in the fine garments that matched his own dignity, and did
not reproach him for any of his sins.

Further, when he found the one sheep that had strayed from
God's flock, wandering in the mountains and hills, he brought it
back to the fold, but not by driving it to exhaustion. Instead, he
placed it on his own shoulders and compassionately restored it
safely to the flock.

So also he cried out, "Come to me, all you that toil and are heavy
of heart. Accept my yoke" (Matt. 11:28–29), by which he meant
his commands, or rather, the whole way of life that he taught us in
the Gospel. He then speaks of a burden, but that is only because
repentance seems difficult. In fact, however, "My yoke is easy," he
assures us, "and my burden is light" (Matt. 11:30).

Maximus the Confessor

✦ 73 ✦

PATIENCE WITH WRETCHES LIKE US (I)

I have seen another evil under the sun, and it weighs heavily on mankind: God gives some people wealth, possessions and honor, so that they lack nothing their hearts desire, but God does not grant them the ability to enjoy them, and strangers enjoy them instead. This is meaningless, a grievous evil. (Ecclesiastes 6:1–2)

I desired honor, money, and marriage, but you mocked me. I suffered as these desires went unfulfilled, which was a clear grace from your hand, as you would not allow me to grow fond of anything but you.

Look into my heart, Lord, as you have willed that I should recall all this and confess to you. Let my soul cleave to you, which you have freed from the poison of death. How wretched it was! You irritated my despair, so that at all cost I would be converted to you and healed by you, who are above all and sustain all.

How wretched I was at that time, and how lovingly you dealt with me, to make me aware of my wretchedness, especially the day I was preparing a speech praising the emperor, in which I intended to lie repeatedly, and which lies were to be applauded by those who knew I lied. My heart was stricken with worry, and my mind consumed in its thoughts. [Continued in next entry ...]

Augustine

❖ 74 ❖

PATIENCE WITH WRETCHES LIKE US (II)

A person can do nothing better than to eat and drink and find satisfaction in their own toil. This too, I see, is from the hand of God, for without him, who can eat or find enjoyment? (Ecclesiastes 2:24–25)

But then, while walking along one of the streets of Milan, I observed a poor beggar — whose belly was full at the time — joking and joyous. I sighed and spoke to my friends about the many sorrows resulting from our stupidity, and that for all the stress we endure by dragging our unhappiness about in search for true happiness, prodded by various desires, we merely magnify our unhappiness, all in an effort to gain what the beggar easily attained, and what we probably would never get! For what he had obtained through a few coins thrown to him, I was scheming for by sinful and pathetic actions: the joy of a temporary happiness. Obviously he did not have true joy, but I was seeking an even falser joy. And the truth is that he was joyous, and I anxious; he was free from care, and I full of worry.

And if anyone asked me if I would rather be merry or fearful, I would reply, "Merry." If I were asked if I would rather be the beggar or myself, I would have said, "Myself," but only out of perversity and ignorance. For I should prefer to be joyous and uneducated rather than miserable and learned, as I was. And my learning was employed for pleasing men and not for teaching. Therefore you broke my bones with the rod of your correction.

Augustine

⚜ 75 ⚜

BAPTISM

And this water symbolizes baptism that now saves you also—not the removal of dirt from the body but the pledge of a clear conscience toward God. It saves you by the resurrection of Jesus Christ. (1 Peter 3:21)

Through Christ we received new life and we consecrated ourselves to God. Those who believe that what we teach is true, and who give assurance of their ability to live according to that teaching, are taught to ask God's forgiveness for their sins by prayer and fasting, and we pray and fast with them. We then lead them to a place where there is water and they are reborn: they are washed in the water in the name of God, the Father and Lord of the whole universe, of our Savior Jesus Christ, and of the Holy Spirit. This is done because Christ said, "Unless you are born again you will not enter the kingdom of heaven" (John 3:3).

The apostles taught us the reason for this ceremony of ours. Our first birth took place without our consent, and we grew up in the midst of wickedness. So in order not to remain children of necessity and ignorance, we need a new birth of which we would be conscious, and which would be our own free choice. We need, too, to have our sins forgiven. This is why the name of God, the Father and Lord of the whole universe, is pronounced in the water over anyone who chooses to be born again and who has repented of his sins. We call upon God by this name alone, for God so far surpasses our powers of description that no one can give a name to him.

The person receiving this enlightenment is also baptized in the name of Jesus Christ, who was crucified under Pontius Pilate, and in the name of the Holy Spirit, who through the prophets foretold everything concerning Jesus.

Justin Martyr

✛ 76 ✛

VANITY OF WORDS
AND WEALTH (I)

Guard your steps when you go to the house of God.
Go near to listen rather than to offer the sacrifice of fools,
who do not know that they do wrong. (Ecclesiastes 5:1)

It is a good thing to only speak a little and to speak from a calm and rightly balanced heart. For it is not right to say things that are foolish and absurd, or anything that happens to cross your mind. We ought to know and reflect on the fact that, though we are far from heaven, we speak in God's hearing and that it is good for us to speak without offense. For just as all kinds of dreams and visions result from a distracted mind, so too is senseless talking the result of foolishness.

Moreover, make sure that the promises you make with a vow are fulfilled, since a property of fools is their unreliability. So be true to your word, since it is better not to promise or vow to do something than it is to promise something and fail to do it. And you should by all means avoid using ugly and profane words, knowing that God will hear them. The men and women who use their mouths to sin give God an excuse to wipe out their lives. Just as constantly day-dreaming is vanity, so is babbling all the time.

The fear of God is humanity's salvation, though it is rarely found. Therefore, do not be surprised when you see the poor being oppressed or judges prosecuting the innocent. [Continued in next entry ...]

Gregory Thaumaturgus

⊹ 77 ⊹

VANITY OF WORDS
AND WEALTH (II)

Everyone comes naked from their mother's womb,
and as everyone comes, so they depart. (Ecclesiastes 5:15)

Of course property acquired by violence is a dangerous and unholy possession, but even lusting after money will bring a man no satisfaction, nor love from his neighbors, even if he ends up rich. This is also vanity. However, goodness brings joy to whoever strives for it, makes them strong, and allows them to see the truth in all things.

It is important to remember that the pursuit of wealth always causes anxiety. A poor man or woman, even if they are a slave and unable to feed themselves, can at least enjoy sleep; but lusting after money will cause sleepless nights and mental anxieties. And what could be more absurd than enduring the trouble to gather wealth and the worry over keeping it, only to guarantee more evils coming into your life?

Moreover, this wealth will be gone at some point or another, whether a person has children or not; and every person is doomed to die, despite their wishes, and will return to the earth in the same condition in which they were born. The fact that they are destined to leave the earth empty-handed will make their pursuits all the more pathetic: they fail to consider that an end is appointed for life, and that they toil for no good reason, and labor on behalf of the wind instead of their own real interest, and waste their whole lives with sin, irrationality, and anxiety.

On the other hand, it is one of God's gifts that a person is able to gladly reap the fruit of their labor and receive rightfully gained possessions from God. This person is neither afflicted with troubles nor a slave of evil thoughts, but spends their lives doing good deeds, having a hopeful heart, and rejoicing in God's gifts.

Gregory Thaumaturgus

✛ 78 ✛

LOVING OUR ENEMIES

Jesus asked him, "Judas, are you betraying the Son of Man with a kiss?" (Luke 22:48)

Christ showed us a wonderful tolerance for evil done against him when he kissed the traitor Judas and even spoke kind words to him. He did not say what he could have said: "You despicable traitor! Is this how you pay me back for the great kindness I am doing for you?" But amazingly he simply says, "Judas," using his proper name, the address used by someone with compassion for the other person, not an address of anger. And he did not call himself, "your Master, the Lord, your helper," but instead simply said, "the Son of Man," that is, the tender and meek one. It was as if he meant to say, "Even if I was not your Master and Lord, would you still betray someone so innocent and with such affection for you? Someone who loved you so much that he kisses you at the moment of your betrayal, a kiss which you arranged to be the signal of your treachery?" Blessed are you, Lord! What a great example of endurance of evil, and of humility, you have shown us in yourself.

Sometimes spiritual wounds are incurable. It is as if the sense of hearing within the wound were dead, because it is not moved to change by exhortations addressed to it — not because it cannot, but because it will not. This was what happened in the case of Judas. And yet Christ, although he knew all these things beforehand, did not at any time stop offering his counsel and love to Judas. Therefore we should follow this example and seek to recover those who have strayed from the flock, even if it appears that our counsels are doing no good.

Dionysius of Alexandria

⊹ 79 ⊹

THE BENEFITS
OF READING SCRIPTURE

All Scripture is God-breathed and is useful for teaching, rebuking,
correcting and training in righteousness, so that the servant of God may
be thoroughly equipped for every good work. (2 Timothy 3:16–17)

Prayer purifies us, reading instructs us. Both are good when both are possible. Otherwise, prayer is better than reading.

If a man wants to be always in God's company, he must pray regularly and read regularly. When we pray, we talk to God; when we read, God talks to us.

All spiritual growth comes from reading and reflection. By reading we learn what we did not know; by reflection we retain what we have learned.

Reading the Holy Scriptures confers two benefits. It trains the mind to understand them; it turns people's attention from the follies of the world and leads them to the love of God.

Two kinds of study are called for here. We must first learn how the Scriptures are to be understood, and then see how to expound them with profit and in a manner worthy of them. People must first be eager to understand what they are reading before they are fit to proclaim what they have learned.

The conscientious readers will be more concerned to carry out what they have read than merely to acquire knowledge of it. For a smaller sin is being ignorant of virtue, and a bigger sin failing to practice the virtue we know. In reading we aim at knowing, but we must put into practice what we have learned in our course of study.

Isidore of Seville

⊰ 80 ⊱

SPEAKING TRUTH

For the lips of a priest ought to preserve knowledge, because he is
the messenger of the LORD Almighty and people seek instruction
from his mouth. (Malachi 2:7)

A spiritual guide should be silent when discretion requires it and speak when words are of service. Unwise speech can lead people into error, and an unwise silence can leave in error those who could have been taught. Pastors will hesitate to say what is right because they fear losing the favor of people. Such leaders are not zealous pastors who protect their flocks, but are like mercenaries who flee when wolves appear and take refuge in silence.

Defending the flock and advancing against the enemy require bold resistance to the powers of this world. To stand fast in battle on the day of the Lord means opposing the wicked enemy out of love for what is right.

The Lord says to his unfaithful people, "Your prophets saw false and foolish visions and did not point out your wickedness, that you might repent of your sins" (Lam. 2:14). The Word of God accuses them of seeing false visions because they are afraid to reproach people for their faults, and therefore give their flock an empty promise of safety. Because they fear people and not God, they keep silent and fail to point out sinners' wrongdoing.

Anyone appointed a pastor undertakes the task of preaching, so that with his voice he might prepare his people before the terrible judge comes. But if he does not know how to preach, what will this mute say to his people? This was the message the Holy Spirit conveyed when he descended in the form of tongues on the first pastors, for he causes whomever he has filled to speak out spontaneously.

Gregory the Great

✢ 81 ✢

WEALTH IN SERVICE
TO RIGHTEOUSNESS

They sold property and possessions to give to anyone who had need.
(Acts 2:45)

Money that benefits our neighbors should not be thrown away. Money is a possession because it is possessed, and it is a good because it is useful and given to us by God for our use. It is in our hands, and under our power, and is a material instrument for good purposes for someone who knows how to use it. If you use it skillfully, it is a benefit; but if you lack skill, your money itself is not to blame. This is the nature of the instrument of wealth.

Are you able to use money well? Then it is a servant of righteousness. Do you use it poorly? In this case it is a minister of wrongdoing. Its nature is to be subservient, not to rule. So anything that is neither good nor evil in itself should not be blamed, but whatever has the power to voluntarily choose good or evil is responsible for a thing's use. The mind of humankind is what has the power to judge and choose, and has freedom and self-determination regarding how it treats other things.

So do not destroy your wealth, but instead destroy the passions in your soul, which make your use of money turn sinful. This way, as you become virtuous and good, you can make good use of your money. The rejection and selling of all possessions I therefore understand as referring to the sinful passions of the soul.

Clement of Alexandria

✢ 82 ✢

KEEP YOUR EYES ON CHRIST

The wise have eyes in their heads, while the fool walks in the darkness.
(Ecclesiastes 2:14)

You can see no darkness if you are surrounded by light; likewise, you can see no trivialities if your eyes are on Christ. When your eyes are on the head and origin of the whole universe, they look at virtue in all its perfection; they see truth, justice, immortality, and everything else that is good, for Christ is goodness itself.

People are often considered stupid and useless when they pursue the supreme Good through intense contemplation of God, but Paul boasted of this and admitted he was a fool for Christ's sake. The reason he said "We are fools for Christ's sake" (1 Cor. 4:10) was that his mind was free from all earthly preoccupations. It was as though he said, "We are blind to the life here below because our eyes are raised toward the one who is our head."

And so, without board or lodging, he traveled from place to place, destitute, naked, exhausted by hunger and thirst. When people saw him in captivity, flogged, shipwrecked, led about in chains, they could hardly help thinking that he was a pitiable sight. Nevertheless, even while he suffered all this at the hands of humans, he always looked toward his head and asked, "What can separate us from the love of Christ? Can affliction or distress? Can persecution, hunger, nakedness, danger or death?" (Rom. 8:35). In other words, "What can force me to take my eyes from Christ and to turn them toward hateful things?"

He bids us follow his example: "Seek the things that are above" (Col. 3:1), which is another way of saying, "Keep your eyes on Christ."

Gregory of Nyssa

✣ 83 ✣

RUN TO THE LIGHT

Dear friends, now we are children of God, and what we will be has not yet been made known. But we know that when Christ appears, we shall be like him, for we shall see him as he is. (1 John 3:2)

When all Scriptures are no longer necessary for our illumination, and when we, with the prophets and apostles, shall together behold the true and precious light without such written aids, what shall we see? With what shall our minds be nourished? What will give joy to our gaze? From where will the gladness come which eye has not seen and ear has not heard, which has not even been conceived by the heart of man (1 Cor. 2:9)? What shall we see?

I implore you to live with me, believe with me, and run with me; let us long for the heavenly country, let us sigh for our heavenly home, let us truly feel that we are strangers here. What shall we see there? You will come to the fountain, with whose water you have already been sprinkled. Instead of the ray of light that was sent into your twisted and darkened heart, you will see the light itself in all its purity and brightness. You are being cleansed now in order to see and experience this light.

I feel that your spirits are being raised up with mine to the heavens above. I am about to lay aside this book, and you are soon going away, each to his own place. It has been good for us to share the common light, good to have enjoyed ourselves, good to have been glad together. When we part from one another, let us not depart from him.

Augustine

✢ 84 ✢

EVEN THE WATCHMEN NEED MERCY (I)

No one serving as a soldier gets entangled in civilian affairs,
but rather tries to please his commanding officer. (2 Timothy 2:4)

"Son of man, I have made you a watchman for the house of Israel" (Ezek. 3:17). Note that a man whom the Lord sends forth as a preacher is called a watchman. A watchman always stands up high so that he can see what is coming from far off. Anyone appointed to be a watchman for the people must stand at this height for all his life to help them by his foresight.

It is very hard for me to say this, because with these very words I denounce myself. I cannot preach with any competence, and even if I sometimes do succeed, I still struggle to live my life according to my own preaching.

I am forced to consider the affairs of the church and the monasteries. I must weigh the lives and acts of individuals. I am responsible for the concerns of our citizens. I must worry about the invasions of roving bands of barbarians and beware of the wolves that lie in wait for my flock. I must act as an administrator in order to have my people fed continuously. I must put up with robbers and cheats without losing patience, and at times I must deal with them in total charity. [Continued in next entry ...]

Gregory the Great

✢ 85 ✢

EVEN THE WATCHMEN NEED MERCY (II)

Preach the word; be prepared in season and out of season; correct, rebuke and encourage—with great patience and careful instruction.
(2 Timothy 4:2)

I do not deny my responsibility; I recognize that I am slothful and negligent, but perhaps if I acknowledge my faults the just judge will pardon me. Back when I was in the monastery, I could curb my pointless talking and usually become absorbed in my prayers. Since I assumed the burden of pastoral care, my mind can no longer be relaxed; it is concerned with so many different things!

With my mind divided and torn to pieces by so many problems, how can I meditate or preach wholeheartedly without neglecting the ministry of proclaiming the Gospel? Moreover, in my position I often have to communicate with worldly men. At times I speak freely with them about worldly things, since if I am always severely judging them then they would avoid me, and I could never effect a good change in them. As a result I often listen patiently to chatter. And because I too am weak, I find myself drawn little by little into meaningless conversation, and I begin to talk about matters that at one time I would have avoided. What once I found tedious I now enjoy!

So who am I to be a watchman, for I do not stand on the mountain of action but lie down in the valley of weakness? Thank the Lord that the all-powerful Creator and Redeemer of humankind can give me convincing and effective speech in spite of my weaknesses; and because I love him, I do not hesitate to speak of him.

Gregory the Great

✢ 86 ✢

THE GLORIFICATION OF THE BODY

For we know that since Christ was raised from the dead, he cannot die again; death no longer has mastery over him. (Romans 6:9)

The dead, now under the dominion of him who has risen to life, are no longer dead but alive. When believers are raised from the dead and freed from decay, they shall never again see death, for they will share in Christ's resurrection just as he himself shared in their death.

Do not let the fact that people still die and bodies still decay in death impact your faith. For in Christ we have received the first-fruits and have received the pledge of all the blessings to come; with Christ we have already reached the heights of heaven and have taken our place beside the one who has raised us up with himself, as Paul says: "In Christ God has raised us up with him, and has made us sit with him in the heavenly places" (Eph. 2:6).

The fulfillment is coming and will be ours on the day predetermined by the Father. For this is the decree of the Father of the ages: the gift, once given, is secure, so do not doubt it!

I need not remind you that the Lord rose from the dead with a spiritual body, since Paul bears witness that our bodies are "sown as animal bodies" and "raised as spiritual bodies" (1 Cor. 15:44). We will share in Christ's glorious transfiguration, as he has kindly gone before us as our leader.

He has already brought his own body to the Father as the first-fruits of our nature — he will also bring the whole body to fulfillment. For he promised this when he said: "I, when I am lifted up, will draw all men to myself" (John 12:32).

Anastasius of Antioch

✦ 87 ✦

PRAYER IS POWERFUL

True worshipers will worship the Father in the Spirit and in truth, for
they are the kind of worshipers the Father seeks. (John 4:23)

Prayer is the spiritual offering that has done away with the sacrifices of old.

We are true worshipers and true priests. We pray in spirit, and so offer in spirit the sacrifice of prayer. Prayer is an offering that belongs to God and is acceptable to him: it is the offering he has asked for, the offering he planned as his own.

We must dedicate this offering with our whole heart, we must fatten it on faith, tend it by truth, keep it unblemished through innocence and clean through chastity, and crown it with love. We must escort it to the altar of God in a procession of good works to the sound of psalms and hymns. Then it will gain for us all that we ask of God.

Since God asks for prayer offered in spirit and in truth, how can he deny anything to this kind of prayer? How great is the evidence of its power, as we read and hear and believe!

In former times, prayer was able to rescue from fire and beasts and hunger, even before it received its perfection from Christ. How much greater then is the power of Christian prayer? No longer does prayer bring an angel of comfort to the heart of a fiery furnace, or close up the mouths of lions, or transport food from the fields to the hungry. But it gives the armor of patience to those who suffer, who feel pain, who are distressed. It strengthens the power of grace, so that faith may know what it is gaining from the Lord, and understand what it is suffering for the name of God.

Tertullian

✥ 88 ✥

BE LIKE THE SHEPHERD

Again Jesus said, "Simon son of John, do you love me?"
He answered, "Yes, Lord, you know that I love you."
Jesus said, "Take care of my sheep." (John 21:16)

You were made in the image of God. If you wish to resemble him, then follow his example. Since the very name *Christian* is a profession of God's love for humanity, imitate the love of Christ.

Reflect for a moment on the wealth of his kindness. Before he came as a man to live among us, he sent John the Baptist to preach repentance and to teach its practice. John himself was preceded by the prophets, who taught the people to repent, to return to God, and to amend their lives. Then Christ himself came, and with his own lips cried out: "Come to me, all you who labor and are overburdened, and I will give you rest" (Matt. 11:28). How did he receive those who listened to his call? He readily forgave them their sins; he freed them instantly from all that troubled them. The Word made them holy; the Spirit set his seal on them. The old Adam was buried in the waters of baptism; the new man was reborn in the power of grace.

What was the result? Those who had been God's enemies became his friends, those estranged from him became his sons and daughters, those who did not know him came to worship and love him.

So let us be shepherds like the Lord. We must meditate on the Gospel, and as we witness Christ's example of compassion and loving kindness, we will become learned in these virtues.

Asterius of Amasea

⤙ 89 ⤚

HOPE IN THE UNSEEN

*"But," he said, "you cannot see my face,
for no one may see me and live." (Exodus 33:20)*

Along the seacoast, you may see mountains facing the sea. At the top a projection forms a ledge overhanging the depths below. If a person were to look down from that ledge, he or she would be overcome by dizziness. In the same way my soul grows dizzy when it hears the voice of the Lord saying, "Blessed are the pure of heart, for they shall see God" (Matt. 5:8).

The vision of God is offered to those who have purified their hearts. Yet no one has seen God at any time. The words of Saint John confirm this (John 1:18; 1 John 4:12), and they are echoed in Saint Paul's lofty thought (1 Tim. 6:16). God is that smooth, steep, and sheer rock, where the mind can find no secure resting place or get a grip to lift ourselves up. In the view of Moses, he is inaccessible. In spite of every effort, our minds cannot approach him. We are cut off by the words, "No man can see God and live" (Ex. 33:20). And yet, to see God is eternal life. But John, Paul, and Moses, pillars of our faith, all testify that it is impossible to see God. My soul is dizzy contemplating the depths of these statements! If God is life, then if you do not see God you do not see life. Yet God cannot be seen; the apostles and prophets, inspired by the Holy Spirit, have testified to this. What hope does humanity have?

Yet God does raise and sustain our faltering hopes. He rescued Peter from drowning and made the sea into a firm surface beneath his feet (Matt. 14:29 – 31). He does the same for us; the hands of the Word are stretched out to us when we are out of our depth, struck by waves, and lost in speculation. Grasped firmly in his hands, we shall be without fear.

Gregory of Nyssa

✤ 90 ✤

VINCENT, DEACON AND MARTYR

I have told you these things, so that in me you may have peace.
In this world you will have trouble. But take heart!
I have overcome the world. (John 16:33)

Remember how Christ our Lord in the Gospel exhorted his disciples. The very King of martyrs equips his troops with spiritual weapons, explains their battles, offers them support, and promises them their reward.

You will suffer persecution in this world, but it cannot overwhelm you and cannot overcome you. The world sets up a twofold battle line against Christ's army: temptations to lead us astray and terrors to break our spirit. Hence if pleasures do not hold us captive, and if brutality does not frighten us, then the world is overcome. On both fronts Christ rushes to our aid, and the Christian is not conquered. If you think of Vincent's martyrdom as only human endurance, then his act is unbelievable from the outset. But first recognize the power to be from God, and it ceases to be a source of wonder.

Savagery was being unleashed upon the martyr's body while serenity came from his lips—harsh cruelties were being inflicted on his limbs while assurance rang out in his words—so that it appears that by some miracle one person suffered while another spoke peacefully. And in fact this was true: another person was speaking. Christ promises this to those who would suffer for him, for he said, "Do not give thought to how or what you are to speak. For it is not you who speaks, but the Spirit of your Father who speaks within you" (Matt. 10:19–20). So as the Spirit spoke through him, his enemies were confused and convicted, and his flesh was strengthened and comforted.

Augustine

⭒ 91 ⭒

GOD ADORNS US WITH GOOD WORKS

For we are God's handiwork, created in Christ Jesus to do good works, which God prepared in advance for us to do. (Ephesians 2:10)

So what shall we do, brothers and sisters? Should we become lazy in doing good, and stop practicing love? God forbid us to follow such a course! Instead let us eagerly seek to perform every good work, with our minds ready.

For the Lord himself rejoices in his works. By his infinitely great power he established the heavens, and by his incomprehensible wisdom he populated them with stars and planets. He also divided the earth from the surrounding water and anchored it to the immovable foundation of his own will. The animals that live upon it were commanded into existence by his Word. Likewise, when he had formed the sea and the living creatures within it, he established their proper boundaries by his power.

Most amazing of all, with his holy and undefiled hands he formed man and woman, who are the most excellent of his creatures; and they were blessed with God's own image. For God said, "Let us make man in our image, and after our likeness. So God made man; male and female he created them" (Gen. 1:26–27). Having finished these things, he approved them and blessed them, and said, "Increase and multiply" (Gen. 1:28).

It is clear, then, how all righteous people have been adorned with good works and how the Lord adorns himself with his works and rejoices in them. With this example guiding us, let us not delay to do the Lord's will and pursue the work of righteousness with all our strength.

Clement of Rome

✢ 92 ✢

PRAYER IS SPIRITUAL FOOD

Rejoice always, pray continually, give thanks in all circumstances; for this is God's will for you in Christ Jesus. (1 Thessalonians 5:16–18)

Prayer and communion with God is a supreme good: it is a partnership and union with God. Just as the eyes of the body are enlightened when they see light, our spirit is lit up by his infinite light when it is intent on God. I do not mean the rote prayers said without thinking, but prayer from the heart, not confined to a schedule, but continuous throughout the day and night.

Our spirit should be eager to reach out toward God not only in meditation, but also when it is doing its everyday activities, caring for the needy, performing works of charity, and giving generously to the ministries of others. Our spirit should long for God and call him to mind, so that our works may be seasoned with the salt of God's love, so our offerings to the Lord are flavorful. We can enjoy the benefits of prayer in every aspect of our lives if we devote ourselves to it.

Prayer casts light on our spirit, gives true knowledge of God, and mediates between God and people. Prayer raises the spirit up to heaven, where it tenderly clings to God and cries for the milk that only God can provide. Prayer turns to God for its satisfaction and receives better gifts than anything the world can offer.

John Chrysostom

✤ 93 ✤

CHRIST IS VICTIM AND PRIEST

God himself will provide the lamb for the burnt offering, my son.
(Genesis 22:8)

Isaac himself carries the wood for his own holocaust: this is a figure of Christ. For Christ carried the burden of the cross himself, and yet to carry the wood for the holocaust is really the duty of the priest. So Christ is then both victim and priest. This is the meaning of the expression "they set out together" (Gen. 22:6). For when Abraham, who was to perform the sacrifice, carried the fire and the knife, Isaac did not walk behind him, but with him. In this way he showed that he exercised the priesthood equally with Abraham.

What happened next? "Isaac spoke to his father Abraham, 'Father' he said" (Gen. 22:7). This plea from the son was at that instant the voice of temptation. Do you not think the voice of the son who was about to be sacrificed struck a responsive chord in the heart of the father? Although Abraham did not waver because of his faith, he responded with a voice full of affection.

The careful yet loving response of Abraham moves me greatly. I do not know what he saw in spirit, because he did not speak of the present but of the future: "God himself will provide the lamb." His son asks what is to happen now, but Abraham's reply concerns the future. Indeed the Lord himself provided a lamb, in Christ.

God emulates man with magnificent generosity. Abraham offered to God his mortal son who did not die; God gave up his immortal Son who died for all of us. Therefore, Christ himself is both victim and priest according to the spirit. For he offers the victim to the Father according to the flesh, and he is himself offered on the altar of the cross.

Origen

❖ 94 ❖

CAST YOUR CARES ON HIM

But those who hope in the LORD will renew their strength.
They will soar on wings like eagles; they will run and not
grow weary, they will walk and not be faint. (Isaiah 40:31)

There is good reason for my solid hope in Christ, because you, Father, will heal all my weaknesses through him, who sits at your right hand and intercedes for us. If it were not so, I would despair, for my many weaknesses are severe; but even more severe is your healing power. We would be in despair if we thought that you were far from us, and if your Word had not become flesh and lived among us. I was once filled with terror by my sins and burdened with misery and was turning over in my mind a plan to flee into solitude; but you forbade me and strengthened me by your words: "For this purpose Christ died for all, that they who are alive might not live for themselves but for him who died for them" (2 Cor. 5:15).

I cast my care upon you, Lord, so that I may live, and "I will contemplate the wonders you have revealed" (Ps. 40:5). You know how stupid and weak I am: teach me and heal me. Your only Son, "in whom are hidden all treasures of wisdom and knowledge" (Col. 2:3), has redeemed me with his blood. "Let not the proud disparage me" (Ps. 123:4), for I am mindful of my ransom. I eat it, I drink it, I dispense it to others, and as a poor man I long to be filled along with those who are fed. And then, "let those who seek him praise the LORD" (Ps. 22:26).

Augustine

✛ 95 ✛

POSSESSIONS SHOULD NOT POSSESS

*My prayer is not that you take them out of the world but that you
protect them from the evil one. They are not of the world,
even as I am not of it. (John 17:15–16)*

I want to tell you to forsake everything worldly, but I cannot presume to do that. Yet if you cannot give up everything that you have in this world, at least keep it in such a way that you are not kept prisoner by the world. Whatever you possess must not possess you, and whatever you own must be under your soul's power; for if your soul is overpowered by desire for the things of this world, it will be totally at the mercy of its possessions.

In that regard, we make use of temporal things, but our hearts are set on what is eternal. Temporal goods help us on our way, but our desire must be for those eternal realities, to which we are headed. We should have nothing but a passing interest in what happens in the world, but focus the eyes of our soul on the world to come; our whole attention must be devoted to our goal.

Whatever is evil must be utterly eradicated, wrenched away from both our actions and our thoughts. No sexual immorality, no desire to experience sin, no hint of ambition must keep us from the Lord's table. Even further, our minds should hardly remember even the good deeds we perform in this life. With all this, the physical things which give us pleasure will serve our bodily needs without hindering the soul's progress.

Gregory the Great

⁘ 96 ⁘

PRIEST, SACRIFICE, AND TEMPLE

Otherwise, would they [sacrifices] not have stopped being offered? For the worshipers would have been cleansed once for all, and would no longer have felt guilty for their sins. But those sacrifices are an annual reminder of sins. It is impossible for the blood of bulls and goats to take away sins. (Hebrews 10:2–4)

The animal sacrifices which our forefathers were commanded to offer to God foreshadowed the most acceptable gift of all: the compassionate Son of God offering himself in his human nature for our sake.

The Apostle teaches that Christ "offered himself for us to God as a fragrant offering and sacrifice" (Eph. 5:2). The true God and the true high priest entered the holy of holies for our sake and once for all, taking with him not the blood of bulls and goats, but his own blood. This was foreshadowed by the high priest of old when each year he would take blood and enter the holy of holies.

Christ in himself, and he alone, embodied all that was necessary to achieve our redemption. He is at once priest and sacrifice, God and temple. He is the priest through whom we have been reconciled, the sacrifice by which we have been reconciled, the temple in which we have been reconciled, the God with whom we have been reconciled. He alone is priest, sacrifice, and temple because he is God in the form of a servant; but he is not alone as God, for he is God with the Father and the Holy Spirit.

Fulgentius of Ruspe

⤙ 97 ⤚

IMMENSE LOVE FOR GOD

I love the LORD, for he heard my voice; he heard my cry for mercy.
(Psalm 116:1)

I knew someone who was sad that he could not love God like he wanted to, but who nevertheless loved God so much that his soul was always gripped with desire for God, for God's glory to manifest itself in him, and for him to be nothing in comparison to God. He could not even hear verbal praise or be shown that he loved God well, since his overwhelming humility meant that he never thought of his own dignity or status. He buried any glory that might come his way in the depth of his love for God, so that he only saw himself as a useless servant: he was divorced from a sense of his own dignity by his desire for lowliness. We ought to emulate him: to flee from any honor or glory that is offered to us, for the sake of our immense love for God who has so loved us.

A man like this lives in this life but at the same time does not live in it, for although he still inhabits his body, he is constantly leaving it in spirit because of the love that draws him toward God. Once God's love releases him from self-love, the flame of divine love burns steadily in his heart and he remains united to God by an irresistible longing. As Saint Paul says: "If we are taken out of ourselves it is for the love of God; if we are brought back to our senses it is for your sake" (2 Cor. 5:13).

Diadochus of Photice

✢ 98 ✢

READY TO DIE FOR THE FAITH OF THE NATIONS

Why are you weeping and breaking my heart? I am ready not only to be
bound, but also to die in Jerusalem for the name of the Lord Jesus.
(Acts 21:13)

If I am worthy, I am ready also to give up my life, without hesitation and most willingly, for his name. I want to spend myself in that country, even in death, if the Lord should grant me this favor. I am deeply in his debt, for he gave me the great grace that through me many peoples were reborn in God. They were made perfect by confirmation, and from among this group of new believers clergy were ordained—one people gathered by the Lord from the ends of the earth. As God had prophesied of old through the prophets: "The nations shall come to you from the ends of the earth, and say: 'How false are the idols made by our fathers: they are useless'" (Jer. 16:19). In another prophecy he said: "I have set you as a light among the nations, to bring salvation to the ends of the earth" (Isa. 49:6).

It is among that people that I want to wait for the promise made by him, who assuredly never tells a lie. He makes this promise in the Gospel: "They shall come from the east and west, and sit down with Abraham, Isaac and Jacob" (Matt. 8:11). This is our faith: believers are to come from the whole world.

Patrick

⚜ 99 ⚜

THE LIVING CHRIST

"Aeneas," Peter said to him, "Jesus Christ heals you. Get up and roll
up your mat." Immediately Aeneas got up. (Acts 9:34)

If the gods of the unbelievers are unable to drive Christ away,
then their disbelief in the resurrection has no support of the facts.
Rather, he shows that their gods are truly dead. We agree that a
dead person can do nothing; yet the Savior works mightily every
day, drawing people to religion, persuading them to virtue, teaching them about immortality, increasing their thirst for heavenly
things, revealing the knowledge of the Father, inspiring strength
in the face of death, revealing himself to each, and disarming the
power of idols. The gods and evil spirits of the unbelievers can do
none of these things, but actually become dead at Christ's presence,
and all their showiness is for nothing. By the sign of the cross all
magic is stopped, all sorcery confounded, all the idols abandoned
and deserted, and all senseless pleasure ceases, as the eye of faith
looks up from earth to heaven.

So whom should we call dead? Should we call Christ dead, who
effects all this? But the dead have no power to effect anything. Or
should we call death dead, which effects nothing whatsoever, but
lies as lifeless and ineffective as the evil spirits and idols are? The
Son of God, "living and effective" (Heb. 4:12), is active every day
and effects the salvation of all; but it is proved daily that death is
stripped of all its strength, and it is the idols and evil spirits that are
dead, not he. No room for doubt remains, therefore, concerning the
resurrection of his body.

Athanasius

✢ 100 ✢

CHRIST THE ETERNAL LAMB

*Then came the day of Unleavened Bread on which
the Passover lamb had to be sacrificed. (Luke 22:7)*

We should understand, beloved, that the Easter mystery is at once old and new, transitory and eternal, corruptible and incorruptible, mortal and immortal. In terms of the Law it is old; in terms of the Word it is new. In its figure it is passing, in its grace it is eternal. It is corruptible in the sacrifice of the lamb, incorruptible in the eternal life of the Lord. It is mortal in his burial in the earth, immortal in his resurrection from the dead.

The Law indeed is old, but the Word is new. The type is transitory, but grace is eternal. The lamb was corruptible, but the Lord is incorruptible. He was slain as a lamb; he rose again as God. "He was led like a sheep to the slaughter" (Isa. 53:7; Acts 8:32), yet he was not a sheep. He was silent as a lamb, yet he was not a lamb. The type has passed away; the reality has come. The lamb gives place to God, the sheep gives place to a man, and the man is Christ, who fills the whole of creation. The sacrifice of the lamb, the celebration of the Passover, and the prescriptions of the Law have been fulfilled in Jesus Christ. Under the old Law, and still more under the new dispensation, everything pointed toward him.

Both the Law and the Word came forth from Zion and Jerusalem, but now the Law has given place to the Word, the old to the new. The commandment has become grace, the type a reality. The lamb has become a Son, the sheep a man, and man, God.

Melito of Sardis

✣ 101 ✣

MEDICINE MADE FROM HEAVENLY FRUITS

But the fruit of the Spirit is love, joy, peace, forbearance, kindness, goodness, faithfulness, gentleness and self-control. (Galatians 5:22–23)

Let us deal kindly with our adversaries and persuade them of what is profitable for them. For we do not wish to aggravate, but rather heal; we set no ambush for them, but warn them as our duty demands. Kindness often convinces those whom neither force nor argument will overcome. Our Lord cured with oil and wine the man who, going down from Jerusalem to Jericho, fell among thieves (Luke 10:30–37), instead of treating him with the harsh remedies of the law or the sternness of prophecy.

Let anyone who wishes to be made whole come to him. Treat them with the medicine made in heaven that he has brought down from his Father, having prepared it from the juices of heavenly fruits that do not wither. This is from no earthly plant, for nature does not possess this mixture. For such a wondrous purpose he took our flesh!

How would I have benefited if he had simply bared the arm of his power and only displayed the fullness of his godhead? Why would he have taken human nature upon himself except to be tempted under the condition of my weakness? Mercifully he was tempted, and did suffer with me, with the purpose that I might know how to defeat temptation and how to escape when surrounded.

Peter saw this medicine and left his nets, his instruments of security and gain, and renounced the lusts of the flesh as one might abandon a leaky ship that sinks in the water of many passions. It is truly a mighty remedy, one that not only removes the scar of an old wound, but cuts the root and source of sin. Our faith is richer than all treasure-houses! Our remedy heals our wounds and sins!

Ambrose

❖ 102 ❖

INCREASING OUR CAPACITY FOR CHRIST (I)

But one thing I do: Forgetting what is behind and straining toward
what is ahead, I press on toward the goal to win the prize for which
God has called me heavenward in Christ Jesus. (Philippians 3:13–14)

We have been promised that "we shall be like him, for we shall see him as he is" (1 John 3:2). These words are the best that speech can do, and now we must apply the meditation of the heart. Although they are the words of Saint John, what are they in comparison with the divine reality? And how can we, so greatly inferior to John in wisdom, add anything of our own? But even John tells us that we have received an anointing by the Holy One, who teaches us inwardly more than our tongue can speak. Let us turn to this source of knowledge, building up our desire to see Christ, since it cannot yet be satisfied.

The whole life of a good Christian is in fact an exercise in holy desire. You do not yet see what you long for, but your desire to see him prepares you for when he finally comes, and you may be satisfied.

Imagine you need to fill a container with a large amount of something. You therefore begin the process of stretching your bag or wineskin or whatever it is. Why? Because you know the quantity you will have to put in it and your eyes tell you there is not enough room. By stretching it, therefore, you increase the capacity of the wineskin, and this is how God deals with us. Just by making us wait he increases our desire, which enlarges the capacity of our soul for Christ, enabling it to receive what is soon to be given to us. [Continued in next entry ...]

Augustine

✢ 103 ✢

INCREASING OUR CAPACITY FOR CHRIST (II)

"What no eye has seen, what no ear has heard, and what no human mind has conceived"—the things God has prepared for those who love him. (1 Corinthians 2:9)

By desiring heaven we exercise and expand the powers of our soul. However, this exercise will be effective only to the extent that we free ourselves from infatuation with this world. Let me return to the example I have already used, of filling an empty container. God intends to fill each of you with what is good, so cast out what is bad! If he wishes to fill you with honey and you are full of sour wine, where will the honey go? The vessel must be emptied of its contents and cleaned out. Indeed, it must be cleaned even if you have to work hard and scour it. It must be made fit for the new thing, whatever it may be.

We can go on speaking figuratively of honey, gold, or wine—but whatever analogy we use cannot express the reality we will receive, and that reality is God. As if the sound of that one syllable conveys the full breadth of our heart's desire—whatever we say is always less than the full truth. We must grow ourselves into a container fitting for Christ, so that when he comes he may fill us with his presence. "Then we shall be like him, for we shall see him as he is" (1 John 3:2).

Augustine

✠ 104 ✠

WALK WITH CHRIST TO JERUSALEM

Here is my servant, whom I uphold, my chosen one in whom I delight; I will put my Spirit on him, and he will bring justice to the nations. He will not shout or cry out, or raise his voice in the streets. (Isaiah 42:1–2)

Let us go together to meet Christ on the Mount of Olives. Today he returns from Bethany and proceeds freely toward his holy and blessed passion, to consummate the mystery of our salvation. He came down from heaven to raise us from the depths of sin and now comes of his own free will to make his journey to Jerusalem. Meek and humble, he comes without pomp or ostentation.

Let us accompany him as he approaches his passion, and imitate those who met him then, not by covering his path with garments, olive branches, or palms, but by prostrating ourselves before him through humility and obedience.

In his humility Christ entered the dark regions of our fallen world, with gladness made himself low for our sake, and with gladness lived among us and shared our nature in order to raise us up to himself. His love for man will never rest until he has raised our earthbound nature to glory, and made it one with his own in heaven.

So let us not spread garments or lifeless branches before his feet, which delight the eye for a few hours and then wither, but instead offer ourselves, clothed in his grace. Now that the crimson stains of our sins have been washed away in the saving waters of baptism and we have become white as pure wool, let us present the conqueror of death not with mere branches of palms, but with the real rewards of his victory.

Andrew of Crete

✤ 105 ✤

THE SNARES OF THE FLESH

Can a man scoop fire into his lap without his clothes being burned?
Can a man walk on hot coals without his feet being scorched?
(Proverbs 6:27–28)

If our body has seen the flame, let us not obsess over that flame in our heart. Let us not put this fire into our bones, let us not place chains on ourselves, let us not join in conversation with what might be the cause of unholy desires within us.

Joseph saw the fire when the woman eager for adultery spoke to him (Gen. 39:7). She wished to catch him with her words. She set the snares of her lips but was not able to capture the chaste man. For the voice of modesty, the voice of gravity, the rein of caution, the care for integrity, and the discipline of chastity broke the woman's chains — that unchaste person could not entangle him in her net. The words of a licentious woman are the snares of lust, and her hands the bonds of lust; but his chaste mind could be taken by neither snares nor bonds. Because he did not admit the fire into his mind, his body was not burnt.

Clearly our mind is the cause of our guilt. And so the flesh is innocent but is often the minister of sin. Do not let the desire of beauty overcome you. Many nets and many snares are spread by the devil. The glance of a harlot is a snare for a man who lusts after her. Our own eyes are nets to us, which is why it is written: "Do not be taken with your eyes" (Prov. 6:25). We spread nets for ourselves in which we are entangled and pinned down.

Ambrose

⊹ 106 ⊹

GOD'S MANY GIFTS

What shall I return to the LORD for all his goodness to me?
(Psalm 116:12)

What words can adequately describe God's gifts? They are so numerous that they defy numbering. They are each so great that any of them demands our total gratitude.

But even if our words cannot do them justice, there is one gift which we cannot be silent about. God fashioned man and woman in his own image and likeness; he gave them knowledge of himself; he endowed them with the ability to think, which raised them above all living creatures; he allowed them to delight in the beauties of paradise and gave them dominion over everything upon earth.

Then, when they were deceived by the serpent and fell into sin, suffering, and death, God did not forsake them. He first gave them the law to help them; he set angels over them to guard them; he sent the prophets to denounce vice and to teach virtue; he restrained people's evil and assisted their virtue through warnings and promises. He frequently taught man and woman the ends of vice and virtue through the examples of other people. Moreover, when they continued in disobedience after all this, God did not desert them. No, we were not abandoned by the goodness of the Lord. Even the insults we hurled at our Benefactor by despising his gifts did not lessen his love for us.

Basil the Great

⚜ 107 ⚜

DEATH'S POWER IS BROKEN

Our friend Lazarus has fallen asleep; but I am going there
to wake him up. (John 11:11)

Our faith tells us that whoever believes in Christ will never die; our faith is that Christ is not dead, nor will we ever be. The Lord himself will come down from heaven, the archangel's voice and the trumpet will sound, and those who are united with Christ in death will rise.

The hope of resurrection encourages us because we will see again whomever we lost on earth. He is so powerful that it is easier for him to raise someone from the dead than it is for us to wake someone who is sleeping! Even as we assure ourselves of these things, we burst into tears; we still struggle to trust and hope in Christ. This is the sad human condition; without Christ life is utterly empty.

Death! You separate those who are joined in marriage, and you cruelly divide those who are united in friendship. But your power is broken. Your terrible burden has been destroyed by Christ, who sternly threatened you through Hosea: "Death! I shall be your death" (Hos. 13:14). And we join with the Apostle in deriding you: "Death! Where is your victory? Death! Where is your sting?" (1 Cor. 15:55).

Your conqueror redeemed us. He gave himself over to wicked people in order to transform the wicked into dear friends. It would take too long to narrate all of the comforts that Scripture gives us, but by focusing on the glory of our Redeemer we have sufficient hope for our resurrection. Through faith we know that we are already risen from the dead, as the Apostle writes: "If we have died with Christ, we believe that we are at the same time living with him" (Rom. 6:8).

Braulio

✢ 108 ✢

GRATITUDE
AND GENEROSITY (I)

Every good and perfect gift is from above. (James 1:17)

Recognize to whom you owe the fact that you exist, that you breathe, that you understand, that you are wise, and above all that you know of God and hope for the kingdom of heaven and the vision of glory—now darkly as in a mirror but then with greater fullness and purity (1 Cor. 13:12). You have been made a son or daughter of God, a coheir with Christ. Where did you get all this, and from whom?

Let me turn to what is of less importance: the visible world around us. What benefactor has enabled you to look out upon the beauty of the sky, the sun in its course, the circle of the moon, the countless number of stars, with the harmony and order that they exhibit, like the music of a harp? Who has blessed you with rain, with the art of farming, with different kinds of food, with the arts, with houses, with laws, with states, with a life of humanity and culture, with friendship and the easy familiarity of family?

Who has given you dominion over animals, those that are pets and those that provide you with food? Who has made you lord and master of everything on earth? In short, who has endowed you with all that makes humans superior to all other living creatures?

Is it not God? And is it not he who asks you in turn to be generous above all other creatures and for the sake of all other creatures? We have received so many wonderful gifts from him—will we refuse to give him this one thing, our generosity? Is that not shameful? Though he is God and Lord he is not afraid to be known as our Father. Will we respond by denying our brothers and sisters? [Continued in next entry ...]

Gregory of Nazianzus

⁘ 109 ⁘

GRATITUDE
AND GENEROSITY (II)

*If I have seen anyone perishing for lack of clothing, or the needy
without garments ... then let my arm fall from the shoulder,
let it be broken off at the joint. (Job 31:19, 22)*

Brothers, sisters, and friends, we should not allow ourselves to
misuse what has been given to us by God's gift. If we do, we
will hear Saint Peter say, "Be ashamed of yourselves for holding on
to what belongs to someone else. Resolve to imitate God's justice,
and no one will be poor." We should not labor to heap up and hoard
riches while others remain in need. If we do, the prophet Amos will
speak out against us with sharp and threatening words: "Listen,
you that say: When will the new moon be over, so that we may start
selling? When will the sabbath be over, so that we may start opening our treasures?" (Amos 8:5).

Let us put into practice the supreme and primary law of God.
He sends down rain on just and sinful alike, and causes the sun to
rise on everyone without distinction. To all earth's creatures he has
given the broad earth, the springs, the rivers, and the forests. He
has given the air to the birds, and the waters to those who live in
the water. He has amply given to all creatures the basic needs of
life, not as a private possession, not restricted by law, not divided
by boundaries, but as common to all and in abundance. His gifts
are not deficient in any way, because he wanted to give equal blessings to things equally cherished and to show the abundance of his
generosity.

Gregory of Nazianzus

⊰ 110 ⊱

PREFER NOTHING OVER CHRIST

By myself I can do nothing; I judge only as I hear, and my judgment is just, for I seek not to please myself but him who sent me. (John 5:30)

We add: "Your will be done, on earth as it is in heaven" (Matt. 6:10). Since the devil hinders us from obeying God's will in all things, both in thought and deed, we pray and ask that God's will be done in us. For this to happen, we need God's good will—that is, his help and protection—since no one is strong in him or herself but is kept safe only by the grace and mercy of God. Even the Lord, showing the weakness of the humanity he bore, said, "Father, if it is possible, let this cup pass from me," and showing his disciples an example that they should not do their own will but God's, went on to say, "nevertheless, let it not be my will, but yours" (Matt. 26:39).

Christ both did and taught God's will. Humility in dealings with others; steadfastness in faith; modesty in words; justice in deeds; mercifulness in works; discipline in morals. To never wrong another, but to bear a wrong when it is done; to keep peace with your neighbors; to love God with all your heart; to love God because he is a Father but fear him because he is God; to prefer nothing over Christ because he preferred nothing over us; to cling inseparably to his love; to stand faithfully and bravely by his cross; to defend his honor when his name is maligned; to show confidence in suffering; to show patience in death, which rewards our crown—this is what it means to be coheirs with Christ, to do what God commands, and to fulfill the Father's will.

Cyprian of Carthage

✦ III ✦

POVERTY ON EARTH AND WEALTH IN HEAVEN

At once they left their nets and followed him. (Matthew 4:20)

It cannot be doubted that the poor can more easily attain the blessing of humility than those who are rich. In the case of the poor, the lack of worldly goods is often accompanied by a quiet gentleness, whereas the rich are more prone to arrogance. Nevertheless, many wealthy people are disposed to use their abundance not to swell their own pride but to perform works of benevolence. They consider their greatest gain what they spend to alleviate the distress of others.

This virtue is open to all people, no matter what their class or condition because all can be equal in their willingness to give, however unequal they may be in earthly fortune. Indeed, their inequality in regard to worldly means is unimportant, provided they are found equal in spiritual possessions. Blessed, therefore, is that poverty which is not trapped by the love of temporal things and does not seek to be enriched by worldly wealth, but desires rather to grow rich in heavenly goods.

The apostles were the first after the Lord himself to provide us with an example of this generous poverty, when they all equally left their belongings at the call of the heavenly Master. By an immediate conversion they were turned from the catching of fish to become fishers of people, and by their own example they won many others to the imitation of their own faith. In these first sons of the church there was but one heart and one soul among all who believed. Abandoning all their worldly property and possessions in their dedicated poverty, they were enriched with eternal goods, and in accordance with the apostolic preaching, they rejoiced to have nothing of this world and to possess all things with Christ.

Leo the Great

✢ 112 ✢

HE HAS PAID OUR RANSOM

Yet the LORD longs to be gracious to you; therefore he will rise up
to show you compassion. For the LORD is a God of justice.
Blessed are all who wait for him! (Isaiah 30:18)

"I appeal to you by the mercy of God," (Rom. 12:1). This appeal is made by Paul, or, rather, it is made by God through Paul, because of God's desire to be loved rather than feared, to be a Father rather than a Lord. God appeals to us in his mercy to avoid having to punish us in his righteousness.

Listen to the Lord's appeal: "In me, I want you to see your own body, your members, your heart, your bones, your blood. You may fear what is divine, but why not love what is human? You may run away from me as the Lord, but why not run to me as your Father? Perhaps you are filled with shame for causing my bitter passion. Do not be afraid. This cross inflicts a mortal injury, not on me, but on death. These nails no longer pain me, but only deepen your love for me. I do not cry out because of these wounds, but through them I draw you into my heart. My body was stretched on the cross as a symbol, not of how much I suffered, but of my all-embracing love. The same is shown by the shedding of my blood: it is the price I have paid for your ransom. So come, return to me and learn to know me as your Father, who repays good for evil, love for injury, and boundless charity for piercing wounds."

Peter Chrysologus

⤋ 113 ⤉

SECOND CENTURY
WORSHIP SERVICE

*They devoted themselves to the apostles' teaching and to fellowship,
to the breaking of bread and to prayer. (Acts 2:42)*

On Sunday we have a common assembly of all our members, whether they live in the city or the outlying districts. The recollections of the apostles or the writings of the prophets are read, as long as there is time. When the reader has finished, the overseer of the assembly speaks to us; he urges everyone to imitate the examples of virtue we have heard in the readings. Then we all stand up together and pray.

At the conclusion of our prayer, bread and wine and water are brought forward. The overseer offers prayers and gives thanks to the best of his ability, and the people give assent by saying, "Amen." The Eucharist is distributed, everyone present communicates, and the deacons take it to those who are absent.

The wealthy, if they wish, may make a contribution, and they themselves decide the amount. The collection is placed in the custody of the overseer, who uses it to help the orphans and widows and anyone who may be in distress, whether because they are sick, in prison, or away from home. In a word, he takes care of all who are in need.

We hold our common assembly on Sunday because it is the first day of the week, the day on which God put darkness and chaos to flight and created the world, and because on that same day our Savior Jesus Christ rose from the dead. For he was crucified on Friday and on Sunday he appeared to his apostles and disciples and taught them the things that we have passed on for your consideration.

Justin Martyr

✢ 114 ✢

CHRIST WAS MADE
A CURSE FOR US

By his wounds you have been healed. (1 Peter 2:24)

Let us consider the benefits of right belief. It is good for me to know that for my sake Christ bore my sickness, submitted to the weaknesses of my body, was made sin and a curse, was humbled and made a servant, all for me. He is for me the Lamb, the Vine, the Rock, the Servant, the Son of a handmaid, and for my sake not knowing the day and the hour of judgment (Matt. 24:36).

How could he, who has made days and times, be ignorant of the day? How could he not know the day, when he has declared both the time and reason of the judgment to come? Consider that he was made a curse, not in respect to his godhead, but his flesh, for it is written: "Cursed is every one that hangs on a tree" (Deut. 21:23; Gal. 3:13). Since he hung in the flesh, he who bore our curses in the flesh became a curse in the flesh. He wept so that you, men and women, might not weep long. He endured insults so that you might not grieve over insults thrown at you.

A glorious remedy—to have the consolation of Christ! He bore these things with extraordinary patience for our sakes—and we cannot even bear them with ordinary patience for the glory of his name! Who cannot learn to forgive when attacked, knowing that Christ prayed for those who persecuted him, even from the cross? Do you not see that Christ's weakness is your strength? Why question him on what is good for us? His tears wash us, his weeping cleanses us.

Ambrose

✤ 115 ✤

GRIEF WITH EVERLASTING HOPE (I)

But Stephen, full of the Holy Spirit, looked up to heaven and saw the glory of God, and Jesus standing at the right hand of God. (Acts 7:55)

[From a letter to a widow:] If it is not your new title of *widow* that distresses you, but the loss of such a good husband, then I grant that there have been few men like him, so affectionate, so gentle, so humble, so sincere, so understanding, so devout. It would be appropriate to be sorrowful if he had perished completely and stopped existing; but if he has only sailed to heaven and journeyed to his true king, then you should not mourn for him! For this death is not death, but only a translation from worse to better, from earth to heaven, from men to angels, and to him who is the Lord of angels.

So in proportion to the grief you feel over losing a man so worthy, you should rejoice that he has departed in safety and honor and has passed from this season of danger to the place of tranquility. Is it not somewhat strange to acknowledge that heaven is superior to earth and yet to weep over those who are brought there?

If your husband had lived a shameful life contrary to the Gospel, it would be right to lament both his life and his death. But insofar as he was a friend of God, we should take pleasure in both how he lived and how he passed on. This attitude is confirmed in the words of blessed Paul, who said, "to depart and to be with Christ which is far better" (Phil. 1:23). [Continued in next entry . . .]

John Chrysostom

✢ 116 ✢

GRIEF WITH EVERLASTING HOPE (II)

Therefore, since we are surrounded by such a great cloud of witnesses,
let us throw off everything that hinders and the sin that so easily
entangles. And let us run with perseverance the race marked out for us.
(Hebrews 12:1)

[From a letter to a widow:] The power of love is such that it embraces, unites, and fastens together not only those who are present with us, but also those who are far away; and the soul's affection cannot be broken by time, nor space, nor anything else. But since you especially wish to see him face-to-face, honor him by letting no other man touch your bed and do your best to keep a life of purity. Do this and you will one day depart to be with him, to dwell with him not for five years like you did here, nor one hundred or one thousand, but for endless ages.

After all, it is not a family or legal relationship that qualifies you for the heavenly inheritance, but a similarity in the way of living between you and heaven's residents. Look at how Lazarus and Abraham both found rest in their heavenly home, although they were strangers to each other — their common faith unites them and many other saints besides them. Therefore, if you exhibit the same manner of life as your husband, you will see him again in heaven, only this time with a beauty and splendor far beyond the earthly beauty he had when he left. The beauty of our present bodies does not compare to that of our future bodies. The bodies of the saints in heaven are so glorious and bright that our present eyes are unable to look upon them. We are given hints of this from Moses' face, which shone with an intolerable glory in front of the Israelites (Ex. 34:29–30), and the face of Christ which shone far more brilliantly than his (Matt. 17:2).

John Chrysostom

⤙ 117 ⤚

PROPER BEHAVIOR
FOR WIDOWS (I)

*For the LORD your God is God of gods and LORD of lords, the great
God, mighty and awesome, who shows no partiality and accepts no
bribes. He defends the cause of the fatherless and the widow, and loves
the foreigner residing among you, giving them food and clothing.
(Deuteronomy 10:17–18)*

Regarding the honors that widowhood enjoys in the sight of
God, the Father says the following through the prophet Isaiah:
"Act justly to the widow and to the orphan; and come, let us reason,
says the LORD" (Isa. 1:17–18). The Father's defense of the orphan
and widow is in proportion to their lack of human support, since
they are left in the hands of divine mercy. Even the widow's helper
is honored with the widow herself and shall "reason with the Lord"!

Such honor is not even given to virgins. Although in their case
perfect sexual integrity and sanctity shall reward the closest vision
of the face of God, the widow has a more toilsome task: it is easy not
to crave what you have never known and to turn away from what
you have never desired. More glorious in God's eyes is the temperance that gives up its rights, which knows what it gives up.

The virgin may possibly be considered happier, but the widow
has a harder obedience; the former is praised for having always
kept "the good," the latter for finding and preserving "the good
for herself." In the former it is grace, and in the latter virtue, that is
crowned. [Continued in next entry ...]

Tertullian

✦ 118 ✦

PROPER BEHAVIOR
FOR WIDOWS (II)

*No widow may be put on the list of widows unless she is over sixty, has
been faithful to her husband, and is well known for her good deeds, such
as bringing up children, showing hospitality, washing the feet of the
Lord's people, helping those in trouble and devoting herself to all kinds
of good deeds. (1 Timothy 5:9–10)*

For some things are a gratuitous grace of God, and some the
result of our own working. The gifts granted by the Lord are
governed by his grace; the things for which we strive are attained
by earnest pursuit. Therefore, earnestly pursue the virtue of con-
tinence, which is how modesty manifests itself; industry, which
helps women not to be "busybodies" (1 Tim. 5:13); frugality, which
scorns the world.

Be part of communities and conversations worthy of God,
remembering the short verse that Paul quotes, "Bad company
corrupts good character" (1 Cor. 15:33). Gossip, laziness, drinking excessively, and covetous friends do the greatest damage to
the goals of widowhood. Gossip makes words that assault modesty; laziness erodes one's discipline; drunkenness leads to any and
every evil; and covetous friends encourage rivalry and lust. Women
like this cannot even speak of the goodness of having one husband.
Their "god," as the Apostle says, "is their belly" (Phil. 3:19), and
also what is quite near the belly.

Tertullian

✦ 119 ✦

WEAPONS
TO WIN SALVATION

What is mankind that you are mindful of them,
human beings that you care for them? (Psalm 8:4)

What is this new mystery surrounding me? I am both small and great, both lowly and exalted, both mortal and immortal, both earthly and heavenly. I am to be buried with Christ and to rise again with him, to become a coheir with him, a son of God, and indeed to be one with God himself.

This is what the great mystery means for us; this is why God became man and became poor for our sake: it was to raise up our flesh, to recover the divine image, to re-create humankind, so that all of us might become one in Christ who perfectly became in us everything that he is himself. So we are no longer "male and female, barbarian and Scythian, slave and free" (Col. 3:11)—distinctions deriving from the flesh—but are to bear within ourselves the seal of God, by whom and for whom we were created. We are to be formed and molded by him in such a way that we will belong to his one family.

If only we could be what we hope to be, by the great kindness of our generous God! He asks so little and gives so much, in this life and in the next, to those who love him sincerely. In a spirit of hope and out of love for him, let us bear and endure all things and give thanks for everything we suffer, since even our weak minds can see that these things are weapons to win salvation.

Gregory of Nazianzus

✤ 120 ✤

SHADOWS OF THINGS TO COME

The LORD said to Moses, "Make a snake and put it up on a pole; anyone who is bitten can look at it and live." (Numbers 21:8)

He established a law for the people governing the construction of the tabernacle and the building of the temple, the choice of Levites, the sacrifices, the offerings, the rites of purification, and the rest of what belonged to worship.

He himself needs none of these things. Even before Moses existed he had within himself every fragrance of all that is pleasing. Yet he sought to teach his people, even though they were always ready to return to their idols. He kept calling them to what was primary by means of what was secondary, that is, by foreshadowings of the reality—from things of time to things of eternity, from things of the flesh to things of the spirit, from earthly things to heavenly things.

As he said to Moses: "You will fashion all things according to the pattern that you saw on the mountain" (Ex. 25:40). For forty days Moses was engaged in remembering the words of God, the heavenly patterns, the spiritual images, the foreshadowings of what was to come.

Saint Paul says, "They drank from the rock that followed them, and the rock was Christ" (1 Cor. 10:4). After speaking of the things that are in the law he continues: "All these things happened to them as symbols: they were written to instruct us, on whom the end of the ages has come" (1 Cor. 10:11).

Through foreshadowings of the future they were learning reverence for God and perseverance in his service. The law was therefore a school of instruction for them, and a prophecy of what was to come.

Irenaeus

⤕ 121 ⤖

STANDING FIRMLY ON THE ROCK

God is our refuge and strength, an ever-present help in trouble.
(Psalm 46:1)

The waters have risen and severe storms rage, but we do not fear drowning because we stand firmly upon a rock. Let the sea rage—it cannot break the rock. Let the waves rise—they cannot sink the boat of Jesus. What should we fear? Death? "Life to me means Christ, and death is gain" (Phil. 1:21). Exile? "The earth and its fullness belong to the LORD" (Ps. 24:1). Theft or poverty? "We brought nothing into this world, and we will surely take nothing out of it" (1 Tim. 6:7). The world's threats are powerless against me, and its blessings are insignificant. I have no fear of poverty and no desire for wealth. I am not afraid of death, and I only continue living for your good. So regarding your present fear, the message I give you is to have confidence.

Do you not know that the Lord said, "Where two or three are gathered in my name, there I am among them" (Matt. 18:20)? Do you think he would be absent, then, when so many of you are gathered together, united in love? I have his promise; I am surely not going to rely on my own strength! I have what he has written; it is my support, my security, my peaceful refuge. Let the world be in upheaval. I hold to his promise and read his message; that is my protecting wall and stronghold. What message do I hold on to? "Know that I am with you always, until the end of the world" (Matt. 28:20).

John Chrysostom

✢ 122 ✢

THE FACE OF JESUS

But I cry to you for help, LORD; in the morning my prayer comes before
you. Why, LORD, do you reject me and hide your face from me?
(Psalm 88:13–14)

We think that God has turned his face away from us when we find ourselves suffering, so that shadows overwhelm our feelings and darken our eyes, stopping us from seeing the truth's brilliance.

A person's face shines out more than the rest of his or her body, and it is by the face that we perceive strangers and recognize our friends. How much more, then, is the face of God able to bring illumination to whomever he looks at!

The apostle Paul has something important to say about this, as about so many other things. He is a true interpreter of Christ for us, bringing him to our understanding through well-chosen words and images. He says: "It is the same God that said, 'Let there be light shining out of darkness,' who has shone in our minds to radiate the light of the knowledge of God's glory, the glory in the face of Christ" (2 Cor. 4:6). We have heard where Christ shines in us: he is the eternal brilliant illumination of our souls, whom the Father sent into the world so that his face would shine on us and reveal to us eternal and heavenly truths—we who had before been plunged in earthly darkness.

"Why do you turn your face away?" Let us understand it like this: even if you do turn your face away from us, Lord, its light is still imprinted upon us. We hold it in our hearts and our deepest feelings are transformed by its light.

For if you truly turn your face away, Lord, no one can survive.

Ambrose

✢ 123 ✢

SEEING GOD
IN YOUR NEIGHBOR

Is it not to share your food with the hungry and to provide the poor
wanderer with shelter — when you see the naked, to clothe them, and
not to turn away from your own flesh and blood? (Isaiah 58:7)

These two commandments ought to be very familiar to you;
they should spring to your mind when I mention them, and
never be absent from your hearts: "Love God with your whole
heart, your whole soul, and your whole mind, and your neighbor
as yourself" (Matt. 22:37 – 39). These two commandments must
always be in your thoughts and in your hearts, treasured, acted on,
and fulfilled. Love of God is the first to be commanded, but love of
neighbor is the first to be put into practice.

Since you do not yet see God, you glimpse the vision of God by
loving your neighbor. By loving your neighbor you prepare your
eyes to see God.

Consider what is said to you: "Love God." If you say to me,
"Show me whom I am supposed to love," what can I say except
what Saint John says: "No one has ever seen God!" (John 1:18;
1 John 4:12). But so you do not worry that you are completely
cut off from the sight of God, he says, "God is love, and he who
remains in love remains in God" (1 John 4:16). Therefore love your
neighbor, and observe the power by which you love him or her —
there you will see God, as far as you are able.

In loving and caring for your neighbor you are on a journey to
the Lord. We have not yet reached his presence, but we have our
neighbor at our side. We are all pilgrims, so support your companions as we walk together toward the kingdom of God, with whom
we wish to remain forever.

Augustine

✦ 124 ✦

SAVING HIS ENEMIES

It is not the healthy who need a doctor, but the sick. I have not come
to call the righteous, but sinners. (Mark 2:17)

Brethren, we ought to regard Jesus Christ as God and judge of the living and the dead. We should not regard our Savior in a small way, otherwise we obtain little from him. Moreover, people who think the name of Jesus insignificant commit sin, and we also sin if we do not realize the magnitude of that from which we have been called, who has called us, and to what place, and how much suffering Jesus Christ endured on our account.

How shall we repay him? What fruit can we bear that would be worthy of this gift? Imagine our debt for the benefits he has given us! He has enlightened our minds; he has called us sons and daughters as a father does; he saved us when we were about to perish. How then shall we praise him, and how repay him for his gifts?

Spiritually blind, we worshiped stones and pieces of wood, things made by human hands, and our whole life was death. We were in utter darkness and completely blind. Then, by his will, we were rescued from the cloud of sin and recovered our sight. For he saw our many errors and the damnation that awaited us, and knowing that apart from him we had no hope of salvation, he pitied us, and in his mercy saved us. He called us when we were not his people and willed us to become his people.

It is a great and wonderful work to uphold those who are falling, rather than those who already stand firm. Christ willed to save people who were in danger of losing their souls, and he has been the salvation of many. When we were on the point of perishing, he came and called us.

Second-Century Writer

⊹ 125 ⊹

OFFERINGS ARE A PURE SACRIFICE

I have received from Epaphroditus the gifts you sent. They are a fragrant offering, an acceptable sacrifice, pleasing to God. (Philippians 4:18)

The oblation of the church, which the Lord taught was to be offered throughout the whole world, has been regarded by God as a pure sacrifice and is acceptable to him. Not that he needs sacrifice from us, but the one who makes the offering receives glory in it, provided that his or her gift is accepted. Through a gift both honor and love are shown to a king. God does nothing without purpose, and nothing without its meaning and reason. In this way the people of Israel used to dedicate tithes of their possessions. But those who have been given the freedom of Christ devote what they possess to the Lord's use. They give it all to him and not simply what is less important to them; and they give cheerfully and freely because they hope for greater things, like the poor widow who put her whole livelihood into God's treasury (Mark 12:41–44).

We must make an offering to God, and as we do we must be found pleasing to God the Creator, in sound teaching, in sincere faith, in firm hope, and in passionate love, for we are offering back to him the firstfruits of the new creation, his children. Only the church can offer this pure oblation to the Creator when it offers it in thanksgiving.

We offer to him what is his, and by this we proclaim communion and unity, and profess our belief in the resurrected Christ. Just as the earthly bread becomes the Eucharist when we ask God to so bless it, so too do our bodies, in receiving the Eucharist, take on the incorruptibility of Christ, for they have the hope of resurrection.

Irenaeus

✢ 126 ✢

WHAT EASTER BRINGS

"Don't be alarmed," he said. "You are looking for Jesus the Nazarene,
who was crucified. He has risen! He is not here. See the place where
they laid him." (Mark 16:6)

The passion of our Savior is the salvation of mankind. The reason why he desired to die for us is that he wanted believers to live with him forever. In the fullness of time it was his will to become what we are, so that we might inherit the eternity he promised and be with him in heaven.

There is a superb grace given by these heavenly mysteries, the gift that Easter brings, the most longed for feast of the year. This day marks the beginning of newly formed creatures: children born from the life-giving church, born anew with the simplicity of little children, and crying out with the evidence of a purified mind and heart.

The Easter festival brings the grace of holiness from heaven to people. Through the repeated celebration of the sacred mysteries they receive the spiritual nourishment of the sacraments. Fostered in the very heart of the church, the fellowship of one community worships the one God, adores the holiness of his triple name, and together with the prophet sings the psalm that belongs to this yearly festival: "This is the day the LORD has made; let us rejoice and be glad" (Ps. 118:24). And what is this day? The dawn of this day is the light of the Lord Jesus Christ himself, the Author of light, who brings the sunrise and the beginning of new life. He says of himself, "I am the light of day; whoever walks in daylight does not stumble" (John 8:12). That is to say, whoever follows Christ in all things will come by this path to the throne of eternal light.

Early Church Presbyter

⁜ 127 ⁜

HUNGERING FOR THE TRUE FOOD

Take delight in the LORD, and he will give you the desires of your heart.
(Psalm 37:4)

What does it mean to be drawn by desire? The heart has its own desires; it takes delight, for example, in the bread from heaven. A poet might say, "Everyone is drawn by his own desire," but would not say "drawn by necessity" or "by compulsion." It is pleasure that draws. Therefore anyone who finds pleasure in truth, in happiness, in justice, and in everlasting life, is drawn to Christ, for Christ is all these things.

Anyone who loves knows what I mean. Anyone who is full of longing, who is hungry, who is a pilgrim and parched with thirst in the desert of this world, eager for a drink of water in the eternal homeland — show me someone like that, and he or she knows what I mean.

Show a leafy branch to a sheep, and it is drawn to it. If you show sweets to a little boy, he is drawn to them. He runs to them because he is drawn, drawn by love, drawn without any physical compulsion, drawn by a chain attached to his heart. "Everyone is drawn by his own desire." This is true, because we know earthly delights succeed in drawing people to them. And if this is so, how much more does Christ draw us, as he is revealed and set before us by the Father? What does the soul desire more than truth and joy? For what else could satisfy our hungering spiritual palate than the divine fruits of wisdom, justice, truth, and eternal life?

Augustine

✦ 128 ✦

DARK PROGRESSION OF COVETOUSNESS (I)

You shall not covet your neighbor's house. You shall not covet your neighbor's wife, or his male or female servant, his ox or donkey, or anything that belongs to your neighbor. (Exodus 20:17)

When the vice of greed has gotten hold of the lukewarm soul of a monk, it begins by tempting him with a small sum of money, giving him convincing and almost reasonable excuses for keeping some money for himself. He complains that he is not sufficiently provided for in the monastery, and it can hardly be endured by a healthy person, let alone a sick one. What is he supposed to do if he becomes ill and has no savings to support him in his illness? He says to himself that his allowance is pitiful, and that the other monks are very careless about the sick, and if he does not have something set aside for himself he will certainly die.

He does not have enough clothes and needs money with which to buy more. Worst of all, he says that he cannot possibly stay in the same monastery forever, and that unless he has saved some money for his journey across the sea, he cannot move when he wants to. And stuck in the same place due to his poverty, he will live in misery until the end of his days without making the slightest advance.

Thus, he must keep some money, for he cannot bear the embarrassment of living on the charities of others, as a needy beggar. [Continued in next entry . . .]

John Cassian

DARK PROGRESSION
OF COVETOUSNESS (II)

Those who trust in their riches will fall, but the righteous
will thrive like a green leaf. (Proverbs 11:28)

A nd so when the greedy monk has deceived himself with these thoughts, he strains to think of how he can acquire at least one penny. Then he anxiously searches for some work he can do without the abbot knowing. And finding work and doing it secretly, he gets his hands on some money but torments himself with thoughts of how he can multiply his earnings. He does not know where to deposit it or to whom he could entrust it. Further, he worries about what to buy with it or where to invest it in order to grow it.

When he has figured out his first set of problems, an even stronger craving for money springs up, and he grows even more hungry for coin as his store of money grows larger and larger — for as one's wealth increases so does one's greed for more.

Next he imagines himself at the end of his life — crippled with old age, ailments of all sorts, long and drawn-out suffering — during which he will be unable to support himself unless he has saved a large sum of money in his youth. And so his wretched soul is tormented, held tightly in a serpent's coils, while he nonetheless continues to scheme of unlawful ways to grow his pile of money. [Continued in next entry . . .]

John Cassian

✦ 130 ✦

DARK PROGRESSION OF COVETOUSNESS (III)

It is easier for a camel to go through the eye of a needle than for someone who is rich to enter the kingdom of God. (Mark 10:25)

So the monk's greed gives birth to more greed and it burns in his soul, and being entirely absorbed in the quest for gain, he thinks of nothing but how to get enough money to leave the monastery as quickly as possible, abandoning all ethics whenever there is the tiniest hope of getting money. He does not shy away from lying, slander, theft, breaking promises, and even outbursts of anger.

Any person who forgets his or her faith for the hope of monetary gain has no problem forgetting humility. Money and the desire for money become his or her god, just like the belly is a god for others (Phil. 3:19). This is why the blessed Apostle, talking about the deadly poison of this sin, not only says that it is the root of all kinds of evil (1 Tim. 6:10), but also calls it idol-worship, saying, "And covetousness which is the worship of idols" (Col. 3:5).

I hope you see the wickedness that this sin leads to step-by-step — such wickedness that the Apostle actually calls it the worship of idols and false gods because it ignores the image and likeness of God (which we ought to preserve undefiled in ourselves) and chooses to love images stamped on gold instead of God.

John Cassian

✦ 131 ✦

POWER OF THE FLESH IS BROKEN

*For we know that our old self was crucified with him so that the body
ruled by sin might be done away with, that we should no longer
be slaves to sin. (Romans 6:6)*

We who have a Spirit-given hope of the resurrection possess
that future blessing as if it were already present. We say,
"Our life is controlled by the Spirit now and is not confined to this
physical world that is subject to corruption. While sin was our
master the bonds of death had a firm hold on us, but now with the
righteousness of Christ we have freed ourselves from our former
corruptibility."

"Once we thought of Christ as being in the flesh, but we do not
any longer" (2 Cor. 5:16) says Saint Paul. By this he meant that the
Word became flesh and suffered death in the flesh in order to give
all people life; and though he remains a man, we know that by his
resurrection and ascension he has passed beyond the life of the flesh.

Since Christ has become the source of life for us, we who follow in his footsteps must not think of ourselves as living in the
flesh any longer, but as having passed beyond it. Saint Paul's saying is absolutely true that "when anyone is in Christ he becomes a
completely different person: his old life is over and a new life has
begun" (2 Cor. 5:17). We have been justified by our faith in Christ
and the power of the curse has been broken. Christ's coming to life
again for our sake has put an end to the sovereignty of death. We
have come to know the true God and to worship him in spirit and in
truth, through the Son our mediator, who sends the Father's blessings down upon the world.

Cyril of Alexandria

❖ 132 ❖

PRAYER ACCOMPLISHES MUCH

But God has surely listened and has heard my prayer. (Psalm 66:19)

In the past, prayer was able to bring down punishment, rout armies, and withhold the blessing of rain. Now, however, the prayer of the just turns aside the whole anger of God, keeps vigil for its enemies, pleads for persecutors. Is it any wonder that it can call down water from heaven when it could obtain fire from heaven as well? Prayer is the one thing that can conquer God. But Christ has willed that it should work no evil and has given it all power over good.

Its only art is to call back the souls of the dead from the very journey into death, to give strength to the weak, to heal the sick, to exorcise the possessed, to open prison cells, to free the innocent from their chains. Prayer cleanses from sin, drives away temptations, stamps out persecutions, comforts the fainthearted, gives new strength to the courageous, brings travelers safely home, calms the waves, confounds robbers, feeds the poor, overrules the rich, lifts up the fallen, supports those who are falling, and sustains those who stand firm.

All the angels pray. Every creature prays. Cattle and wild animals pray and bend the knee. As they come from their barns and caves they look up to heaven and call out, lifting up their spirit in their own fashion. The birds too rise and lift themselves up to heaven: they open out their wings, instead of hands, in the form of a cross and give voice to what seems to be a prayer.

What more need be said on this duty of prayer? Even the Lord himself prayed. To him be honor and power forever and ever. Amen.

Tertullian

⊰ 133 ⊱

GIVING OUR LIVES TO CHRIST

For our light and momentary troubles are achieving for us an eternal
glory that far outweighs them all. So we fix our eyes not on what is
seen, but on what is unseen, since what is seen is temporary,
but what is unseen is eternal. (2 Corinthians 4:17–18)

Pray that the Lord would give me the courage and endurance not only to speak, but also to will what is right, so that I may not only be called a Christian, but prove to be one. For if I prove myself to be a Christian by martyrdom, then people will call me one, and my loyalty to Christ will be apparent when I am gone from the world. Our Lord Jesus Christ, now that he has returned to his Father, has more fully revealed himself. Our task is not to persuade the world with arguments; Christianity shows its greatness when it is hated by the world.

As a prisoner I am learning to give up my own wishes. All the way from Syria to Rome I have fought wild beasts, by land and by sea, by day and by night. I am chained to ten leopards—the group of soldiers that guards me—and the better I treat them, the worse they become. By their abuse of me I am trained in discipleship, "but I am not therefore justified" (1 Cor. 4:4).

How happy I will be to face the beasts that are prepared for me! I hope they will make short work of me. Now I am beginning to be a disciple. I hope nothing robs me of my prize, which is Jesus Christ! Fire, the cross, packs of wild animals, lacerations, tortures, broken bones, mangling of limbs, crushing of the whole body, the horrible assaults of the devil—let all these things happen to me, if it means I gain Jesus Christ!

Ignatius of Antioch

✛ 134 ✛

KEEPING SILENT

*For by your words you will be acquitted, and by your words
you will be condemned. (Matthew 12:37)*

Now what should we learn before everything else, but to be silent, that we may later be able to speak wisely? Otherwise my words might condemn me before those of another spare me; for it is written: "By your words you shall be condemned" (Matt. 12:37). Why then should you risk condemnation by speaking quickly, when you can be safer by keeping silent? I have seen many fall into sin by speaking, but hardly anyone by keeping silent; so I find that it is more difficult to know how to keep silent than how to speak wisely. A person is wise, then, who knows how to keep silent. The wisdom of God states: "The LORD has given to me the tongue of learning, that I should know when it is good to speak" (Isa. 50:4). So he or she who has heard from the Lord knows when to speak and when to remain silent. Thus the Scripture states it well: "A wise man will keep silence until there is opportunity" (Sir. 20:7).

The law says: "Hear, Israel, the LORD your God" (Deut. 6:4). It did not say, "Speak," but, "Hear." Eve fell because she said to Adam something she had not heard from the Lord. God says to you: Hear! If you hear, examine your conduct; and if you have fallen, quickly amend your ways. For: "With what does a young man amend his way, except in heeding the word of the LORD?" (Ps. 119:9). So first of all be silent, and listen to others, so that your words do not condemn you.

Ambrose

✢ 135 ✢

REDEEMED TO BE PRIESTS

But you are a chosen people, a royal priesthood, a holy nation, God's special possession, that you may declare the praises of him who called you out of darkness into his wonderful light. (1 Peter 2:9)

"You are a chosen race, a royal priesthood." Moses once gave this praise to ancient Israel (Ex. 19:6), but now the apostle Peter rightly gives it to the Gentiles. Salvation once belonged to the Jews, but the Gentiles have come to believe in Christ, who is the cornerstone of the salvation for all nations.

Peter calls them "chosen" because of their faith, to distinguish them from those who have been rejected by denying the cornerstone. They are "a royal priesthood" because they are united to the body of Christ, the supreme King and true priest. As King he grants them his kingdom, and as high priest he washes away their sins by the offering of his blood. In their royalty they must remember to hope for an everlasting kingdom, and in their priesthood to offer God the sacrifice of obedience.

After Israel had been freed from slavery in Egypt and had crossed the Red Sea and Pharaoh's army had been overwhelmed, they sang a song of triumph to the Lord; in the same way, now that our sins have been washed away in baptism, we should also express joyous gratitude for God's gifts. The Egyptians were Israel's oppression, darkness, and trial; they are therefore an appropriate symbol of the sins that once oppressed us but were destroyed in baptism.

The deliverance of the children of Israel and their journey to the Promised Land corresponds with the mystery of our redemption: we are making our way toward the light of our heavenly home with the grace of Christ showing us the way.

Bede the Venerable

✣ 136 ✣

RELIVING CHRIST'S PASSION

I have been crucified with Christ and I no longer live, but Christ lives in me. The life I now live in the body, I live by faith in the Son of God, who loved me and gave himself for me. (Galatians 2:20)

We must sacrifice ourselves to God, each day and in everything we do, accepting all that happens to us for the sake of the Word, imitating his passion by our sufferings, and honoring his blood by shedding our own. We must be ready to be crucified.

If you are a Simon of Cyrene, take up your cross and follow Christ. If you are crucified beside him like one of the thieves, acknowledge your God like the good thief. For your sake, and because of your sin, Christ himself was regarded as a sinner; for his sake, therefore, you must cease to sin. Worship him who was hung on the cross because of you, even if you are hanging there yourself. Choose to benefit from your shame, and purchase salvation with your death. Enter paradise with Jesus, and discover how far you have fallen. Contemplate the glories there, and leave the other blasphemous thief to die outside.

If you are a Joseph of Arimathea, go to the one who ordered his crucifixion, and ask for Christ's body. Make your own atonement for the sins of the whole world. If you are a Nicodemus, the man who worshiped God by night, bring spices and prepare Christ's body for burial. If you are one of the Marys or Salome or Joanna, weep in the early morning. Be the first to see the stone rolled back, and even the angels perhaps, and Jesus himself.

Gregory of Nazianzus

❖ 137 ❖

THE SONGS
OF THE PILGRIMS

But if Christ is in you, then even though your body is subject to death
because of sin, the Spirit gives life because of righteousness.
(Romans 8:10)

But in the next life, when this body of ours has become immortal and incorruptible, then all trials will be over. Are we to leave our dead bodies behind then? By no means. Listen to the words of Holy Scripture: "If the Spirit of him who raised Christ from the dead dwells within you, then he who raised Christ from the dead will also give life to your own mortal bodies" (Rom. 8:11).

The happiness of the heavenly alleluia, sung in security, with no fear of adversity! We shall have no enemies in heaven, and we shall never lose a friend. God's praises are sung both there and here, but here they are sung by those destined to die, there, by those destined to live forever; here they are sung in hope, there, in hope's fulfillment; here they are sung by pilgrims, there, by citizens of the heavenly country.

So let us sing now, not in order to enjoy a life of leisure, but in order to lighten our labors. You should sing as travelers do — sing, but continue your journey. Do not be lazy, but sing to make your journey more enjoyable. Sing, but keep going. What do I mean by keep going? Keep on making progress. This progress, however, must be in virtue; for there are some, the Apostle warns, whose only progress is in vice. If you make progress, you will be continuing your journey, but be sure that your progress is in virtue, true faith, and right living. Sing then, but keep going.

Augustine

✤ 138 ✤

SEVENS IN CREATION AND CHRIST

These are the words of him who holds the seven stars in his right hand and walks among the seven golden lampstands. (Revelation 2:1)

Look upon the seven horns of the Lamb, the seven eyes of God—the seven eyes are the seven spirits of the Lamb; seven torches burning before the throne of God, seven golden candlesticks, seven young sheep, the seven women in Isaiah, the seven churches in Paul, seven deacons, seven angels, seven trumpets, seven seals to the book, seven periods of seven days in which Pentecost is completed, the seven weeks in Daniel, also the forty-three weeks in Daniel; with Noah, seven of all clean things in the ark, seven revenges of Cain, seven years for a debt to be forgiven, the lamp with seven lips, seven pillars of wisdom in the house of Solomon.

The nativity of God's Son Jesus Christ was how he brought aid to his entire creation and was accomplished by the re-creation of Adam by means of the week. Who does not see in their heart that the day the serpent seduced Eve is the same day the angel Gabriel brought glad tidings to the Virgin Mary; that the day the Holy Spirit overflowed in the Virgin Mary is the same day God made light; that the day Jesus was conceived in the flesh is the same day God made the land and the water; that the day he was first fed by Mary is the same day God made the stars; that the day he was incarnated is the same day God formed man out of the ground; that the day he suffered is the same day Adam fell; and that the day he rose again from the dead is the same day God created light?

Victorinus of Pettau

✢ 139 ✢

WE TOO SHALL CROSS
THE JORDAN

*When you walk through the fire, you will not be burned ... For I am the
LORD your God, the Holy One of Israel, your Savior. (Isaiah 43:2–3)*

The ark of the covenant led the people of God across the Jordan.
The priests and the Levites halted, and the waters, as though
out of reverence to the ministers of God, stopped flowing. They
piled up in a single mass, thus allowing the people of God to cross
in safety. As a Christian, you should not be amazed to hear of these
wonders performed for people of the past. The divine Word promises much greater and more lofty things to you who have passed
through Jordan's stream by the sacrament of baptism. He promises
you a passage even through the sky: "We shall be caught up in the
clouds to meet Christ in heaven, and so we shall always be with the
Lord" (1 Thess. 4:17).

So you must not think that these events belong only to the past,
and that you who now hear the account of them do not experience
anything like them. It is in you that they all find their spiritual fulfillment. You have recently abandoned the darkness of idolatry,
and you now desire to come and hear the divine Law. This is your
departure from Egypt. When you became a believer and began to
obey the laws of the church, you passed through the Red Sea; now
at the various stops in the desert, you give time every day to hear
the Law of God and to see the face of Moses unveiled by the glory of
God. But once you come to the baptismal font and are initiated into
those sacred and venerable mysteries, you will cross the Jordan and
enter the Promised Land. There Moses will hand you over to Jesus,
and he himself will be your guide on your new journey.

Origen

✢ 140 ✢

YOU ARE A HOLY TEMPLE (I)

Don't you know that you yourselves are God's temple and that God's Spirit dwells in your midst? (1 Corinthians 3:16)

My fellow Christians, today is the birthday of this church and an occasion for celebration and rejoicing. It is we, however, who ought to be the true and living temple of God. Nevertheless, it is right to commemorate this feast of the church, our mother, for we know that through her we were reborn in the Spirit. At our first birth, we were vessels of God's wrath, but when we were reborn, we became vessels of his mercy. Our first birth established our death, but our second restored us to life.

Moreover, before our baptism we were sanctuaries of the devil; but after our baptism we were granted the privilege of being temples of Christ. And if we think carefully about the meaning of our salvation, we realize that we are indeed living and true temples of God. "God does not dwell only in structures made by human hands" (Acts 7:48), in homes of wood and stone, but dwells primarily in the souls of men and women, made according to his own image and fashioned by his own hands. Therefore, the apostle Paul says, "The temple of God is holy, and you are that temple" (1 Cor. 3:17). [Continued in next entry . . .]

Caesarius of Arles

❖ 141 ❖

YOU ARE A HOLY TEMPLE (II)

In fact, no one can enter a strong man's house without first tying him up. Then he can plunder the strong man's house. (Mark 3:27)

When Christ came, he banished the devil from our hearts, in order to build a temple for himself there. Because of this, whoever does evil does harm to Christ. So with his help, we should make sure that our evil deeds do not deface our temple. As I said earlier, before Christ redeemed us, we were the house of the devil, but afterward we gained the privilege of being the house of God. God, in his loving mercy, decided to make his home in us!

My fellow Christians, do you wish to celebrate the building of this temple joyfully? Then do not deface the living temples of God in your bodies with evil actions. I will speak clearly, so that everyone understands. Whenever we come to church, we prepare our hearts to be as beautiful as we expect this church to be. Do you wish to find this sanctuary immaculately clean? Then do not tarnish your soul with the filth of sins. Do you wish this sanctuary to be full of light? Of course you do, and God likewise wishes for your souls not to be in darkness, but that the light of good works would shine in you, so that he who dwells in the heavens would be glorified. Just as you enter this church building, God enters into your soul, for he promised, "I shall live in them, and I shall walk the corridors of their hearts" (Jer. 31:33).

Caesarius of Arles

✦ 142 ✦

THE BAPTISM OF CHRIST

Having been buried with him in baptism, in which you were also raised
with him through your faith in the working of God, who raised him
from the dead. (Colossians 2:12)

The Gospel tells us that the Lord went to the Jordan River to be baptized and that he wished to consecrate himself in the river by signs from heaven.

At Christmas he was born a man; today he is reborn sacramentally. Then he was born from the Virgin; today he is born in mystery. When he was born a man, his mother Mary held him close to her heart; when he is born in mystery, God the Father embraces him with his voice when he says, "This is my beloved Son in whom I am well pleased: listen to him" (Matt. 17:5). The mother caresses the tender baby on her lap; the Father serves his Son by his loving testimony. The mother holds the child for the magi to adore; the Father reveals that his Son is to be worshiped by all the nations.

Someone might ask, "Why would a holy man desire baptism?" Listen to the answer: Christ is baptized, not to be made holy by the water, but to make the water holy, and by his cleansing to purify the waters that he touched. For the consecration of Christ involves a more significant consecration of the water.

For when the Savior is washed, all water for our baptism is made clean, purified at its source for the dispensing of baptismal grace to the people of future ages. Christ is the first to be baptized so that Christians will follow after him with confidence.

Maximus of Turin

⊱ 143 ⊰

UNITED WITH CHRIST THE BODY WILL RISE

If the part of the dough offered as firstfruits is holy, then the whole batch is holy; if the root is holy, so are the branches. (Romans 11:16)

The Word of God became man — the Son of God became the Son of Man — in order to unite himself with human beings and make them adopted sons and daughters of God. Only by being united to Christ, who is himself incorruptible, could we be saved from corruption and death; and how else could this union have been achieved if Christ had not first become what we are? How else could our corruptible and mortal bodies have been swallowed up in his incorruptibility and immortality? Therefore, the Son of God, our Lord, the Word of the Father, is also properly called Son of Man; he became the Son of Man by being born of Mary, a member of the human race.

A virgin conceived a child and bore a son who is called Emmanuel, which means "God with us." He came down to the earth here below in search of the sheep that were lost, which were in fact his own creatures, and then ascended back to heaven to offer to the Father and entrust to his care the human race that he had found again. The Lord himself became the firstfruits of the resurrection of humankind, and when the time of judgment is complete, the rest of the body, to which we all belong, will rise from the grave just as the head has done. And just as a body does, the heavenly church will grow and be strengthened in all its joints and ligaments, and each member will have its own proper place in the body.

Irenaeus

✢ 144 ✢

REMEMBER WHERE YOU CAME FROM

For he has rescued us from the dominion of darkness and brought us into the kingdom of the Son he loves, in whom we have redemption, the forgiveness of sins. (Colossians 1:13–14)

It is right that you should think of Jesus Christ as God—as the Judge of the living and the dead. It is not good to think lightly of our salvation, for if we think little of him, we can only hope to obtain little from him. And if we are careless about these things, as if they were not very important, we commit sin. We must not be ignorant about the place from which we were called, and by whom, and to what place, and how much Jesus Christ chose to suffer for our sakes. What will we return to him? Or what would be a worthy fruit to give back to him?

After all, he is responsible for many great benefits! He has graciously given us light; as a Father, he has called us sons and daughters; he saved us when we were about to perish. How should we praise him? And what should we return to him for everything we have received? Formerly we were ignorant, worshiping stones and wood and gold, the works of human hands; and our whole life was nothing besides death. We were utterly blind and enveloped in darkness but have received sight and by his grace been freed from the cloud that concealed the truth. When he saw the errors we were drowning in, he had compassion on us and mercifully saved us, seeing the destruction we were headed for, and that we had no hope of salvation except by him. For he called us when we were dead, and willed that we should be given a real existence.

From the Second Epistle of Clement

⊹ 145 ⊹

DEATH MADE DEAD (I)

I will deliver this people from the power of the grave; I will redeem
them from death. (Hosea 13:14)

A very strong proof of the conquest and destruction of death by the cross is given by an interesting fact. All of Christ's disciples despise death; they take the offensive against it, and instead of fearing it, by the sign of the cross and by faith in Christ they trample on it as on something dead. Before the Savior came, even the holiest of men were afraid of death and mourned the dead as people gone forever. But now that the Savior has raised his body, death is no longer terrible, and all those who believe in Christ tread it underfoot as nothing. They prefer to die rather than to deny their faith in Christ, knowing full well that when they die they do not perish, but in fact live and become incorruptible through the resurrection.

Now that the pains of death are removed, the devil — who once took joy in death — is the only one who remains truly dead. There is proof of this too. Men prior to their belief in Christ think death is horrible and are afraid of it; but once converted, they despise it so completely that they go eagerly to meet it and become witnesses of the Savior's resurrection from it. Even children hurry to die this way; women also train themselves by bodily discipline to meet it. Death has become so weak that even women who used to be shaken by it, now mock it as a dead thing robbed of all its strength. [Continued in next entry ...]

Athanasius

✤ 146 ✤

DEATH MADE DEAD (II)

The last enemy to be destroyed is death. (1 Corinthians 15:26)

Death has become like a tyrant who has been completely conquered by the legitimate monarch; bound hand and foot, the passers-by sneer at him, hit him, and abuse him, as they are no longer afraid of his cruelty and rage because of their king's conquest. That is how death has been conquered and branded for what it is by the Savior on the cross. It is bound hand and foot; all who are in Christ trample it as they pass, and his witnesses mock it, scoffing and saying, "O death, where is your victory? O grave, where is your sting?" (1 Cor. 15:55).

Do you think this is a weak proof of the impotence of death? Or is it a small indication of the Savior's victory when young boys and girls who are in Christ look beyond this present life and train themselves to die? No! It is strong proof. Everyone is by nature afraid of death and of bodily destruction; the marvel of marvels is that the person with faith in the cross despises this natural fear and, for the sake of the cross, is no longer cowardly in the face of it.

If, then, it is by the sign of the cross and by faith in Christ that death is trampled underfoot, clearly it is Christ himself who is the arch-victor and has robbed death of its power. Death used to be strong and terrible, but now, since the time of the Savior and the death and resurrection of his body, it is despised; Christ and his cross have destroyed and vanquished death forever.

Athanasius

✢ 147 ✢

BE LIKE SHEEP, DOVES, AND SNAKES (I)

The gatekeeper opens the gate for him, and the sheep listen to his voice. He calls his own sheep by name and leads them out. When he has brought out all his own, he goes on ahead of them, and his sheep follow him because they know his voice. (John 10:3–4)

As long as we are sheep, we overcome and emerge victorious, despite being surrounded by countless wolves. But if we turn into wolves, we are overcome, for we lose the shepherd's help. After all, he feeds the sheep and not the wolves and will abandon you if you do not let him show his power in you.

What he says is this: "Do not be upset that I ask you to be as sheep and doves when I send you out among the wolves. I could have managed things quite differently and sent you, not to suffer evil nor to yield like sheep to the wolves, but to be fiercer than lions. But the way I have chosen is right. It will bring you greater praise and at the same time manifest my power."

That is what he told Paul: "My grace is enough for you, for in weakness my power is made perfect" (2 Cor. 12:9). He says this same thing to you. For when he says, "I am sending you out like sheep" (Matt. 10:16), he implies, "But do not lose heart over this, because I know, and I am certain, that no one will be able to overcome you." [Continued in next entry ...]

John Chrysostom

◆ 148 ◆

BE LIKE SHEEP, DOVES, AND SNAKES (II)

*Everyone has heard about your obedience, so I rejoice because of you;
but I want you to be wise about what is good, and innocent about
what is evil. (Romans 16:19)*

But the Lord does want you to contribute something, so he adds, "You must be clever as snakes and innocent as doves" (Matt. 10:16). Now you may ask yourselves, "What good is our cleverness in the face of so many dangers? What can a sheep's cleverness accomplish among the wolves—and so many of them! However innocent the dove, what good does it do him, with so many hawks swooping down on him?"

What kind of cleverness is the Lord requiring here? The cleverness of a snake. A snake will surrender everything and will put up no fight even if its body is being cut to pieces, provided it can save its head. So the Lord is saying that you must surrender everything but your faith: money, body, even life itself. For faith is the head and the root; keep that, and you could lose everything else and still have an abundance.

Therefore the Lord counseled the disciples not to be just clever or just innocent; rather he joined them together so that they become a unique virtue. He insisted on the cleverness of a snake so that you might avoid deadly wounds, and he insisted on the innocence of a dove so that you might not take revenge on those who injure you. Cleverness is useless without innocence.

Do not believe that this teaching is beyond your power. More than anyone else, the Lord knows the nature of created things; he knows that moderation, and not ferocity, beats back a fierce attack.

John Chrysostom

⊰ 149 ⊱

DEATH IS A PASSOVER

The world has been crucified to me, and I to the world. (Galatians 6:14)

We should understand Paul to mean that this death by crucifixion takes place in this life, and that this death is a blessing. Death must be active within us if life also is to be active within us. True life is life after death, a life that is a blessing. This blessing of life comes after victory, when the contest is over, when we no longer need to struggle against the body that leads to death. It seems to me that this "death" is more powerful than "life." I accept the authority of the Apostle when he says, "Death is therefore active within us, but life is active within you" (2 Cor. 4:12). The "death" of one man established life for countless multitudes of peoples! He therefore teaches us to seek out this kind of death even in life, so that the death of Christ may shine forth in our lives — that blessed death by which our outward self is destroyed and our inmost self renewed, and our earthly dwelling crumbles away while a home in heaven opens to us.

The Lord allowed death to enter this world so that sin might come to an end. But he gave us the resurrection of the dead so that our nature might not end in death; death brings guilt to an end, and the resurrection enables our nature to continue forever.

"Death" is a Passover to be made by all humankind. You must keep facing it with perseverance. It is a Passover from corruption, from mortality to immortality, from rough seas to a calm harbor. The word "death" must not trouble us; the blessings that come from a safe journey should bring us joy. What is death but the burial of sin and the resurrection of goodness?

Ambrose

✢ 150 ✢

KNOWING AS
HE KNOWS ME

You have searched me, LORD, and you know me. You know when I sit and when I rise; you perceive my thoughts from afar. (Psalm 139:1–2)

Lord, you know me. Let me know you. Let me come to know you even as I am known. You are the strength of my soul; enter it and make it a place suitable for your dwelling, a house "without spot or blemish" (Eph. 5:27). This is my hope and my prayer. In this hope I rejoice, and it is right to rejoice in it. As sinners we tend to lament the things that do not deserve our tears and be unaffected by things that deserve our sorrow. "For behold, you have loved the truth, because the one who does what is true enters into the light" (John 3:21). Help me do this truth both when I am alone and before many witnesses.

Lord, the depths of a person's conscience lie exposed before your eyes. Could I hide anything from you, even if I did not want to confess it to you? If I tried I would only be hiding you from myself, not myself from you.

Whoever I am, Lord, I lie exposed to your scrutiny. I have already spoken of the profit I gain when I confess to you. But I do not confess with mere bodily speech, but with the words of my soul and the cry of my mind, which you hear and understand. When I am wicked, my confession to you is an expression of displeasure with myself. But when I do good, I confess that this goodness comes from you. "For you, LORD, bless the just man" (Ps. 5:12), but first you "justify the wicked" (Rom. 4:5). And so I confess to you in silence, but not in silence. My voice is silent but my heart cries out.

Augustine

✣ 151 ✣

TO A YOUNG PASTOR

Be diligent in these matters; give yourself wholly to them,
so that everyone may see your progress. (1 Timothy 4:15)

I was struck by the godliness of your mind, as if it were anchored to the immovable rock, and I rejoice that God blessed me with seeing your blameless face. I exhort you to press forward on your journey in the grace that now clothes you, and for you to exhort all people to salvation. Perform your office with both bodily and spiritual diligence. Strive for unity, for there is nothing better. Help all people, as the Lord also helps you, and treat them all with love — as you have been doing. Pray unceasingly. Beg for the wisdom that you do not have, and be watchful to prevent the spirit from slumbering. Speak to each person individually, just like God himself, and bear the sufferings of all as our Savior did. The greater your toil, the greater your gain.

It is no credit to you if you simply love your good disciples; try also to conquer the bad ones with your gentleness. Remember that not all wounds are healed in the same way — where the pain is acute, apply soothing remedies. "Be wise as the serpent" in all things but always "harmless as the dove" (Matt. 10:16). This is why you are both body and spirit — so that you can be tender with visible things and pray that invisible things be revealed to you. This way you will lack nothing and abound in every gift. You are needed in these critical times, as a ship needs a helmsman and the storm-tossed sailor needs a harbor. Be strict with yourself, like a good athlete of God. The prize is immortality and eternal life, as you know. I offer myself up as a sacrifice on your behalf — myself and these chains, which you yourself have kissed.

Ignatius of Antioch

✛ 152 ✛

COMPLAINING
AND COMPARING (I)

This is a sign to them that they will be destroyed, but that you will be
saved—and that by God. For it has been granted to you on behalf
of Christ not only to believe in him, but also to suffer for him.
(Philippians 1:28–29)

Whenever we suffer some affliction, we should regard it as both a punishment and as a correction. Our Holy Scriptures themselves do not promise us peace, security, and rest. On the contrary, the Gospel makes no secret of the troubles and temptations that await us, but it also says that "he who perseveres to the end will be saved" (Matt. 24:13). This life has produced suffering since the time of Adam, when the first man was cursed and received the just sentence of death, from which Christ our Lord has delivered us.

So we must not grumble, my brothers and sisters, for as the Apostle says: "Some of them murmured and were destroyed by serpents" (1 Cor. 10:9–10). Do we endure any affliction that was not endured by our fathers and mothers before us? How can we even compare our sufferings with what we know of theirs? And yet you hear people complaining about the present day and age because things were so much better in former times. I wonder what would happen if they could be taken back to the days of their ancestors— they would be complaining then as they do now. You may think past ages were good, but it is only because you are not living in them. [Continued in next entry . . .]

Augustine

✤ 153 ✤

COMPLAINING AND COMPARING (II)

*Who is going to harm you if you are eager to do good? But even if
you should suffer for what is right, you are blessed. Do not fear
their threats; do not be frightened. (1 Peter 3:13–14)*

You have now been freed from the curse, and have believed in
the Son of God, and have been instructed in the Holy Scriptures—and yet you think the days of Adam were good? And your
ancestors bore the curse of Adam, to whom God addressed with
the words, "With sweat on your brow you shall eat your bread;
you shall till the earth from which you were taken, and it will yield
thorns and thistles" (Gen. 3:18–19). This is what he deserved and
what he had to suffer; this is the punishment assigned to him by the
just judgment of God.

So how can you think that the past ages were better than your
own? From the time of that first Adam to the time of his descendants today, man's lot has been labor and sweat, thorns and thistles.
Have we forgotten the flood and the disastrous times of famine and
war, which have been recorded precisely in order to keep us from
complaining to God about our own times? Just think what those
past ages were like! Is there anyone who does not shudder to hear
or read about them? They do not justify the complaints we moan
about our own time but actually teach us how much we have to be
thankful for.

Augustine

✦ 154 ✦

HEARTS AND MINDS THAT SEE GOD

I have a message from God in my heart concerning the sinfulness of the wicked: There is no fear of God before their eyes. (Psalm 36:1)

If you say, "Show me your God," I will say to you, "Show me what kind of person you are, and I will show you my God." Show me then whether the eyes of your mind can see, and the ears of your heart hear.

It is like this. Those who can see with the eyes of their bodies are aware of what is happening in this life on earth. They distinguish light and darkness, black and white, ugliness and beauty, elegance and inelegance, proportion and lack of proportion, excess and defect. The same is true of the sounds we hear: high or low or pleasant. So it is with the ears of our heart and the eyes of our mind in their capacity to hear or see God.

God is seen by those who have the capacity to see him, provided that they keep the eyes of their minds open. All have eyes, but some have eyes that are shrouded in darkness, unable to see the light of the sun. Because the blind cannot see it, it does not follow that the sun does not shine. The blind must trace the cause back to themselves and their eyes.

A person's soul should be clean, like a mirror reflecting light. If there is rust on the mirror, one's face cannot be seen in it. In the same way, no one who has sin within can see God.

But if you want, you can be healed. Hand yourself over to the doctor, and he will open the eyes of your mind and heart. Who is to be the doctor? It is God, who heals and gives life through his Word and wisdom.

Theophilus of Antioch

✣ 155 ✣

THE PRECIOUS TEMPLE
OF THE POOR

Woe to you, teachers of the law and Pharisees, you hypocrites! You give
a tenth of your spices — mint, dill and cumin. But you have neglected
the more important matters of the law — justice, mercy and faithfulness.
You should have practiced the latter, without neglecting the former.
(Matthew 23:23)

What use is it to stack Christ's table with golden cups when Christ himself is dying of hunger? First, feed him when he is hungry; only after should you use what is left to adorn his table. Will you buy a golden cup but not give a cup of water? What is the use of laying the table with expensive fabrics but not wrapping Christ himself with the clothes he needs? What benefit is there in that? If you saw him going hungry but left him like that, and instead surrounded his table with gold, would he be grateful or angry? What if you saw him in worn-out rags and frozen from cold, and instead of clothing him you set up golden columns for him, saying you were doing it in his honor? Would he not think you were mocking him?

Apply this to Christ when he comes along the road as a pilgrim looking for shelter. You do not take him in as your guest, but you decorate the floors and walls and tables of churches. You provide silver chains for lamps, but you cannot even look at him as he lies chained in prison. Again, I am not forbidding you to supply these adornments; I am urging you to provide the other things as well, and actually to provide them first. No one has ever sinned by not providing ornaments, but whoever neglects their neighbor asks for hell, with its inextinguishable fire and torment in the company of the demons. Therefore do not adorn the church and ignore your impoverished brother, for he is the most precious temple of all.

John Chrysostom

✢ 156 ✢

THE SCRIPTURES ARE FOR LOVERS OF LEARNING

The law of the LORD is perfect, refreshing the soul. The statutes of the LORD are trustworthy, making wise the simple. (Psalm 19:7)

All Scripture, then, is "given by inspiration of God and is also assuredly profitable" (2 Tim. 3:16). Therefore the task of searching the Scriptures is beautiful and beneficial for the soul. For just as the "tree planted by the channels of waters gives fruit in its season" (Ps. 1:3), the soul that is watered by the divine Scriptures flourishes with orthodox belief and is adorned with actions pleasing to God like the tree with its evergreen leafage. For through the Holy Scriptures we are trained in action that is pleasing to God and in peaceful reflection. In them we find both exhortation to every virtue and dissuasion from every vice. So if you love learning you will be very wise by attending to the Scriptures.

Remember, it is by God's care and toil that all things are accomplished, since he is a giver and full of grace. "For every one that asks receives, and he that seeks finds, and to him that knocks it shall be opened" (Luke 11:10). Therefore let us knock at the fair garden of the Scriptures, so fragrant and sweet and blooming, with its multitude of spiritual and divinely-inspired birds singing in the trees, laying hold of our hearts, comforting the mourners, calming the angry and filling them with everlasting joy.

John of Damascus

✢ 157 ✢

MARY AND MARTHA (I)

"Martha, Martha," the Lord answered, "you are worried
and upset about many things." (Luke 10:41)

Our Lord's words teach us that though we labor among the many distractions of this world, we should have only one goal. For we are just travelers on a journey without a real home; we are on our way, and have not yet arrived in our native land; we are in a state of longing, not yet of fulfillment. So let us continue on our way and carry on without rest, so that we may ultimately arrive at our destination.

Martha and Mary were sisters, related not only by blood but also by their faith in Jesus. They stayed close to our Lord and served him harmoniously when he stayed with them. Martha welcomed him as she would a traveler. But Jesus was no ordinary traveler: the maid-servant received her Lord, the broken woman her Savior, the creature her Creator, to serve him bodily food while she was fed by the Spirit. For the Lord willed to put on the form of a slave and to be fed by his own servants, out of condescension and not out of need. For it was indeed condescension to present himself to be fed; since he was in the flesh he would be hungry and thirsty.

In this way the Lord was received as a guest who "came to his own and his own did not receive him; but whoever did receive him, he gave them the power to become sons of God" (John 1:11–12). He adopted his servants and made them his brothers and sisters, ransomed the captives, and made them his coheirs. [Continued in next entry ...]

Augustine

✢ 158 ✢

MARY AND MARTHA (II)

But few things are needed—or indeed only one. Mary has chosen what is better, and it will not be taken away from her. (Luke 10:42)

No one of you should say, "Blessed are they who have deserved to receive Christ into their homes!" Do not complain that you were born in a time when you can no longer see God in the flesh. He did not in fact take this privilege from you, since he says, "Whatever you have done to the least of my brothers, you did to me" (Matt. 25:40).

And you, Martha, are blessed for your good service, and you seek the reward of peace for your labors. On earth you are occupied with nourishing the body, admittedly a holy one. But when you come to the heavenly homeland, will you find a traveler to welcome, someone hungry to feed, or thirsty to whom you may give drink, someone ill whom you could visit, or quarreling whom you could reconcile, or dead whom you could bury?

No, there will be nothing like that there. What you will find there is what Mary chose. There we shall not feed others, but be fed ourselves. Thus what Mary chose in this life will be realized there in its fullness; she was smelling the fragrance of that rich banquet, the Word of God. Do you wish to know what we will have there? The Lord himself tells us when he says of his servants, "Truly, I say to you, he will make them sit at the table and he will serve them" (Luke 12:37).

Augustine

✣ 159 ✣

TAKING REFUGE BESIDE THE FOUNTAIN

When you give it to them, they gather it up; when you open your hand, they are satisfied with good things. (Psalm 104:28)

"We have died with Christ" (Rom. 6:8). We carry in our bodies the sign of his death, so that the living Christ may also be revealed in us. The life we live now is not our ordinary life, but the life of Christ: a life of sinlessness, of chastity, of simplicity and every other virtue. We have risen with Christ; therefore let us live in Christ and ascend with him and so disarm the serpent that means to bite us in the heel.

Let us take refuge from this world. You can do this in spirit, even if you are kept here in body. Your soul must hold fast to Christ, you must follow after him in your thoughts, you must tread his footsteps by faith. You must take refuge in him. He is your refuge and your strength. David addresses him in these words: "I fled to you for refuge, and I was not disappointed" (Ps. 25:20).

Since God is our refuge, God who is in heaven and above the heavens, we must take refuge from this world where he is—where there is peace, where there is rest from toil, where we can celebrate the great Sabbath, as Moses said: "The Sabbaths of the land will provide you with food" (Lev. 25:6). To rest in the Lord and see his joy is like a banquet and full of gladness and tranquility.

Let us take refuge like deer beside the fountain of waters. Like David, let our soul thirst for the fountain. What fountain? Listen to David: "With you is the fountain of life" (Ps. 36:9). Let our souls say to this fountain: When shall I come and see you face-to-face? For the fountain is God himself.

Ambrose

✢ 160 ✢

STAY FOCUSED
IN SPIRITUAL WARFARE

And this is my prayer: that your love may abound more and more
in knowledge and depth of insight, so that you may be able to discern
what is best and may be pure and blameless for the day of Christ.
(Philippians 1:9–10)

Those who struggle in spiritual battle ought to keep their souls free from tumultuous waves of distraction. If they do this, the mind will be able to distinguish among the various thoughts that come to it. The good thoughts, sent by God, can be stored in the treasure-house of their memory. The evil thoughts, sent by the devil, can be thrown out. In just the same way, when the sea is calm, the fisherman can see to the bottom of it and practically no fish can escape his net; but if it is stirred up by winds and storms, it goes from translucent to murky, and then even the craftiest fisherman is wasting his time.

Only the Holy Spirit can purify the mind, just as when a house is being robbed, the stolen goods can only be recovered if a strong man bursts in and disarms the burglar. Therefore we should keep our souls at peace so that the Holy Spirit is welcome there, and he can always keep our lamp of wisdom lit—for when it is, the dark and bitter impulses of the devil will be easy to see, and they will be pathetic and powerless as they are caught in that holy and glorious light.

This is why Saint Paul says "Do not extinguish the Spirit" (1 Thess. 5:19)—that is, do not sadden the Holy Spirit with evil acts and thoughts, or his light may cease to protect you.

Practice this and your mind will perceive and desire the consolations that God offers. It has an unfading memory of the taste of God's love, and so it can always seek what is best.

Diadochus of Photice

✢ 161 ✢

HE ARRIVED IN A
LOWLY CONDITION

*Who, being in very nature God, did not consider equality with God
something to be used to his own advantage; rather, he made himself
nothing by taking the very nature of a servant, being made
in human likeness. (Philippians 2:6–7)*

Christ is humble-minded and not someone who exalts himself over his flock. Our Lord Jesus Christ, the scepter of the majesty of God, did not come in the pomp of pride or arrogance, even though he easily could have, but arrived in a lowly condition, as the Holy Spirit had declared he would. For he said, "LORD, who has believed our report, and to whom is the arm of the LORD revealed?" (Isa. 53:1).

We have declared this message to you in his presence: he came as a child, like a thirsty root in the ground. He had no form of glory — we saw him, and he was not beautiful (v. 2). His eminence was hidden from us, and he was lacking even in comparison to an ordinary man. He was a man exposed to scars and sufferings, and acquainted with grief; his face was turned away; he was hated and not held in high honor (v. 3).

He bore our iniquities, and was sorrowful for our sake, but we assumed that it was his own fault that he was persecuted, afflicted, and killed (v. 4)! In fact, he was wounded for our transgressions, and bruised for our iniquities. He carried the costly punishment for our peace, and his scars were the means of our healing (v. 5).

We have all, like sheep, gone astray (v. 6). But the Father has delivered the Son over to death for our sins, and the Son does not even open his mouth in his sufferings. He was brought like a sheep to the slaughter, and like a lamb says nothing before the shearer, so Christ does not open his mouth (v. 7).

Clement of Rome

✤ 162 ✤

CHRIST PLUNDERS HELL (I)

*At noon, darkness came over the whole land until three
in the afternoon. (Mark 15:33)*

Something strange is happening — there is a great silence and stillness on earth today [Holy Saturday]. The whole earth keeps silence because the King is asleep. The earth trembled and is still because God has fallen asleep in the flesh, and he has raised up all who have ever slept since the world began. God has died in the flesh and hell trembles with fear.

He has gone to search for our first parents, as for lost sheep. Greatly desiring to visit those who live in darkness and in the shadow of death, he has gone to free the captives Adam and Eve from sorrow, he who is both God and the Son of Eve. The Lord approached them bearing the cross, the weapon that had won him the victory. When Adam saw him, he struck his breast in terror and cried out to everyone, "My Lord be with you all!" Christ answered him: "And with your spirit." He took him by the hand and raised him up, saying: "Awake, sleeper, and rise from the dead, and Christ will give you light" (Eph. 5:14).

"I am your God, who for your sake has become your son. Out of love for you and your descendants, by my own authority I now command all who are held in bondage to come forth, all who are in darkness to be enlightened, all who are sleeping to arise. I order you, sleeper, to awake. I did not create you to be held a prisoner in hell. Rise from the dead, for I am the Life of the dead. Rise up, work of my hands, you who were created in my image. Rise, let us leave this place, for you are in me and I in you; together we form one body and cannot be separated." [Continued in next entry ...]

Fourth-Century Writer

✢ 163 ✢

CHRIST PLUNDERS HELL (II)

The curtain of the temple was torn in two from top to bottom.
(Mark 15:38)

"For your sake I, your God, became your son; I, the Lord, took the form of a slave; I, whose home is above the heavens, descended to the earth and beneath the earth. For your sake, for the sake of humanity, I became like a helpless human. For the sake of you, who left a garden, I was betrayed to the Jews in a garden.

"See on my face how they spat upon me, which I took to restore to you the life I once breathed into you. See there the marks of the blows I received in order to refashion your warped nature in my image. On my back see the marks of the scourging I endured to remove the burden of sin that weighs upon your back. See my hands, nailed firmly to a tree, for you who once wickedly stretched out your hand to a tree.

"I slept on the cross and a sword pierced my side for you, who slept in paradise and brought forth Eve from your side. My side has healed the pain in yours. My sleep will rouse you from your sleep in hell. The sword that pierced me has sheathed the sword that was turned against you.

"Rise, let us leave this place. The enemy led you out of the earthly paradise. I will not restore you to that paradise, but will enthrone you in heaven. I forbade you the tree that was a symbol of life, but I, who am Life itself, am now one with you. I appointed cherubim to guard you as slaves are guarded, but now I make them worship you as God. The bridal chamber is adorned, the banquet is ready, the eternal dwelling places are prepared, the treasure-houses of all good things lie open. The kingdom of heaven has been prepared for you from all eternity."

Fourth-Century Writer

✢ 164 ✢

BE ROOTED IN DISCIPLINE

My son, do not despise the LORD's discipline, and do not resent his
rebuke, because the LORD disciplines those he loves, as a father
the son he delights in. (Proverbs 3:11–12)

Discipline is the safeguard of hope, the bond of faith, the guide on the way to salvation, the cause and nourishment of good attitudes, the teacher of virtue. Discipline lets us always abide in Christ and live continually for God and attain the heavenly promises and the divine rewards. To follow her is wholesome, and to turn away and neglect her is deadly.

So if God rebukes those whom he loves for the purpose of mending their ways, believers and especially pastors should love those whom they rebuke and not hate them. This was demonstrated by God through the prophet Jeremiah, who spoke of our times when he said, "And I will give you shepherds according to my heart: and they shall feed you with the food of discipline" (Jer. 3:15).

Therefore, if Holy Scripture frequently prescribes discipline everywhere in its pages, and the whole foundation of our faith rests on fear and obedience, what could be more appropriate than for us to urgently desire that you cling to discipline? What more could we wish for than for you to stand with strongly planted roots, with your houses built solidly upon the rock of the divine precepts, and unshaken by the storms and whirlwinds of the world so that you might arrive at the rewards of God?

Cyprian of Carthage

⤖ 165 ⤔

REWARDS FOLLOW OUR DUTIES

Since ancient times no one has heard, no ear has perceived, no eye has seen any God besides you, who acts on behalf of those who wait for him.
(Isaiah 64:4)

The good servant is confident of the bread he will receive for his labor, but the wicked and lazy servant cannot look his employer in the face. So it is our duty to be eager for goodness, since everything is from God. Since we believe in him with all our heart, we should obey him and not be idle or careless about good works. Our boasting and our confidence must rest in him. Let us be subject to his will. Look at the example of the host of angels, thousands and thousands who minister to him and stand ready to do his will, who rightly call him holy (Dan. 7:10; Isa. 6:3). We too should cry out to him continuously, with one voice and one mind, to share in his great and glorious promises.

How blessed and how wonderful are God's gifts! Life with immortality, glory with righteousness, truth with confidence, self-control with holiness—these are the gifts of which we have some understanding. What are the other gifts that he has in store for us? Only the Creator and Father of the ages knows their greatness and splendor.

We should therefore zealously strive to be among those who wait for him, so that we may share in the promised gifts. How should we do this? By fixing our mind on God through faith, by seeking diligently what is pleasing to him, by fulfilling his blameless will and following the way of truth, and casting off anything that is unholy.

Clement of Rome

✛ 166 ✛

PRAISING GOD
AT ALL TIMES

I will extol the LORD at all times; his praise will always be on my lips.
(Psalm 34:1)

Our thoughts in this life should rest on the praise of God, because in praising God we shall rejoice forever in the life to come; and no one can be ready for the next life unless he or she trains for it now. So we praise God during our earthly life and at the same time submit our petitions. Our praise is expressed with joy, our petitions with yearning. We have been promised something we do not yet possess, but the promise was made by the ultimate promise-keeper, so we trust him and are glad; yet we still long for it, because our gift is delayed.

Now, therefore, brothers and sisters, we urge you to praise God. That is what we are all telling each other when we say, "Alleluia." You say to your neighbor, "Praise the Lord!" and he says the same to you. We are all urging one another to praise the Lord, and all thereby doing what we urge the other to do. And remember, we praise not only with our lips and voices, but with our whole being: our minds, our lives, and all our actions.

We are praising God now, here in church; but when we depart from here, it may appear as if we cease to praise God. But provided we do not cease to live a good life, we shall always be praising God. If you never turn aside from the good life, your tongue may be silent but your actions will cry aloud, and God will perceive your intentions; for as our ears hear each other's voices, God's ears hear our thoughts.

Augustine

✣ 167 ✣

GOD HAS NO NEEDS

*If I were hungry I would not tell you, for the world is mine, and all that
is in it. Do I eat the flesh of bulls or drink the blood of goats?
(Psalm 50:12–13)*

In the beginning God created Adam, not because he needed man,
but because he wanted to have someone on whom to bestow his
blessings. Before Adam was, and even before all of creation was, the
Word was glorifying the Father in whom he dwelt and was himself
being glorified by the Father. The Word himself said, "Father, glorify
me with that glory I had with you before the world was" (John 17:5).

Nor did the Lord need our service. He commanded us to follow him, but this was the gift of salvation. To follow the Savior is
to share in salvation; to follow the light is to enjoy the light. Those
who are in the light are not the source of the light, but are themselves illuminated and enlightened by the source. They add nothing
to the light; rather, they are beneficiaries, for they are enlightened
by the light.

The same is true of service to God: it adds nothing to God, nor
does God need the service of man. Rather, he gives life and immortality and eternal glory to those who follow and serve him. He confers a benefit on his servants in return for their service and on his
followers in return for their loyalty, but he receives no benefit from
them. He is rich, perfect and in need of nothing.

The reason why God requires service from people is this:
because he is good and merciful he desires to confer benefits on
those who persevere in his service. Humanity needs communion
with God just as much as God needs nothing, that is, absolutely.

Irenaeus

⊹ 168 ⊹

A ROYAL PRIESTHOOD

For we were all baptized by one Spirit so as to form one body —
whether Jews or Gentiles, slave or free — and we were all
given the one Spirit to drink. (1 Corinthians 12:13)

Although the universal church of God is constituted of distinct orders of members, still, in spite of the many parts of its holy body, the church subsists as an integral whole, just as the Apostle says: "We are all one in Christ" (Gal. 3:28). No difference in office is so great that anyone can be separated, through lowliness, from the head. In the unity of faith and baptism, therefore, our community is undivided. There is a common dignity, as the apostle Peter says in these words: "And you are built up as living stones into spiritual houses, a holy priesthood, offering spiritual sacrifices which are acceptable to God through Jesus Christ" (1 Pet. 2:5). And again: "But you are a chosen people, a royal priesthood, a holy nation, a people set apart" (1 Pet. 2:9).

For all, regenerated in Christ, are made kings by the sign of the cross; they are consecrated priests by the oil of the Holy Spirit, so that beyond the special service of our ministry as priests, all spiritual and mature Christians know that they are a royal race and are sharers in the office of the priesthood. For what is more kinglike than to find yourself ruler over your body after having surrendered your soul to God? And what is more priestly than to promise the Lord a pure conscience, and to offer him the passions of the flesh on the altar of your heart?

Leo the Great

✢ 169 ✢

GOD'S WILL TO SAVE

There will be more rejoicing in heaven over one sinner who repents than over ninety-nine righteous persons who do not need to repent. (Luke 15:7)

God's will is to save us, and nothing pleases him more than our coming back to him with true repentance. The heralds of truth and the ministers of divine grace have told us this from the beginning, repeating it in every age. Indeed, God's desire for our salvation is the primary and preeminent sign of his infinite goodness. Precisely in order to show that there is nothing closer to God's heart than this, the divine Word of God the Father, with untold humility, lived among us in the flesh, suffered, and died; he said all that was necessary to reconcile us to God the Father when we were at enmity with him, and to restore us to the life of blessedness from which we had been exiled. He healed our physical infirmities by miracles. He freed us from our sins, many and grievous as they were, by suffering and dying, taking them upon himself as if he were answerable for them, though he was sinless himself. He also taught us in many different ways that we should wish to imitate him by our own kindness and genuine love for one another.

So it was that Christ proclaimed that he had come to call sinners to repentance, not the righteous, and that it was not the healthy who required a doctor, but the sick. He declared that he had come to look for the sheep that was lost, and that it was to the lost sheep of the house of Israel that he had been sent. Speaking more obscurely in the parable of the silver coin, he tells us that the purpose of his coming was to reclaim the royal image, which had been coated with the filth of sin.

Maximus the Confessor

✢ 170 ✢

FOLLOWING HIM MEANS SELF-DENIAL (I)

Whoever wants to be my disciple must deny themselves
and take up their cross and follow me. (Mark 8:34)

The Lord's command seems difficult and painful, that whoever wishes to follow him must deny themselves. But his command is not really difficult or painful, since he himself helps us to do what he commands. For the verse of the psalm addressed to him was truly spoken: "Because of the words of your lips I have dealt with hardships" (Ps. 17:4). Also true are his own words: "My yoke is mild and my burden is light" (Matt. 11:30). For love makes whatever is difficult easy in his commands.

What does it mean, "let them take up their cross"? It means they must endure many things that are painful; that is the way they must follow Jesus. When they begin to follow Christ in his life and teachings, many will contradict them and try to stop them, or dissuade them, even those who call themselves Christ's disciples. These people are like Christ's followers who tried to stop the blind men from calling out to him (Matt. 20:31).

So if you want to follow Christ, you will take these threats and obstacles as honors, and fashion them into the cross; you must endure it, carry it, and not give way under it. And so in the church—the place of the good, the reconciled, and the saved— which completely follows Christ, he has said to everyone: "If anyone wishes to follow me, let them deny themselves." [Continued in next entry ...]

Augustine

❧ 171 ❧

FOLLOWING HIM MEANS SELF-DENIAL (II)

But rejoice inasmuch as you participate in the sufferings of Christ,
so that you may be overjoyed when his glory is revealed. If you are
insulted because of the name of Christ, you are blessed, for the Spirit
of glory and of God rests on you. (1 Peter 4:13–14)

This is a command for both virgins and brides to obey, for widows and for married women, for monks and for married men, or for the clergy and for the laity. The whole church, the entire body, all the members in their distinct and varied functions, must follow Christ. She who is totally unique, the dove, the spouse who was redeemed and bought by the blood of her bridegroom, is to follow him.

There is a place in the church for the chastity of the virgin, for the temperance of the widow, and for the modesty of the married. Indeed, all her members have their place, and this is where they are to follow Christ, in their role and in their way of life. They must deny themselves; that is, they must surrender themselves to Christ. They must take up their cross by enduring whatever pain the world brings for Christ's sake.

Let us love him who alone can neither deceive nor be deceived, who alone will not fail us. Let us love him because his promises are true. Our faith sometimes falters because we are not rewarded immediately. But hold out, be steadfast, endure, bear the delay, and you have carried the cross.

Augustine

❖ 172 ❖

THE TROPHY RAISED AGAINST DEMONS

Remember the wonders he has done, his miracles,
and the judgments he pronounced. (Psalm 105:5)

Let me tell you something remarkable about how Christ gained his victory. Christ conquered the devil using the same weapons that the devil used to win in the garden. The symbols of our fall were the virgin Eve, the tree of the knowledge of good and evil, and Adam's penalty of death. In God's victory, instead of Eve there was Mary; instead of the tree, the wood of the cross; instead of Adam's death, the death of Christ.

Do you see that the devil was defeated by the means he used in the first place? By a tree the devil deceived Eve, and by a tree Christ defeated him. The first tree buried Adam in the earth as captive; the second tree raised Christ up as a victor. The first death condemned those who followed, but the second death saved those who came before.

And this victory was won without any effort or contribution of our own. We did not bloody any weapons, or stand on the battle line, or suffer any injury, or even sweat, and yet we won the victory. It was the Lord's combat, but the crown is ours. And since it is our victory, let us like soldiers sing joyously of our achievement and praise our captain.

The cross is our trophy raised against the demons, our shield against sin, and the sword Christ used to pierce the serpent. The cross is the Father's will, the glory of the only begotten Son, the joy of the Spirit, the pride of the angels, the guarantee of the church, the boast of Paul, the fortress of the saints, and the light of the entire world.

John Chrysostom

✣ 173 ✣

AN UNSPEAKABLE MYSTERY

I delight to sit in his shade, and his fruit is sweet to my taste.
(Song of Solomon 2:3)

Good Shepherd, you who carry the whole flock on your shoulders, where do you pasture your sheep? For the entire human race, which you lift onto your shoulders, is a single sheep. Show me the place where there are green pastures and restful waters, lead me out to nourishing grass, and call me by name so that I can hear your voice, for I am your own sheep. And through that voice calling me, give me eternal life.

"Tell me, you whom my soul loves" (Song 1:7). This is how I address you, because your true name is above all other names; it is unspeakable and a mystery to all rational creatures. So the name I use for you is simply the statement of my soul's love for you, and this is a good name for making your goodness known. Though I am very dark you loved me, and you laid down your life for me, so how could I not love you? There is no greater love imaginable than this, that you should purchase my salvation at the cost of your life.

Show me, says the bride, where you tend your sheep, so that I may find the saving pasture and be filled with heavenly nourishment. For whoever does not eat this food cannot enter eternal life. Let me run to you, the spring, and taste the divine drink that you pour out for the thirsty, offering water from your side opened by the spear. Whoever drinks of this becomes "a fountain of water springing up to eternal life" (John 4:14).

This is what the bride speaks, anxious about the beauty God has given her and seeking to learn how her beauty may continue forever.

Gregory of Nyssa

⁘ 174 ⁘

WITNESS AND TESTIFY
WITH ACTIONS

This is how you can recognize the Spirit of God: Every spirit that
acknowledges that Jesus Christ has come in the flesh is from God.
(1 John 4:2)

Just like there are many kinds of persecution, so there are many kinds of martyrdom. Every day you are a witness to Christ. You were tempted by the spirit of fornication but feared the coming judgment of Christ and did not want the purity of your mind and body to be defiled: you are a martyr for Christ. You were tempted by the spirit of greed to seize the property of a child and violate the rights of a defenseless widow but remembered God's law and saw your duty to help and not act unjustly: you are a witness to Christ.

Christ wants witnesses like this to stand ready, as Scripture says: "Do justice for the orphan and defend the widow" (Isa. 1:17). You were tempted by the spirit of pride but saw the poor and the needy and looked with loving compassion on them, and fostered humility rather than arrogance: you are a witness to Christ. More importantly, your witness was not in word only but also in deed.

Who gives greater witness than one who acknowledges that the Lord Jesus has come in the flesh and keeps the commandments of the Gospel? Those who hear the Word but do not act deny Christ. Even if they acknowledge him with their words, they deny him with their deeds. How many will say to Christ, "Lord, Lord, did we not prophesy and cast out devils and work many miracles, all in your name?" (Matt. 7:22). On that day he will say to them, "Depart from me, all you evildoers" (Matt. 7:23). The true witnesses are those who affirm with their mouths the commandments of the Lord Jesus and obey them with their deeds.

Ambrose

❖ 175 ❖

OUR CHILDREN
AND OUR WEALTH (I)

The righteous lead blameless lives; blessed are their children after them.
(Proverbs 20:7)

By the words "Their angels see my Father's face" (Matt. 18:10) and "For this purpose I have come" (John 12:27) and "This is my Father's will" (Matt 18:14), the Lord calls those who take care of children to a special task.

He has built a protective wall around them. Severe punishments are threatened for whoever causes them harm, and great blessings are promised to whoever protects and cares for them. All this is confirmed by the example of our Father, who takes care of his children. So let us imitate him and do whatever is necessary for our brothers and sisters—his children—however simple or difficult it may seem to us.

We may have to serve some insignificant person, and the job may be taxing, and obstacles may lie in our way, but for the salvation of our brothers and sisters everything must be endured. So from the moment we leave our homes in the morning, let us aim to rescue anyone who is in danger.

Nothing is as precious as a human soul. "For what does it profit a man if he gains the whole world but suffers the loss of his soul?" (Mark 8:36). Yet the love of money has perverted and destroyed all our values; it has driven out the fear of God and holds us in its power, as a usurper holds a throne. We actually neglect the spiritual well-being of ourselves and our children in our desire to become richer. And what is our goal? To leave our wealth to others, who will in turn leave it to others, and then on to their descendants? We are not really owners of our money and possessions—we merely hand them on. What folly! [Continued in next entry . . .]

John Chrysostom

✢ 176 ✢

OUR CHILDREN AND OUR WEALTH (II)

And these words that I command you today shall be on your heart.
(Deuteronomy 6)

Our children become less important than our workers. We admonish our workers for our own financial benefit, but our children receive no instruction or correction, in effect being regarded as less valuable than our workers.

But why even compare our children with other humans? We take better care of our cattle and horses than our children. Those who own a mule make sure to find the best driver for it, not some idiot who is a dishonest and inexperienced drunk. But if our child needs a teacher, we take the first person who comes along, haphazardly and without consideration. Yet no profession is more important than teaching.

For what even remotely compares with guiding the soul and forming the mind and character of a young person? A teacher should be more skilled than a painter, and certainly more virtuous. But we completely neglect this. The one thing that matters to us is that our child learns to speak well—and just for the sake of money! In fact, if a person could become wealthy without being able to speak at all, we would not bother with our language lessons.

Money exercises a tyranny over the world! It invades all of life and forces people to go where it chooses, like slaves. We make verbal attacks against it, but it defeats us by the sheer force of events. Nevertheless, I will not stop attacking it with my mouth, and if I achieve anything, you and I will both be better off.

John Chrysostom

✢ 177 ✢

ALL JUSTICE FULFILLED

Look at my hands and my feet. It is I myself! Touch me and see; a ghost does not have flesh and bones, as you see I have. (Luke 24:39)

I celebrate the glory of Jesus Christ as God, because he is responsible for your wisdom, coming from the perfection of your unshakeable faith. You are like people who have been nailed body and soul to the cross of Jesus Christ, confirmed in love by his blood.

In regard to the Lord, you firmly believe that he was "of the race of David according to the flesh" (Rom. 1:3) but God's Son by the will and power of God; truly born of the Virgin and baptized by John, "that all justice might be fulfilled" (Matt. 3:15); truly nailed to a cross in the flesh for our sake under Pontius Pilate and the Tetrarch Herod; and that we are the fruit of his most blessed passion. By his resurrection he raised up a flag of victory over his saints and is forever the head of his church, one body of Jews and Gentiles. He endured all this for us and our salvation, and he truly suffered and just as truly rose from the dead.

I am convinced that he was united with his body even after the resurrection. When he visited Peter and his companions, he said to them, "Take hold of me, touch me and see that I am not a spirit without a body" (Luke 24:39). Immediately they touched him and believed, and therefore they immediately despised and conquered death. In addition, after his resurrection, the Lord ate and drank with them like a real human being, even though in spirit he was united with his Father.

Ignatius of Antioch

✤ 178 ✤

UNCHANGEABLE GLORIFICATION

In a flash, in the twinkling of an eye, at the last trumpet.
For the trumpet will sound, the dead will be raised imperishable,
and we will be changed. (1 Corinthians 15:52)

Future transformation will be rewarded to those who are united to Christ and his companions by upright lives within the communion of the church. He hints at the nature of the change when he says, "This corruptible body must put on incorruptibility, this mortal body immortality" (1 Cor. 15:53). In other words, in order to obtain the transformation that is the reward of the just, men and women must first undergo a change here on earth, which is God's free gift. Those who have been changed from evil to good in this life are promised the future transformation as a reward.

Through justification and the spiritual resurrection, grace now causes an initial change in them that is God's gift. Later on, through the bodily resurrection, the transformation of the just will be brought to completion, and they will experience a perfect, lasting, unchangeable glorification. The purpose of the change wrought in them is that they may abide in an eternal, changeless state of joy.

Here on earth they are changed by the first resurrection, by which they are converted and enlightened, thus passing from death to life, sinfulness to holiness, unbelief to faith, and evil actions to a holy life. For this reason the second death has no power over them.

Anyone in this life who is converted out of fear of God passes from an evil life to a good one and passes from death to life, and later they will be transformed from a shameful state to a glorious one.

Fulgentius of Ruspe

❖ 179 ❖

THE GENTLE
AND TENDER SPIRIT

There are different kinds of gifts, but the same Spirit distributes them.
There are different kinds of service, but the same Lord. There are
different kinds of working, but in all of them and in everyone
it is the same God at work. (1 Corinthians 12:4–6)

The Spirit makes one person a teacher of divine truth, inspires another to prophesy, gives another the power of casting out devils, enables another to interpret Holy Scripture. The Spirit strengthens one person's self-control, shows another how to help the poor, teaches another to fast and lead a life of asceticism, makes another oblivious to the needs of the body, trains another for martyrdom. His action is different in different people, but the Spirit himself is always the same. The Scripture says, "In each person the Spirit reveals his presence in a particular way for the common good" (1 Cor. 12:7).

The Spirit comes gently and makes himself known by his fragrance. He is not felt as a burden, for he is very light. Rays of light and knowledge emanate from him as he approaches. The Spirit comes with the tenderness of a true friend and protector to save, to heal, to teach, to advise, to strengthen, to console. The Spirit first comes to enlighten the mind of the one who receives him, and then through this one to the minds of others as well.

Just as light strikes the eyes of people who come out of darkness into the sunshine, and suddenly they can see things they could not see before, so too does light flood the souls of people who receive the Holy Spirit, and suddenly they can see things beyond the range of human vision, things previously undreamed of.

Cyril of Jerusalem

✦ 180 ✦

THE PATH IS SET BEFORE US

But if anyone obeys his word, love for God is truly made complete in them. This is how we know we are in him: Whoever claims to live in him must live as Jesus did. (1 John 2:5–6)

Dear brothers and sisters, the commands in the Gospel are truly God's lessons: the foundations on which to build up hope, the supports for strengthening faith, the food that nourishes the heart. They are the rudder that keeps us on the right course, and the protection that keeps our salvation secure. They instruct the receptive minds of believers on earth in order to lead safely to the kingdom of heaven.

God willed that many things should be said by his servants the prophets and willed for them to be listened to by his people. How much greater are the things spoken by the Son! The Word of God himself now confirms the things he at one time said through the prophets. He no longer commands us to prepare the way for his coming: he comes in person and prepares a way for us and directs us toward it. Before, we wandered in the darkness of death, aimlessly and blindly. Now we can see by the light of grace, and are able to continue down the road of life, with the Lord preceding us and directing us.

The Lord has given us many counsels and commandments to help us toward salvation. He has even given us a pattern of prayer, instructing us on how we should pray. He has given us life, and with his accustomed generosity, he has also taught us how to pray. He has made it easy for us to be heard as we pray to the Father in the words taught by the Son.

Cyprian of Carthage

⊹ 181 ⊹

ON THE INCARNATION

But in these last days he has spoken to us by his Son,
whom he appointed heir of all things, and through whom
also he made the universe. (Hebrews 1:2)

We must consider the Word's becoming man and his divine appearing in our midst. That mystery the Jews defame, the Greeks deride, but we adore; and your own love and devotion to the Word will be greater, because in his manhood he seems worth so little. For it is a fact that the more unbelievers pour scorn on him, the more he makes his godhead evident. The things they, as humans, rule out as impossible, he plainly shows to be possible; that which they deride as unfitting, his goodness makes most fit; and things these windbags laugh at as "human" he declares divine by his inherent might. Thus what seem to be his utter poverty and weakness on the cross he uses to embarrass the parade of idols and quietly and secretly wins over the mockers and unbelievers to recognize him as God.

You must understand why it is that the Word of the Father, so great and so high, has been made manifest in bodily form. He has been manifested in a human body for the salvation of us humans, out of the love and goodness of his Father. We will begin with the creation of the world and with God its Maker, for the first fact that you must grasp is this: the renewal of creation has been accomplished by the same Word who made it in the beginning. There is thus no inconsistency between creation and salvation, for the one Father has employed the same agent for both works, effecting the salvation of the world through the same Word who made it in the beginning.

Athanasius

✦ 182 ✦

SHARING THE TITLES
OF CHRIST

I no longer live, but Christ lives in me. (Galatians 2:20)

Paul teaches us the power of Christ's name when he calls him the power and wisdom of God, our peace, the unapproachable light where God dwells, our expiation and redemption, our great high priest, our paschal sacrifice, our propitiation—the radiance of God's glory, the very pattern of his nature, the Creator of all ages, our spiritual food and drink, the rock and the water, the bedrock of our faith, the cornerstone, the visible image of the invisible God. He goes on to speak of him as the mighty God, the head of his body the church, the firstborn of the new creation, the firstfruits of those who have fallen asleep, the firstborn of the dead, the eldest of many brothers. He tells us that Christ is the mediator between God and humankind, the only begotten Son crowned with glory and honor, the Lord of glory, the beginning of all things, the King of justice and of peace, the King of the whole universe, ruling a realm that has no limits.

Paul calls Christ by many other titles too numerous to recall here. Their cumulative force will give some conception of the marvelous content of the name "Christ," revealing to us his inexpressible majesty, insofar as our minds and thought can comprehend it. Since by God's goodness we who are called "Christians" have been granted the honor of sharing this name—the greatest, highest, and most sublime of all names—it follows that each of Christ's titles should be clearly reflected in us. If we are not to lie when we call ourselves "Christians," we must bear witness to this honor by our way of living.

Gregory of Nyssa

✛ 183 ✛

THE FEAR OF THE LORD (I)

The LORD confides in those who fear him;
he makes his covenant known to them. (Psalm 25:14)

Notice that when Scripture speaks of the fear of the Lord it does not leave the phrase in isolation, as if it were a complete summary of faith. No, many things are added to it, or are presupposed by it. From these we may learn its meaning and excellence. In the book of Proverbs, Solomon tells us, "If you cry out for wisdom and raise your voice for understanding, if you look for it as silver and search for it as treasure, then you will understand the fear of the LORD" (Prov. 2:3–5). We see here the difficult journey we must undertake before we can arrive at the fear of the Lord.

We must begin by crying out for wisdom. We must hand over the duty of all decision making to our intellect. We must look for wisdom and search for it. Then we can understand the fear of the Lord.

"Fear" is not to be understood in the sense that we commonly give to it. Fear in the ordinary sense is the trepidation our weak humanity feels when it is afraid of suffering something it does not want to happen. We are afraid, or are made afraid, because of a guilty conscience, the rights of someone more powerful, an attack from someone who is stronger, sickness, encountering a wild beast—suffering evil in any form. This kind of fear is not taught: it happens because we are weak. We do not have to learn what we should fear: objects of fear bring their own terror with them. [Continued in next entry ...]

Hilary of Poitiers

✢ 184 ✢

THE FEAR OF THE LORD (II)

Come, my children, listen to me; I will teach you the fear of the LORD.
(Psalm 34:11)

The fear of the Lord has to be learned because it can be taught. It does not lie in terror, but in something that can be taught. It does not arise from the fearfulness of our nature; it has to be acquired by obedience to the commandments, by holiness of life, and by knowledge of the truth.

For us the fear of God consists wholly in love, and perfect love of God brings our fear of him to its perfection. Our love for God has its own responsibility: to observe his wisdom, to obey his laws, to trust his promises. Listen to what Scripture says: "And now, Israel, what does the LORD your God ask of you except to fear the LORD your God and walk in all his ways and love him and keep his commandments, with your whole heart and your whole soul, so that it may be well for you?" (Deut. 10:12).

The ways of the Lord are many, though he himself is the way. When he speaks of himself he calls himself "the way" and shows us the reason why he called himself that: "No one can come to the Father except through me" (John 14:6).

We should ask for these many ways, to find the goodness of all of them. That is, we shall find the one way of eternal life through the guidance of many teachers. These ways are found in the law, in the prophets, in the gospels, in the writings of the apostles, and in the different good works with which we fulfill the commandments. Blessed are those who walk in these ways in the fear of the Lord.

Hilary of Poitiers

✦ 185 ✦

OLD SACRIFICES, NEW EUCHARIST

For by one sacrifice he has made perfect forever
those who are being made holy. (Hebrews 10:14)

In the time of the Old Testament, patriarchs, prophets, and priests sacrificed animals in Christ's honor, and in honor of the Father and the Holy Spirit as well.

Now in the time of the New Testament the holy catholic church throughout the world never ceases to offer bread and wine, in faith and love, to him and to the Father and the Holy Spirit, with whom he shares one godhead.

The former animal sacrifices looked forward to the flesh of Christ that he would offer for our sins — though himself without sin — and the blood that he would pour out for the forgiveness of our sins. Our celebration commemorates and gives thanks for the flesh of Christ that he offered for us, and the blood that he poured out for us.

The sacrifices of old used signs to point to what would be given to us. In the Eucharist we see plainly what has already been given to us. The old sacrifices foretold the death of the Son of God for sinners. In the Eucharist his death for sinners is proclaimed as accomplished, as the Apostle testifies: "Christ died for the wicked at a time when we were still powerless, and when we were enemies we were reconciled with God through the death of his Son" (Rom. 5:6, 10).

Fulgentius of Ruspe

✢ 186 ✢

THE FIRST AND LAST ADAM

The first man was of the dust of the earth;
the second man is of heaven. (1 Corinthians 15:47)

The holy Apostle has told us that the human race takes its origin from two men, Adam and Christ, who are equal in body but unequal in merit, completely alike in their physical structure but totally different in the origin of their being. He says, "The first man, Adam, became a living soul, the last Adam a life-giving spirit" (1 Cor. 15:45).

The first Adam was created by the last Adam, who also gave him his soul and his life. On the other hand, the last Adam was formed by his own action; he did not wait for life to be given to him by someone else, but was himself the one who could give life. The first Adam was formed from dirt that was worthless, but the second Adam was born from a virgin womb that was precious. With the first Adam, earth was changed into flesh, but with the second Adam, flesh was raised up to divinity.

What more can we say? The second Adam stamped his image on the first Adam when he was created. In order to save what he had made in his own image, he took on the name and the headship of the first Adam. The first Adam, the last Adam—the first had a beginning, the last has no end. The last Adam is indeed the first; as he himself says: "I am the first and the last" (Rev. 22:13).

Peter Chrysologus

✦ 187 ✦

GIVE AS YOU ASK TO RECEIVE

Give, and it will be given to you. A good measure, pressed down, shaken together and running over, will be poured into your lap. For with the measure you use, it will be measured to you. (Luke 6:38)

What kind of people are we? When God gives, we gladly receive, but when he begs, we refuse to give. Remember, it was Christ who said, "I was hungry and you gave me nothing to eat" (Matt. 25:42). When the poor are starving, Christ hungers too. Do not neglect to improve the miserable condition of the poor, if you desire your own sins to be forgiven. Christ hungers now, my brothers and sisters; he condescends to feel hunger and thirst in the needy. And what he receives on earth today is what he will return in heaven tomorrow.

What do you wish for, what do you pray for, my dear brothers and sisters, when you come to church? Is it mercy? How can it be anything else? Show mercy, then, while you are on earth, and mercy will be shown to you in heaven. A poor person asks you for something; you ask God for something. He begs for a morsel of food; you beg for eternal life. Give to the beggar so that you may receive from Christ. For Christ says, "Give and it will be given to you" (Luke 6:38). It baffles me that you have the audacity to ask for what you do not want to give. Give when you come to church. Give to the poor. Give them whatever your resources will allow.

Caesarius of Arles

❖ 188 ❖

DIVINE LOVE TRIUMPHS OVER FEAR (I)

After this, the word of the LORD came to Abram in a vision:
"Do not be afraid, Abram. I am your shield, your very great reward."
(Genesis 15:1)

When God saw the world falling to ruin because of fear, he immediately acted to call it back to himself with love. He invited it by his grace, preserved it by his love, and embraced it with compassion. When the earth had become hardened by evil, God sent the flood both to punish and to cleanse it. He called Noah to be the father of a new era, urged him with kind words, and showed that he trusted him; he gave him fatherly instruction about the coming calamity and graciously consoled him with hope for the future. God did not merely issue commands, but shared the work with Noah and filled the ark with the future parents of the whole world. Their loving fellowship removed fear from Noah, and mutual love preserved the fruit of their shared labor.

God called Abraham out of the heathen world, symbolically lengthened his name, and made him the father of all believers. God walked with him on his journeys, protected him in foreign lands, enriched him with earthly possessions, and honored him with victories. He made a covenant with him, saved him from harm, accepted his hospitality, and astonished him by giving him the offspring he thought he would never have. Lavished with so many graces and drawn by the sweetness of divine love, Abraham learned to love God rather than fear him, and love rather than fear inspired his worship. [Continued in next entry ...]

Peter Chrysologus

✤ 189 ✤

DIVINE LOVE TRIUMPHS OVER FEAR (II)

My heart says of you, "Seek his face!" Your face, LORD, I will seek.
(Psalm 27:8)

God comforted Jacob with a dream during his flight, roused him to combat upon his return, and taught him with a wrestler's embrace not to be afraid of the Lord, but to love him. God spoke to Moses as a father would and with fatherly affection invited him to become the liberator of his people.

In all of these events, the flame of divine love enkindled human hearts. Wounded by love, these men longed to look upon God with their bodily eyes. Yet how could our faulty human vision see God, whom the whole world cannot contain? But the law of love is not concerned with what will be, what ought to be, or what can be. Love does not hold back; it is unreasonable and knows no moderation. Love is inconsolable when it cannot reach its goal and despises all hindrances between it and its object. Love destroys the lover if he cannot obtain what he loves; love aims at its own satisfaction and does not think of right and wrong. Love creates a desire to do the forbidden. Need I go on?

It is intolerable for love not to see the object of its longing. That is why the saints were dissatisfied if they could not see the Lord. A love that desires to see God may not be altogether reasonable, but it is the evidence of filial love. It gave Moses the boldness to say, "If I have found favor in your eyes, show me your face" (Ex. 33:17–18). It inspired the Psalmist to make the same prayer: "Show me your face" (Ps. 69:17; 102:2). Even the pagans made their images for this purpose—they wanted actually to see what they mistakenly revered.

Peter Chrysologus

✣ 190 ✣

ATONEMENT AND
THE TRUE HIGH PRIEST

*This is my blood of the covenant, which is poured out for many
for the forgiveness of sins. (Matthew 26:28)*

Once a year the high priest, leaving the people outside, entered
that place where no one except the high priest could enter. In
it was the mercy seat, and above the mercy seat were the cherubim
as well as the ark of the covenant and the altar of incense.

Let me turn to my true high priest, the Lord Jesus Christ. In
our human nature he spent the whole year in the company of the
people, the year that he spoke of when he said: "He sent me to
bring good news to the poor, to announce the acceptable year of the
LORD, and the day of forgiveness" (Isa. 61:1–2). Notice how once
in that year, on the day of atonement, he enters into the Holy of
Holies. Having fulfilled God's plan, he passes through the heavens,
enters into the presence of the Father to make him turn in mercy to
the human race, and prays for all who believe in him.

Paul the apostle, knowing of the atonement that Christ makes to
the Father for all people, says this: "He is the atonement for our sins
in his blood, through faith" (Rom. 3:25). We have a day of atonement that remains until the world comes to an end.

God taught the people of the old covenant how to celebrate the
ritual offered to him in atonement for the sins of people. But you
have come to Christ, the true high priest. Through his blood he has
made God turn to you in mercy and has reconciled you with the
Father. You must not think of ordinary blood, but recognize instead
the blood of the Word.

Origen

GIFTED PHYSICIANS

Besides everything else, I face daily the pressure of my concern for all the churches. (2 Corinthians 11:28)

Holy men undergoing tribulation will endure violence and verbal attacks. They resist violence with the shield of patience and combat verbal attacks by firing the sharp arrows of true doctrine. They take the posture of patient contempt for their enemy but are mindful of weaker believers — they oppose the enemy so that no one is led astray but remain blameless so that other brothers do not lose sight of the truly upright life.

But think about how difficult it is to simultaneously endure attacks from without and protect the weak from within. He endures the attacks without, perhaps being whipped and locked up; inwardly he experiences fear, since he worries that his sufferings may be a stumbling block — not to himself but his disciples. For this reason Paul writes to them, "Let no one be shaken by these trials, for you know that they are our lot" (1 Thess. 3:3). While he suffered himself he feared for the fall of others, that seeing him flogged for his faith might stop them from publicly confessing their own.

What an immensely loving heart! He thinks nothing of his own suffering and is concerned only for the disciples' salvation. He brushes off his own bodily wounds and brings healing to the spiritual wounds of others. It is characteristic of holy men that their own painful trials do not make them lose their concern for the well-being of others. They are grieved by their torments, but they nonetheless look out for others and teach them necessary lessons; they are like gifted physicians who are sick themselves. They also suffer injuries but bring others the medicine that cures them.

Gregory the Great

✢ 192 ✢

CHRIST THE OBJECT OF OUR FAITH

He committed no sin, and no deceit was found in his mouth.
(1 Peter 2:22)

Elders should be sympathetic and merciful to everyone, bring back those who have wandered, and visit the sick; they must not neglect widows and orphans or the poor, always providing for what is good in the sight of God and of people. They should refrain entirely from anger, partiality, and prejudice; greediness should be wholly alien to them. Nor should they be rash in believing something said against another, nor too severe in judging others, since they know that we are all debtors through sin.

If, then, we pray to the Lord to forgive us, we must in turn forgive. For we live under the eye of our Lord and God, and "we must all stand before the judgment seat of God, each to give an account of himself" (Rom. 14:10–12). Let us then serve God with fear and awe. The Lord's command is also the command of the apostles who preached the Gospel to us, to say nothing of the prophets who foretold the Lord's coming.

For anyone who does not confess that Jesus has come in the flesh is the antichrist. And anyone who refuses to admit the testimony of the cross is of the devil. Whoever perverts the Lord's words to suit his or her own desires and denies that there is a resurrection or a judgment is the firstborn of Satan.

So let us persevere in the pledge of our righteousness and in our hope, that is, in Christ Jesus. He endured everything for our sake so that we might live in him. Let us then imitate his constancy; if we should suffer because of his name, let us give him that glory. For this is the personal example he has given us—this is the object of our faith.

Polycarp

❖ 193 ❖

FROM THE LIFE AND PASSION OF CYPRIAN (I)

Where can I go from your Spirit? Where can I flee from your presence?
(Psalm 139:7)

Banishment followed the good and benevolent actions of Cyprian [bishop of Carthage], for injustice always brings evil on a holy man. So a man who had worked for the city's safety, its plague victims, and its welfare was ostracized from it. He had toiled so that the living might not suffer the horrors of hell, with vigilance and unacknowledged goodness, and cared for the sick when the rest of the country considered the city to be too far gone to help. With what wickedness they treated this man!

But let the world, which considers banishment a punishment, hear this. To them, their country is very dear, and they share the name of their parents; but we hate even our parents if they try to persuade us against God. To them, it is a severe punishment to live outside their own city; to Christians, the whole world is their home — even if they are banished to some hidden and far-off place, as long as they have God, they are never in exile.

In another way, even while serving God, Christians are strangers in the world even in their own city. For through the Holy Spirit's power their former person is left behind and their sinful desires are suppressed, and among their fellow citizens and even parents they are like strangers. Besides all this, although to the world it might look like a punishment, we suffer these trials as a proof of our virtue, and in this way it is not a punishment but a glory. [Continued in next entry ...]

Pontius of Carthage

✦ 194 ✦

FROM THE LIFE AND PASSION OF CYPRIAN (II)

Now Stephen, a man full of God's grace and power, performed great
wonders and signs among the people. Opposition arose, however, from
members of the Synagogue of the Freedmen (as it was called) — Jews of
Cyrene and Alexandria as well as the provinces of Cilicia and Asia —
who began to argue with Stephen. But they could not stand up against
the wisdom the Spirit gave him as he spoke. (Acts 6:8 – 10)

So the judge read Cyprian's sentence from his tablet without understanding its spiritual significance. It was a sentence worthy of the
bishop and his witness, a glorious sentence, in which he was called a
standard-bearer of the Christian sect, and an enemy of the gods, and
one who was to be punished as an example to his people — and that
discipline would be established with the shedding of his blood.

Nothing could be more complete, nothing more true, than this
sentence. For everything that was said, although said by a heathen, was divine. And we should not be surprised, since priests
are known to prophesy of an imminent martyrdom. He had been a
standard-bearer, who taught others how to bear Christ's standard;
he had been an enemy of the gods, and commanded their idols to
be destroyed. Moreover, he was an example to his friends since he
was the first in the province to consecrate the firstfruits of martyrdom, when many would soon follow him. And through his blood
discipline would be established, but it was the discipline of martyrs,
who would emulate him in glory by the discipline of giving up their
lives for the faith. [Continued in next entry . . .]

Pontius of Carthage

✢ 195 ✢

FROM THE LIFE AND PASSION OF CYPRIAN (III)

I saw that the woman was drunk with the blood of God's holy people,
the blood of those who bore testimony to Jesus. When I saw her,
I was greatly astonished. (Revelation 17:6)

Besides being an example to all good men, Cyprian was also the first in Africa to decorate his priestly crown with the blood of martyrdom, since he was the first martyr since the apostles. We know this from the episcopal order recorded at Carthage, which has no good men or priests suffering death for the faith. Although God recognizes true devotion in holy men before martyrdom, Cyprian was the first priest to decorate his garments with the glorious blood of martyrdom. The city in which he lived and accomplished many noble deeds was also where he attained a perfect crown by imitating his Lord in death.

What will I do now? Between joy at his passion and grief at remaining behind, my mind is pulled in different directions, and contrary feelings are burdening my weak heart. Should I grieve that I was not his associate? But I must triumph in his victory. Shall I triumph at his victory? Yet I still grieve that I am not his companion. I must confess what you are already aware of, that it was my intention to be martyred with him. I rejoice in his glory, but mourn that I am not with him in heaven.

Pontius of Carthage

196

GOD'S ROBUST WORD

Man does not live on bread alone but on every word that comes from the mouth of the L*ORD*. *(Deuteronomy 8:3)*

Lord, who can comprehend even one of your words? We lose more of it than we hold on to, like people drinking from a flowing spring. For God's Word offers different truths depending on the capacity of the listener, and he has painted his message in many colors, so that whoever listens to it can hear what is appropriate for him or her. There are all kinds of treasures buried inside, so that each of us might grow rich in seeking them out.

And so whenever you discover some part of the treasure, you should not think that you have exhausted God's Word. Instead you should feel that this was all the wealth that you were able to find in it. Nor should you say that the Word is weak and unfruitful simply because all you happened to find was one portion. You should actually give thanks for its riches precisely because you could not capture it all.

So be glad that you are overwhelmed by the Word, not saddened because God is too much for you. A thirsty person is happy when drinking, not depressed because he or she cannot exhaust the spring! So let this spring quench your thirst, and do not try to quench the spring with your drinking. If you can satisfy your thirst without exhausting the spring, then when you are thirsty again you can drink from it once more.

Be thankful then for what you have received, and do not be saddened at all that such an abundance still remains. What you have received is your present share, while what is left will be your inheritance. What you cannot receive now because of weakness will be given to you later if you persevere.

Ephrem the Syrian

⊰ 197 ⊱

THE LETHARGY OF SIN

I myself in my mind am a slave to God's law, but in my sinful nature
a slave to the law of sin. (Romans 7:25)

With the baggage of the world was I kept numb, like when asleep; and my efforts to think of you were like trying to wake myself up — still overpowered with heavy drowsiness, I would fall back to sleep again. And though no one wants to sleep forever, since people think more clearly in waking life, they also tend to delay getting up when there is a heaviness in their bodies, and though they end up dissatisfied with themselves, they yield to their sleepiness and fall back into sleep — so too was my wrestling with your pursuit of me, as I knew it was better to give myself over to your love than to wallow in my own greed. The rightness of choosing you was certain, but I was enslaved by my pleasure-seeking.

And I could not answer your calling to me, "Awake, you that sleep, and arise from the dead, and Christ shall give you light" (Eph. 5:14). And you confirmed your words to me in all parts of life, but I, though convicted by the truth, had nothing at all to reply, but the slurring and sleepy words: "Soon, soon, Lord; leave me a little while." But my "soon, soon" did not mean now; and my "leave me a little while" went on for a long while.

My intellectual delight in your law was pointless when another law in my flesh warred against the law of my mind and brought me into captivity to the law of sin which ruled my body. For the law of sin is the prison of habits into which the mind is drawn and held, even against its will. Wretched man that I am! Who shall deliver me from the body of death but your grace only, through Jesus Christ our Lord (Rom. 7:21–25)?

Augustine

❖ 198 ❖

FROM PROSTITUTE TO VIRGIN

*And that is what some of you were. But you were washed,
you were sanctified, you were justified. (1 Corinthians 6:11)*

Jericho is besieged and surrounded but has yet to fall. How is it to be conquered? Not with arrows or swords or battering ram. Nothing is deployed but the priests' trumpets, and the walls of Jericho crumble.

In Scripture we often find Jericho used as a symbol of the world. And so this Jericho — this world — must fall. The consummation of this present age has long been prophesied by the sacred books.

How will this consummation come about? By what means? Scripture tells us, "at the sound of the trumpet" (1 Cor. 15:52; 1 Thess. 4:16). Then, therefore, our Lord Jesus will come with trumpets to conquer Jericho and throw it down, so that out of all its people there will survive only the prostitute and her household. Our Lord Jesus will come down with the sound of the trumpet.

May he save that one woman who gave nourishment to his spies, who received his apostles in trust and obedience and hid them in her roof. But let us not retell this story and still label her with the name of her past sin. She may have been a prostitute once, but now she is a chaste virgin, joined to her chaste spouse, who is Christ. Listen to what Saint Paul says about her: "I arranged for you to marry Christ so that I might give you away as a chaste virgin to this one husband" (2 Cor. 11:2).

Do you want to know more about how the prostitute ceased to be a prostitute? To enable her to escape the destruction of Jericho she received a powerful sign of safety from the spies, the scarlet rope. For it is through the blood of Christ that the whole church is saved.

Origen

✦ 199 ✦

JOY IN RECOVERING SINNERS

But we had to celebrate and be glad, because this brother of yours was dead and is alive again; he was lost and is found. (Luke 15:32)

God, why is it that people rejoice more at the salvation of a soul formerly lost and brought out of great danger than if there had always been hope for the sinner? For you also, merciful Father, rejoice more over one sinner that repents than over ninety-nine that need no repentance. We listen with joy whenever we hear in the Scriptures how the lost sheep is brought home again on the shepherd's shoulders, while the angels rejoice (Luke 15:4–7); and when the drachma is restored to your treasury, the neighbors rejoicing with the woman who found it (Luke 15:9–10); and when in your house the story is read of your younger son who was dead and is alive again, and was lost and is found (Luke 15:11–32).

What happens in the soul when it delights more at recovering the thing it loves than if it had always possessed it? Indeed, other things manifest this truth from all parts of life. The victorious commander triumphs; yet he only conquered because he fought and rejoices more because he escaped great peril. The storm tosses the voyagers, and threatens them with shipwreck, and everyone goes pale thinking death is near; but suddenly the sky and sea grow calm, and they rejoice in proportion to their former fear. A loved one is sick, and her heart is barely beating, and all her family are overcome with grief; but she recovers, and though not able to walk with her former strength, there is greater joy than before when she walked perfectly well.

Augustine

✢ 200 ✢

THE NEW
AND GLORIOUS DAY (I)

Suddenly Jesus met them. "Greetings," he said. They came to him,
clasped his feet and worshiped him. (Matthew 28:9)

The reign of life has begun, the tyranny of death is ended. A new birth has taken place, a new life has come, a new order of existence has appeared, and our very nature has been transformed! This birth is not brought about "by human generation, by the will of man, or by the desire of the flesh, but by God" (John 1:13).

If you wonder how, I will explain in clear language. Faith is the womb that conceives this new life, and baptism the rebirth by which brings it into the light of day. The church is its nurse, her teachings are its milk, and the bread from heaven is its food. It is brought to maturity by the practice of virtue; it is wedded to wisdom; it gives birth to hope. Its home is the kingdom; its rich inheritance the joys of paradise; its end is not death, but the blessed and everlasting life prepared for those who are worthy.

"This is the day the LORD has made" (Ps. 118:24), a day far different from those made when the world was first created and which are measured by the passage of time. This is the beginning of a new creation. On this day, as the prophet says, God makes "a new heaven and a new earth" (Isa. 65:17). [Continued in next entry . . .]

Gregory of Nyssa

✤ 201 ✤

THE NEW
AND GLORIOUS DAY (II)

Therefore, if anyone is in Christ, the new creation has come:
The old has gone, the new is here! (2 Corinthians 5:17)

What is this new heaven? It is the cosmos of our faith in Christ. What is the new earth? A good heart, a heart like the earth, which drinks up the rain that falls on it and yields a rich harvest. In this new creation, the sun is a pure life, the stars are the virtues, the air is pervasive goodness, and the sea is "the depths of the riches of wisdom and knowledge" (Rom. 11:33). The sound doctrine of divine teaching is the grass and plants that feed God's flock, the people whom he shepherds; the keeping of the commandments is the fruit borne by the trees.

On this day the true man is created, the man made in the image and likeness of God. For "this day the LORD has made" (Ps. 118:24) is the beginning of the new world. The prophet says this day is not like other days, nor is this night like other nights. But still we have not spoken of the greatest gift it has brought us. This day destroyed the pangs of death and brought to life the firstborn of the dead.

"I ascend to my Father and to your Father, to my God and to your God" (John 20:17). What wonderfully good news! Christ, who became like us in order to make us his brothers and sisters, now presents his own humanity to his true Father in order to draw his family up after him.

Gregory of Nyssa

✦ 202 ✦

VIRTUE MANIFESTS LOVE

Love is patient, love is kind. It does not envy, it does not boast, it is not proud. It does not dishonor others, it is not self-seeking, it is not easily angered, it keeps no record of wrongs. Love does not delight in evil but rejoices with the truth. (1 Corinthians 13:4–6)

We are told that the law of God is manifold. Why? Because love's concern for others is reflected in all the virtues. The people ruled by this love show their patience by bearing wrongs with peace, and their kindness by generously repaying good for evil. Jealousy is foreign to them. It is impossible to envy worldly success when they have no worldly desires. They are not conceited. What they desire is internal; outward blessings do not tempt them. Their conduct is blameless, for they can do no wrong by devoting themselves entirely to love of God and neighbor. They are not ambitious. They seek the welfare of their souls and nothing else. They are not selfish. Since they know they can take nothing with them, they are indifferent to their own possessions.

Only the things they will have forever do they consider their own. They are not quick to take offense. Revenge never crosses their minds even when provoked. Their endurance here will increase their rewards in heaven. They harbor no evil thoughts. Hatred is alien to hearts that love only goodness. Poisonous thoughts can find no entry. They do not gloat over other people's sins. An enemy's fall does not please them since they love all men and women, and they long for their salvation.

On the other hand, they are gladdened by an upright life. Since they love others as themselves, they take as much pleasure in the good of others as if their progress were their own.

Gregory the Great

⤞ 203 ⤝

WICKEDNESS IS EASY

Make every effort to enter through the narrow door, because many,
I tell you, will try to enter and will not be able to. (Luke 13:24)

The path to heaven is difficult and hilly, entangled with dreadful thorns, and made rough with jutting stones; it takes great labor to traverse it, and your feet will be worn out, and all the while you must take great precautions against falling. But along this path God has placed justice, temperance, patience, faith, chastity, self-restraint, unity, knowledge, truth, wisdom, and the other virtues; but alongside these goods there is poverty, disgrace, labor, pain, and all kinds of hardship.

And whoever has their hopes set on heaven, which is better than any earthly good, will be unattached to earthly things, and therefore lightly equipped and without impediment. Thus they may overcome the difficulty of the way. For anyone that is filled with self-importance or lust for power or greed for wealth is bound to fail on the heavenly path with its challenges.

It is easier for the wicked to succeed in their desires only in this way: because their road slopes downward. Likewise it is difficult for the good to attain to their wishes because they walk along a difficult upward path. Therefore the righteous, since they have chosen a hard and rugged path, will become objects of contempt, derision, and hatred. They will likely be poor, disrespected, unpopular, victimized, but will endure all the grievous things which come their way. But if they patiently continue to the end, the crown of virtue will be given to them, and God will reward them with immortality for their many trials for the sake of righteousness.

That is how short-lived earthly pleasures are followed by eternal evils, and momentary earthly evils by eternal goods.

Lactantius

✤ 204 ✤

GOD'S GRACE SETS US FREE

Dear friends, I urge you, as foreigners and exiles, to abstain from sinful desires, which wage war against your soul. (1 Peter 2:11)

We see that death is gain, life is loss. Paul says, "For me life is Christ, and death is gain" (Phil. 1:21). What does "Christ" mean here except to put the flesh to death and receive the breath of life? Let us then die with Christ, to live with Christ. We should have a familiarity with death, a daily desire for it. By this kind of detachment our soul will learn to free itself from the desires of the flesh. Our soul must soar above earthly lusts to a heavenly place and hold fast to the place they cannot come near.

It must take on the likeness of death to avoid the punishment of death. Our fallen nature is at war with our reason and subjects it to sin and error. What is the remedy? "Who will set me free from this body of death? The grace of God, through Jesus Christ, our Lord" (Rom. 7:24–25).

We have a doctor to heal us — let us use the remedy he prescribes. The remedy is the grace of Christ, the gift of his punished and killed body given to us. So let us be exiles from our own bodies in order to reside in the body of Christ. Though we are still in the body, let us not give ourselves to the things of the body. We must not reject the body's natural needs, but we must desire the gifts of grace before all else.

Ambrose

·✥ 205 ✥·

CONFIDENCE THROUGH GOOD DEEDS

But now, Job, listen to my words; pay attention to everything I say.…
I am the same as you in God's sight; I too am a piece of clay. (Job 33:1, 6)

A rrogant teachers have this characteristic: they do not know how to teach humbly, and they cannot properly convey the things they understand. Their way of speaking betrays their teaching — they act as if they live on lofty heights, looking down disdainfully on their students. They regard their subjects as inferiors, to whom they do not condescend to listen; in fact, they barely talk with them at all — they simply lay down the law.

On the contrary true doctrine eliminates arrogance through reflection, because right teaching attacks arrogance in the teacher's heart. It ensures that the humility it aims to instill in the listeners' hearts is actually preached by a humble man. For humility, the mother of virtues, teaches by word and demonstrates by example. The goal of true doctrine is to express humility among disciples more by deeds than by words.

When Paul tells his disciples, "These things command and teach with all power" (1 Tim. 4:11), he means the credibility that comes with good behavior rather than the domineering exercise of power. When one practices first and preaches afterward, one is really teaching with power. One's doctrine loses credibility if one's conscience condemns his heart. So Paul is not speaking of the power of fancy rhetoric but of the confidence gained by good deeds. It is said of the Lord, "He taught with authority unlike the scribes and the Pharisees" (Matt. 7:29). In a unique and sovereign way, he spoke with the power of his own goodness since he had no sin. His sinless human nature wielded the authority given to it by his divine nature.

Gregory the Great

✛ 206 ✛

CHRIST ABOLISHED DEATH

For we know that since Christ was raised from the dead, he cannot die again; death no longer has mastery over him. (Romans 6:9)

Christ saw that corruption continued to hold us closer, because it was the penalty for our transgression; he saw, too, how unthinkable it would be for the Law to be repealed before it was fulfilled. He saw how the surpassing wickedness of men and women was mounting up against them and also their universal liability to death.

All this he saw and, pitying us humans, was moved with compassion for our limitations, unwilling to endure death having mastery. Instead of letting his creatures and the work of his Father perish, and we humans come to nothing, he took to himself a body, a human body just like our own. He took our body, and not just that, he took it directly from a spotless, stainless virgin, without the agency of a human father — a pure body, untainted by intercourse with a man. Thus, taking a body like our own, because all our bodies were liable to the corruption of death, he surrendered his body to death and offered it to the Father. He did this out of sheer love for us so that in his death all might die and that the law of death would be abolished. By fulfilling in his body its appointed task, death was emptied of its power over us. He did this so that he might give incorruption back to men and women who had fallen into corruption and make them alive through death by their appropriation of his body and by the grace of his resurrection. Thus he made death disappear from them as totally as straw in a fire.

Athanasius

✣ 207 ✣

OVERWHELMING DELIGHTS

It will be good for those servants whose master finds them watching when he comes. (Luke 12:37)

How I wish that he would enkindle me with the fire of divine love! The flames of his love burn beyond the stars; my longing for his overwhelming delights burns within me!

I ask you, Father, in the name of Jesus Christ, your Son and my God, for the love that does not fail so that my lantern, burning within me and giving light to others, may always be lit and never extinguished.

Jesus, our most loving Savior, take pleasure in lighting our lanterns so that they might burn forever in your temple, receiving eternal light from you, the eternal light, to lighten our darkness and to ward off the darkness of the world.

Give your light to my lantern, my Jesus, so that by its light I may see the Holy of Holies, which receives you as the eternal priest entering among the columns of your great temple. May I ever see only you, look on you, and long for you; may I gaze with love on you alone and have my lantern shining and burning always in your presence.

Loving Savior, take pleasure in showing yourself to us who knock so that in knowing you we may love you alone, desire you alone, contemplate only you day and night, and always think of you. Inspire in us the depth of love that is fitting for you to receive as God. Make our love for you pervade our whole being, possess us completely, and fill all our senses so that we know no love besides the love for you, who are everlasting. May our love be so great that the waters of sky, land, and sea cannot extinguish it: "Many waters could not extinguish love" (Song 8:7).

Columbanus

✢ 208 ✢

OUR VOICE IS CHRIST'S (I)

For we do not have a high priest who is unable to empathize
with our weaknesses, but we have one who has been tempted
in every way, just as we are — yet he did not sin. (Hebrews 4:15)

God could give no greater gift to us than to appoint his Word, through whom he created all things, as our head and to join us to him as his body. Doing this made the Word both Son of God and Son of Man, one God with the Father, and one man with all men. The result is that when we speak with God in prayer we pray also to the Son, and when the body of the Son prays so too does the head. Our Lord Jesus Christ, the Son of God, prays for us and in us and is himself the object of our prayers.

He prays for us as our priest, he prays in us as our head, and he is the object of our prayers as our God. Let us then recognize our voice in his, and his voice in ours.

We contemplate his glory and divinity when we listen to these words: "He was in the beginning with God. All things were made through him, and without him nothing was made" (John 1:2 – 3). Here we gaze on the divinity of the Son of God, something supremely great and surpassing all the greatness of his creatures. Every creature is his servant, for it was through him that every creature came to be.

Yet in other parts of Scripture we hear him sighing, praying, and giving praise and thanks. When something is said of the Lord Jesus Christ that seems too human or low or weak, a condition unworthy of God, we must not doubt that he experienced this brokenness, since he did not hesitate to unite himself with us. [Continued in next entry ...]

Augustine

✢ 209 ✢

OUR VOICE IS CHRIST'S (II)

During the days of Jesus' life on earth, he offered up prayers and petitions
with fervent cries and tears to the one who could save him from death,
and he was heard because of his reverent submission. (Hebrews 5:7)

We hesitate to attribute these words [in Hebrews 5:7] to Jesus because our minds are slow to come down to his humble level when we have just been contemplating his divinity. It is as though we were doing him an injustice by acknowledging the words of a man coming from him, when just before we prayed to him as God—we are usually at a loss and try to change the meaning! Yet our minds find nothing in Scripture that does not go back to him, nothing that will allow us to stray from him.

Our thoughts must therefore be refreshed to keep their vigil of faith. We must realize that the one whom we contemplate as God took on himself the nature of a servant; he was made in the likeness of men and seen and touched as a man could be; he humbled himself by being obedient even to accepting death; as he hung on the cross he made the Psalmist's words his own: "My God, my God, why have you forsaken me?" (Matt. 27:46).

We pray to him as God, he prays for us as a servant. In the first case he is the Creator, in the second a creature. He remained unchanged when he took to himself our created nature in order to change it, and made us one person with himself, head and body. So we pray to him, through him, in him, and we speak along with him and he along with us.

Augustine

❖ 210 ❖

GREENER PASTURES

I am the good shepherd; I know my sheep and my sheep know me.
(John 10:14)

The Lord says, "As the Father knows me and I know the Father; and I lay down my life for my sheep" (John 10:15). Clearly he means that laying down his life for his sheep gives evidence of his knowledge of the Father and the Father's knowledge of him. In other words, the love he shows for his sheep, whom he dies for, shows how greatly he loves his Father.

Our Lord's sheep will finally reach their grazing ground, where all who follow him in simplicity of heart will feed on the green pastures of eternity. These pastures are the spiritual joys of heaven. There the elect look upon the face of God with unclouded vision and feast at the banquet of life forevermore.

Beloved brothers and sisters, let us set out for these pastures where there is always a joyful festival with our fellow citizens. Let the thought of their happiness urge us on! Let us stir up our hearts, rekindle our faith, and long eagerly for what heaven has in store for us. If we love we are already on our way. No matter what obstacles we encounter, we must not allow them to turn us aside from the joy of that heavenly feast. Anyone who is determined to reach his or her destination is not deterred by the roughness of the road that leads to it. Nor should we allow worldly success to seduce us, or we will be like foolish travelers who are so distracted by the meadows they pass through that they forget where they are going.

Gregory the Great

✢ 211 ✢

EXAMINE YOURSELF CAREFULLY

If someone slaps you on one cheek, turn to them the other also. If someone takes your coat, do not withhold your shirt from them. (Luke 6:29)

The men and women who know their own faults accept all things cheerfully: misfortune, loss, disgrace, dishonor, and any other kind of adversity. They believe that they are deserving of all these things and nothing can disturb them. No one could be more at peace than these people. Perhaps you will object, "Suppose my brother injures me, but after examining myself I conclude that I have not given him a reason to do so. Why should I blame myself?"

If you examine yourself carefully and with fear of God, you will never find yourself completely innocent. You will discover that you have provoked him by an action or word, or by your manner. If you are not guilty in these ways, you must have hurt that brother somehow at some other time. Or maybe you have been a source of annoyance to some other brother. So you deserve your injury because of the many other sins you have committed on other occasions.

The sister who thinks that she is quiet and peaceful has a passion within her that she does not see. A sister comes up, utters some unkind word, and immediately all the hidden venom and filth come spewing out. If she desires mercy, she must do penance, purify herself, and strive to become perfect. She will see that she should have thanked her sister instead of returning the insult, because her sister has given her a chance to improve herself. It will not be long before she is no longer bothered by these temptations. The more perfect she grows, the less these temptations will affect her. For the more the soul advances, the stronger and more powerful it becomes in bearing the difficulties that it meets.

Dorotheus of Gaza

✢ 212 ✢

THE EUCHARIST

*So then, whoever eats the bread or drinks the cup of the Lord
in an unworthy manner will be guilty of sinning against the body
and blood of the Lord. (1 Corinthians 11:27)*

No one may share the Eucharist with us unless they believe that what we teach is true, unless they are washed in the regenerating waters of baptism for the remission of their sins, and unless they live in accordance with the principles given us by Christ.

We do not consume the Eucharistic bread and wine as if it were ordinary food and drink, for we have been taught that as Jesus Christ our Savior became a man of flesh and blood by the power of the Word of God, so also the food that our flesh and blood takes for its nourishment becomes the flesh and blood of the incarnate Jesus, by the power of his own words contained in the prayer of thanksgiving.

The apostles, in their recollections, which are called gospels, handed down to us what Jesus commanded them to do. They tell us that he took bread, gave thanks, and said, "Do this in memory of me. This is my body" (Luke 22:19). In the same way he took the cup, he gave thanks and said, "This is my blood" (Mark 14:24). The Lord gave this command to them alone. Ever since then we have constantly reminded one another of these things. The rich among us help the poor and we are always united. For all that we receive we praise the Creator of the universe through his Son Jesus Christ and through the Holy Spirit.

Justin Martyr

PREACHING REPENTANCE TO THE DEVIL

Submit yourselves, then, to God. Resist the devil,
and he will flee from you. (James 4:7)

Now, the devil would try to attack Saint Martin of Tours with a thousand malicious schemes and would often thrust himself upon him in a visible form, but in various shapes. Sometimes he would appear as the god Jupiter, and sometimes Mercury or Minerva. He would lob insults and curses, and a crowd of demons would assail him with obscenities. But knowing that all their evil accusations were false and groundless, he was not affected by the charges brought against him.

In one incident, some of the brothers told how they had heard a demon reproaching Martin in abusive terms and interrogating him as to why he had taken certain brothers back into the church — brothers who had lost their baptism by falling into error but had repented. The demon laid out the crimes of each of them; but Martin, resisting the devil firmly, answered him that past sins are cleansed away by the leading of a better life, and that through the mercy of God, those who have given up their evil ways are absolved from their sins. The devil came back at Martin, saying that these guilty men had no hope of forgiveness, and that the Lord extends no mercy to those who have fallen away from the faith. But Martin cried out in these words: "If you yourself, most wretched of creatures, would only cease attacking mankind and repent of your deeds when the day of judgment is at hand, I promise you the mercy of Christ with true confidence in the Lord!" What a holy boldness he demonstrated in the loving-kindness of the Lord!

Sulpitius Severus

⚜ 214 ⚜

LATE HAVE I LOVED YOU

*For you created my inmost being; you knit me together
in my mother's womb. (Psalm 139:13)*

Where did I find you to meet you in the first place? You could not have been in my memory before I knew you. Where could I have found you in order to learn of you, except in yourself, which is far above me? But "place" has no meaning with you, since you are at once so very far and so very close. Truthfully, you are sovereign over all who turn to you in prayer and are able to respond to all concurrently, however many and diverse their pleas are.

Your response is always clear, but not everyone hears it clearly. They all ask after their desires but do not always listen to your answers. Your best servant is the one who wants not to hear his or her own will coming from your mouth, but who willfully embraces what you have said.

Late have I loved you, Beauty so ancient and so new, late
    have I loved you!
Lo, you were within, but I outside, seeking there for you,
    and upon the shapely things you have made.
I rushed headlong — I, misshapen. You were with me, but I
    was not with you.
They held me back far from you, those things which would
    have no being, they were not in you.
You called, shouted, broke through my deafness; you
    flared, blazed, banished my blindness;
You lavished your fragrance, I gasped; and now I pant for
    you; I tasted you, and now I hunger and thirst;
You touched me, and I burned for your peace.

Augustine

✦ 215 ✦

OUR SHEPHERD CARRIES US

Then we your people, the sheep of your pasture, will praise you forever;
from generation to generation we will proclaim your praise. (Psalm 79:13)

Lord, you led me from my father's loins and formed me in my mother's womb. You brought me, a naked babe, into the light of day, for nature's laws always obey your commands.

By the blessing of the Holy Spirit, you prepared my creation and my existence, not because people willed it or flesh desired it, but by your ineffable grace. The birth you prepared for me was such that it surpassed the laws of our nature. You sent me forth into the light by adopting me as your son and you enrolled me among the children of your holy and spotless church.

You nursed me with the spiritual milk of your divine utterances. You kept me alive with the solid food of the body of Jesus Christ, your only begotten Son for our redemption. And he undertook the task willingly and did not shrink from it. Indeed, he applied himself to it as though destined for sacrifice, like an innocent lamb. Although he was God, he became man, and in his human will, became obedient to you, God his Father, unto death, even death on a cross.

In this way you have humbled yourself, Christ my God, so that you might carry me, your stray sheep, on your shoulders. You let me graze in green pastures, refreshing me with the waters of orthodox teaching at the hands of your shepherds. You pastored these shepherds, and now they in turn tend your chosen and special flock.

John of Damascus

✛ 216 ✛

STEPHEN AND PAUL

And Saul approved of their killing him. (Acts 8:1)

The love that brought Christ from heaven to earth raised Stephen from earth to heaven; it was shown first in the King and later shone forth in his soldier. Love was the weapon Stephen used to win every battle, and how he won the crown signified by his name [*Stephanos* means "crown"]. His love of God kept him from backing down from the ferocious mob; his love for his neighbor made him pray for the people stoning him. Love inspired him to rebuke those who erred, to make them amend; love led him to pray for those who stoned him, to save them from punishment. Strengthened by the power of his love, he overcame the raging cruelty of Saul, and his persecutor on earth became his companion in heaven. The ones he could not convert by admonition he tried to gain through prayer, because of his holy and tireless love.

Now Paul rejoices with Stephen, and together they delight in the glory of Christ, together they exalt, together they reign. Stephen went first, killed by the stones thrown by Paul, but Paul followed after, helped by the prayer of Stephen. This is surely the true life, a life in which Paul feels no shame because of Stephen's death, and Stephen delights in Paul's companionship, for love fills them both with joy. Stephen's love prevailed over the cruelty of the mob, and Paul's love covered the multitude of his sins; for both of them it was love that won the kingdom of heaven.

Fulgentius of Ruspe

⊰ 217 ⊱

SPANNING THE JAWS OF DEATH

Through Christ Jesus the law of the Spirit who gives life has set you free from the law of sin and death. For what the law was powerless to do because it was weakened by the flesh, God did by sending his own Son.
(Romans 8:2–3)

The Son of God, who was also the carpenter's glorious Son, laid his cross above death's all-consuming jaws and led the human race into the dwelling place of life. Since a tree had brought about the downfall of humankind, it was upon a tree that humankind crossed over to the realm of life. A bitter branch was grafted to that ancient tree, but a sweet young blossom has now been grafted in: the Lord, whom no creature can resist.

We give glory to you, Lord, who raised up your cross to span the jaws of death like a bridge, by which souls might pass from the region of the dead to the land of the living. We give glory to you, who put on the body of a single mortal man and made it the source of life for every other mortal man and woman. You are incontestably alive. Your murderers sowed your living body in the earth as farmers sow grain, but it sprang up and yielded an abundant harvest of people raised from the dead.

Come then, my brothers and sisters, and let us offer our Lord the great sacrifice of our love, pouring out our treasury of hymns and prayers before Christ, who offered his cross in sacrifice to God for the salvation of us all.

Ephrem the Syrian

⊹ 218 ⊹

TABLETS OF THE HEART (I)

All your children will be taught by the LORD,
and great will be their peace. (Isaiah 54:13)

It would be best for us not to need the aid of the written Word, but to exhibit a life so pure that we would only need the grace of the Spirit instead of books to instruct us; as books are inscribed with ink, our hearts would be inscribed with the Spirit.

That this would be better God has shown, both by his words and his doings. To Noah, and Abraham, and his offspring, and Job, and Moses too, God communicated not by writings, but by himself, finding their minds pure. Only after all the Hebrews had fallen into the pit of wickedness was a written word made.

We can conclude that this was the case not only with the saints in the Old Testament, but also with those in the New. For God did not give anything in writing to the apostles, but instead of written words he promised that he would give them the grace of the Spirit: "He shall bring all things to your remembrance," says the Lord (John 14:26). And so that you would learn that this was far better, listen to what he says by the prophet: "I will make a new covenant with you, putting my laws into their minds, and writing them in their hearts," and, "they will all be taught by God" (Jer. 31:31–33; Isa. 54:13; Heb. 8:8–11; John 6:45). And Paul too, pointing out the same superiority, said that they had received a law "not in tablets of stone, but in fleshy tablets of the heart" (2 Cor. 3:3). [Continued in next entry ...]

John Chrysostom

✦ 219 ✦

TABLETS OF THE HEART (II)

You show that you are a letter from Christ, the result of our ministry,
written not with ink but with the Spirit of the living God, not on tablets
of stone but on tablets of human hearts. (2 Corinthians 3:3)

But since over time people made a shipwreck of God's teachings, some regarding doctrines, others with life and manners, there was again a need to preserve them by having a written word.

Now that we have lost that previous honor, and once again have the need of written words, reflect on how great an evil we would commit by not taking advantage of the remedy given to us in Scripture—we, who ought to live so purely that we should not need written words, but should instead give up our hearts to the Spirit, as if they were books! If it is a fault to turn the Spirit away and to need written words, consider how guilty we would be if we chose to ignore even this assistance. Neglecting Scripture, as if it were created without purpose, and at random, would warrant a greater punishment!

But to ensure that this may not occur, let us listen intently to the things that are written; and let us learn how the Old Law was given on the one hand, and the New Covenant on the other.

John Chrysostom

✤ 220 ✤

JESUS THE LAMP

The city does not need the sun or the moon to shine on it, for the glory of God gives it light, and the Lamb is its lamp. (Revelation 21:23)

The lamp set upon the lampstand is Jesus Christ, the true light from the Father, the light that enlightens every person who comes into the world. In taking our own flesh he has become, and is rightly called, a lamp, for he is the indwelling wisdom and Word of the Father. He is proclaimed in the church of God in accordance with orthodox faith, and he is lifted up and resplendent among the nations through the lives of those who live virtuously in observance of the commandments. So he gives light to all in the house (that is, in this world), just as he himself, God the Word, says, "No one lights a lamp and puts it under a bushel, but on a stand, and it gives light to all in the house" (Matt. 5:15). Clearly he is calling himself the lamp, he who was by nature God and became flesh according to God's saving purpose.

I think the great David understood this when he spoke of the Lord as a lamp, saying, "Your word is a lamp to my feet and a light to my path" (Ps. 119:105). For God delivers us from the darkness of ignorance and sin, and hence he is greeted as a lamp in Scripture.

Lamplike indeed, he alone dispelled the gloom of ignorance and the darkness of evil and became the way of salvation for all humankind. He has designated the holy church as the lamp stand, from which the Word of God sheds light through preaching, and illumines whoever is in this house with the rays of truth, and fills the minds of all people with divine knowledge.

Maximus the Confessor

✢ 221 ✢

THE BEAUTY OF CHRISTIAN MARRIAGE

The wife does not have authority over her own body but yields it to her husband. In the same way, the husband does not have authority over his own body but yields it to his wife. (1 Corinthians 7:4)

No words can describe the beauty of a marriage that the church arranges, the Eucharist strengthens, and a blessing seals — an event that angels attend as witnesses and to which the Father gives his consent. For even earthly fathers attend to give permission for their children's marriages; how much more so our heavenly Father! Indeed, how beautiful the marriage of two Christians, who are one in hope, in desire, in the way of life they follow, in the faith they practice. They are like brother and sister, servants of the same Master. In fact, they were formerly two, made one flesh by God — and where there is one flesh there is also only one spirit. They pray together, worship together, and fast together, instructing, encouraging, and strengthening one another. Side by side they visit God's church and partake of God's Banquet; side by side they face difficulties and persecution and share consolations. They keep no secrets from one another; they never shun each other's company; they never bring sorrow to each other's hearts. They give alms without anxiety; they practice their faith together daily. They need not be embarrassed about making the sign of the cross together, nor silent in asking a blessing of God together.

They sing psalms and hymns to one another, striving to give the most beautiful praise to the Lord. Hearing and seeing this, Christ rejoices. To such a marriage he gives his peace. Where there are two together, there he is also; and wherever he is, evil cannot be.

Tertullian

✢ 222 ✢

SINGLE-MINDED AND STEADFAST

For everything in the world — the lust of the flesh, the lust of the eyes,
and the pride of life — comes not from the Father but from the world.
The world and its desires pass away, but whoever does the will
of God lives forever. (1 John 2:16–17)

Our obligation is to do God's will and not our own. We must remember this if the prayer that our Lord commanded us to pray daily is to have any meaning when we say it. It is not reasonable to pray that God's will be done but then promptly disobey him when he calls us to depart from this world! Instead, we struggle and resist like stubborn slaves and are brought into the Lord's presence lamenting our own deaths, not freely consenting but compelled by necessity. And then we expect to be rewarded with heavenly honors by him whom we willfully resist! Why do we even pray for the kingdom of heaven to come if our earthly bondage is so pleasing? What is the point of praying so often for its arrival if we would rather serve the devil here than reign with Christ in heaven?

The world hates Christians, so why give your love to it instead of Christ, who loves you and has redeemed you? John urgently tells us not to love the world and give in to sensual desires: "Never give your love to the world, or to anything in it. A man cannot love the Father and love the world at the same time" (1 John 2:15).

Our part is to be single-minded, firm in faith, and steadfast in courage, ready for God's will whatever it may be. Banish the fear of death and think of the eternal life that follows. That will show people that we really live our faith.

Cyprian of Carthage

✥ 223 ✥

THE PLACE TO FEED
IN SAFETY

I will bring them out from the nations and gather them from the
countries, and I will bring them into their own land. I will pasture them
on the mountains of Israel. (Ezekiel 34:13)

It was God who brought forth the mountains of Israel, that is to say, the authors of the divine Scriptures. Feed there so that you may feed in safety. Whatever you hear from that source, you should savor. Whatever is foreign to it, reject. Hear the voice of the Shepherd so you do not wander about in the mist. Gather at the mountains of Holy Scripture. The things that will delight your hearts are there; there you will find nothing poisonous, nothing hostile; there the pastures are plentiful. There you will be healthy sheep; you will feed safely on the mountain of Israel.

He concludes by saying, "And I will feed them with judgment" (Ezek. 34:16). He alone feeds the sheep with judgment—for what person can rightly judge another? Our whole life is filled with bad judgments. The person we despaired over is suddenly converted and becomes very good. The person we had high hopes for suddenly fails and becomes very bad. Neither our fear nor our hope is certain.

We hardly know what we ourselves are today. In some ways, we do know—but what we will be tomorrow, we do not know. So the Lord, who assigns what is owed to each of us, feeds his sheep with judgment, giving some things to one group, other things to another, and to each their due. For he knows what he is doing. With judgment he feeds those whom he has judged redeemed. Therefore, he himself feeds his sheep with judgment.

Augustine

✤ 224 ✤

THE HOLY VOICE ON THE MOUNTAINTOP (I)

There he was transfigured before them. His face shone like the sun,
and his clothes became as white as the light. (Matthew 17:2)

Upon Mount Tabor, Jesus revealed to his disciples a heavenly mystery. During his ministry he spoke of the kingdom and of his second coming in glory; but in his love and wisdom, to destroy any doubt they had concerning the kingdom, and to secure their faith in what lay in the future, he gave them a wonderful vision of his glory, a foreshadowing of the kingdom of heaven. It was as if he said to them, "As time goes by you may be in danger of losing your faith. To save you from this I tell you now that 'some standing here listening to me will not taste death until they have seen the Son of Man coming in the glory of his Father'" (Matt. 16:28).

These are the divine wonders we celebrate today; this is the saving revelation given to us upon the mountain; this is the celebration of Christ that has drawn us together. So let us listen to God's holy voice calling us from on high, from the summit of the mountain, so that with the Lord's chosen disciples we may penetrate the deep meaning of these holy mysteries, which are impossible to express with words. Jesus goes before us to show us the way, both up the mountain and into heaven, and we follow him with all speed. On Tabor we yearn for the heavenly vision that will give us a share in his radiance, renew our spiritual nature, and transform us into his own likeness, granting us a share in his godhead and raising us to undreamed of heights. [Continued in next entry ...]

Anastasius of Sinai

✦ 225 ✦

THE HOLY VOICE ON THE MOUNTAINTOP (II)

While he was still speaking, a bright cloud covered them, and a voice from the cloud said, "This is my Son, whom I love; with him I am well pleased. Listen to him!" When the disciples heard this, they fell facedown to the ground, terrified. (Matthew 17:5–6)

Let us run with confidence and joy to enter into the cloud like Moses and Elijah, or like James and John. Let us be dazzled like Peter to behold the divine vision and to be transfigured by that glorious transfiguration. Let us leave the world, rise above the body, detach ourselves from creatures, and turn to the Creator, to whom Peter in ecstasy exclaimed: "Lord, it is good for us to be here" (Matt. 17:4).

It is indeed good to be here, as you have said, Peter. It is good to be with Jesus and to remain here forever. What greater happiness or higher honor could we have than to be with God, to be made like him and to live in his light?

Therefore, since each of us has God in his heart and is being transformed into his divine image, we should also cry out with joy, "It is good for us to be here!" — here where all things shine with divine radiance, where there is joy and gladness and celebration; where there is nothing in our hearts but peace, serenity and stillness; where God is seen. For here, in our hearts, Christ takes up his abode together with the Father, saying as he enters, "Today salvation has come to this house" (Luke 19:9). With Christ, our hearts receive all the wealth of his eternal blessings, and in his shining face on the mountain, we see the firstfruits of the new creation, and an image of the whole world to come.

Anastasius of Sinai

✢ 226 ✢

THE HONOR HE DESIRES

Cornelius stared at him in fear. "What is it, Lord?" he asked.
The angel answered, "Your prayers and gifts to the poor
have come up as a memorial offering before God." (Acts 10:4)

Do you want to honor Christ's body? Then do not ignore him in his nakedness—do not honor him here in the church with expensive clothes while neglecting him outside where he is cold and naked. For he who said, "This is my body" (Matt. 26:26) also said, "You saw me hungry and did not feed me, and inasmuch as you did not do it for the least of my brothers, you did not do it for me" (Matt. 25:42, 45). What we do in the church requires a pure heart, not special clothes, and what we do outside requires great dedication.

So let us be men and women of wisdom and honor Christ as he desires. A person being honored is most pleased with the honor he or she desires, not with the honor we think is best. Peter thought he was honoring Christ when he refused to let him wash his feet; but what Peter wanted was not really an honor, but an insult! Give Christ the honor he requests in the Gospel by giving your wealth to the poor, for God does not want golden decorations in his churches but golden hearts in his followers.

I am not saying that those kinds of gifts are forbidden, but that you give alms along with and before such gifts. He accepts them but is much more pleased with alms. In the former, only the giver benefits; in the latter, the recipient does too. A gift to the church can be seen as a form of vanity, but giving alms is pure kindness.

John Chrysostom

✤ 227 ✤

GIVE BEFORE MEASURING

Here is a boy with five small barley loaves and two small fish,
but how far will they go among so many? (John 6:9)

If the faithful find some store of love's fruit in their hearts, they must not doubt God's presence within them. If God is love, charity should know no limit, for God cannot be confined.

Any time is the right time for works of charity, but these days of Lent provide a special encouragement. Those who want to be present at the Lord's Passover in holiness of mind and body should seek above all to win this grace, for charity contains all other virtues and covers a multitude of sins.

As we prepare to celebrate that greatest of all mysteries, by which the blood of Jesus Christ did away with our sins, let us first of all prepare the sacrificial offerings of acts of mercy. In mercy we give to those who have sinned against us what God has already given to us in his goodness.

Let us extend a more open-handed generosity to the poor and afflicted, so that God may be thanked through many voices, and those in need may be supported by our fasting. No act of devotion on the part of the faithful gives God more pleasure than that which is lavished on his poor. Our charity displays his own fatherly care.

In these acts of giving do not fear a lack of means. There is always something to give where it is Christ who feeds and Christ who is fed. Christ's hand is present, which multiplies the bread by breaking it and increases it by giving it away.

Givers of alms should be free from anxiety and full of joy. Their gain will be greatest when they keep back least for themselves.

Leo the Great

✣ 228 ✣

DRAWING THE SHEEP TO HIMSELF

Surely he took up our pain and bore our suffering, yet we considered him punished by God, stricken by him, and afflicted. (Isaiah 53:4)

When a shepherd sees that his sheep have scattered, he keeps one of them under his control and leads it to the pastures he chooses, and thus he draws the other sheep back to him by means of this one. And so it was when God the Word saw that humanity had gone astray: he took the form of a slave and united it to himself and, by means of it, won over all men and women to him, enticing the sheep that were grazing in bad pastures and exposed to wolves, and leading them to the pastures of God.

This was the purpose for which our Savior assumed our nature — this was why Christ the Lord accepted the sufferings that brought us salvation, was sent to his death, and was committed to the tomb. He broke the grip of the age-old tyranny and promised incorruptibility to those who were prisoners of corruption. For when he rebuilt that temple, which had been destroyed, and raised it up again, he thereby gave trustworthy and firm promises to those who had died and were awaiting his resurrection.

Jesus tells us, "Just as my human nature, which I took from you, has won its resurrection by virtue of the godhead that dwelt in it and with which it was united, and just as this human nature has discarded decay and suffering and passed over to incorruptibility and immortality — in the same way, you too will be set free from the grievous slavery of death. You too will cast aside your corruptible nature and your sufferings and you will be clothed with impassability."

Theodoret of Cyrus

❖ 229 ❖

FINAL PERFECTION OF HIS CITY

So this is what the Sovereign LORD says: "See, I lay a stone in Zion, a tested stone, a precious cornerstone for a sure foundation; the one who relies on it will never be stricken with panic." (Isaiah 28:16).

For many years now God has been watching over this city, always on the alert. He cared for Abraham in his wanderings; he rescued Isaac when he was about to be sacrificed; he blessed Jacob in his time of servitude; he set Joseph over Egypt after he had been sold into slavery; he supported Moses against Pharaoh; he chose Joshua to lead his nation in war; he rescued David from every danger and endowed Solomon with wisdom. He came to the aid of the prophets: he took Elijah up to heaven, chose Elisha, fed Daniel, and stood by and refreshed the three young men in the fiery furnace.

He told Joseph, through an angel, of his virginal conception, strengthened Mary, and sent John ahead to prepare the way. He chose the apostles and prayed for them, saying to his Father, "Holy Father, protect them. While I was with them, I kept them safe by the power of your name" (John 17:11–12). Finally after his passion, he promised us his eternal, watchful protection, in the words, "Behold, I am with you always until the end of the world" (Matt. 28:20).

This is the unfailing protection given to this blessed and holy city — a city built for God, fashioned by the union of many, but seen in each member. And the Lord is the one who must build the city if it is to grow to its appointed size. A building just begun is not the perfect work; final perfection is achieved only through the process of building.

Hilary of Poitiers

❖ 230 ❖

CONFESSION NOW

*Then I acknowledged my sin to you and did not cover up my iniquity.
I said, "I will confess my transgressions to the LORD." And you forgave
the guilt of my sin. (Psalm 32:5)*

If you are a slave to sin then faithfully ready yourself for your second birth into freedom as a child of God. Put aside your wretched servitude to sin and take on the blessed service to the Lord so that you might be a sharer in the inheritance of the kingdom of heaven. Your fallen nature is being torn apart by ugly desires, so strip yourself of it through confession; clothe yourself in your new nature, which is being perfected by the one who created you. Receive the guarantee of the Holy Spirit by faith so that you might enter your eternal home. Be imprinted with the seal of God's kingdom so that you might be recognized by the Master.

When your conscience has been examined and found to be free of all hypocrisy, you will hear the words, "Well done, good and faithful servant" (Matt. 25:23).

The time for confession is now. Confess what you have done, whether by words or actions, whether by day or night. If you confess in this age, you will receive the heavenly treasure on the day of salvation.

Make yourself pure so that you can be a vessel of more abundant grace. Everyone receives remission of sins in the same way, but the Spirit is given differently to everyone, according to his or her faith. You are running this race for your own benefit: run hard, in your own interest.

If you are holding anything against anyone, forget it and let it go. You have come here to receive forgiveness of sins, so you must first forgive whoever has sinned against you.

Cyril of Jerusalem

✦ 231 ✦

BEING BORN AGAIN

Jesus answered, "Very truly I tell you, no one can enter the kingdom
of God unless they are born of water and the Spirit." (John 3:5)

The Holy Spirit renews us in baptism through his godhead, which he shares with the Father and the Son. He finds us in a state of deformity but restores our original beauty and fills us with his grace, leaving us worthy of his love. The Spirit frees us from sin and death and transforms us from the earthly people we were, people of dust and ashes, into spiritual beings; he makes us sharers in the divine glory, sons, daughters, and heirs of God the Father, brothers, sisters, and coheirs with the Son, and appoints us to reign with Jesus and share his glory. The Spirit reopens heaven to us and gladly admits us into paradise, extinguishing the fires of hell with the waters of baptism. We have been given an even greater honor than the angels.

We humans are conceived twice: first by the human body, and second by the divine Spirit. Whoever believes in Christ becomes a child of God by the Holy Spirit and gains kinship with God.

Visibly we come up out of the waters of baptism and are symbolically born again. Invisibly the Spirit of God baptizes both our souls and bodies into himself, and we are made a new creation.

Since we are only vessels of clay, we must first be cleansed in spiritual water and then hardened by spiritual fire, for "God is a consuming fire" (Deut. 4:24). We need the Holy Spirit to perfect and renew us: water to cleanse us and fire to recast us for the furnace, to make us into new people.

Didymus the Blind

✢ 232 ✢

INTERPRETING SCRIPTURE CORRECTLY

Through him all things were made; without him
nothing was made that has been made. (John 1:3)

There is only one God, and we learn about him only from sacred Scripture. It is therefore our duty to learn what Scripture proclaims and investigate its teachings thoroughly. We should believe them in the sense that the Father wills, thinking of the Son in the way he wills, and accepting the teaching on the Holy Spirit the way he wills. Sacred Scripture is God's gift to us, and it should be understood in the way that he intends; we should not do violence to it by interpreting it according to our own preconceived ideas.

God was alone and nothing existed but himself when he determined to create the world. He thought of it, willed it, and spoke the Word that made it. It came into being instantaneously, exactly as he had willed. We know from Scripture that nothing is coeternal with God. Apart from God there was simply nothing else. Yet although he was alone, he was sufficient because he lacked neither reason, wisdom, power, nor counsel. All things were in him and he himself was all. At a moment and in a manner determined by himself, God manifested his Word, and through him he made the whole universe.

When the Word was hidden within God he was invisible to the created world, but God made him visible. First God spoke his voice, making light from light, and then he sent his own mind into the world as its Lord. God made him visible so that the world could be saved by seeing him. This mind that entered our world is the Son of God. All things came into being through him, and he alone is begotten by the Father.

Hippolytus

✢ 233 ✢

SERVING CHRIST IN THE POOR (I)

In all their distress he too was distressed, and the angel of his presence
saved them. In his love and mercy he redeemed them; he lifted them up
and carried them all the days of old. (Isaiah 63:9)

God gave you his own Son, who was put to death for your sake, but you will not even share your bread with him! He is wasting away with starvation, yet you disregard him, even though you would be giving him what is really his, and giving it for your own good! What can be worse than such an injustice?

You are less compassionate than a stone for persisting in this cold-heartedness. He was not satisfied only with dying on a cross for you; he chose to become poor and homeless, a beggar and naked, to be thrown into prison and suffer sickness, so that through these things he might invite you to join him.

"If you will give me nothing for having suffered for you, at least have pity on my poverty. If not that, at least be moved by my sickness and imprisonment. If these do not stir your compassion, at least grant me this small request: I want nothing expensive, just a little bread, shelter, and a few kind words. If all this leaves you unmoved, at least improve your conduct for the kingdom of heaven's sake, for all the rewards I have promised. Is even this impossible for you? Well, perhaps you might pity me when you see me naked and remember how I was naked on the cross, which I suffered for your sake; or if not this, then think of the poverty and nakedness I experience today in the poor." [Continued in next entry . . .]

John Chrysostom

✢ 234 ✢

SERVING CHRIST IN THE POOR (II)

"You wicked servant," he said, "I canceled all that debt of yours because you begged me to. Shouldn't you have had mercy on your fellow servant just as I had on you?" (Matthew 18:32–33)

"I fasted for you and go hungry again for your sake; I thirsted as I hung upon the cross, and I am thirsty again in the poor of today. In one way or another, I am drawing you to myself; for your soul's sake, I will make you compassionate.

"You are indebted to me by uncountable favors, and now I ask that you make some return, but not as a payment that I am owed. I reward you as if you acted out of pure generosity: for your tiniest gestures, I am giving you a kingdom.

"I do not say, 'Put an end to my poverty,' or, 'Give all your wealth to me, since I became poor for you.' All I ask for is a little bread, clothing, and some comfort in my suffering.

"If I am in prison, I do not ask you to set me free; all I ask is that you visit me. In return I shall give you heaven. I released you from your chains; it will be enough if you visited me in mine.

"Of course I could reward you without any of this, but I want to be in your debt, so that in the last days I can proclaim your support of me, saying, 'When I was naked he clothed me, and when I was hungry he fed me' (Matt. 25:35–36). This is why, though I can support myself, I come begging beside your door and stretch out my hand. For I love you exceedingly and desire to eat at your table and share what I have with you."

John Chrysostom

✦ 235 ✦

THE ONE CHURCH

I appeal to you, brothers and sisters, in the name of our Lord Jesus
Christ, that all of you agree with one another in what you say
and that there be no divisions among you, but that you be perfectly
united in mind and thought. (1 Corinthians 1:10)

The church, which has spread everywhere, even to the ends of the earth, received the faith from the apostles and their disciples. By faith we believe in one God, the almighty Father, "who made heaven and earth and the sea and all that is in them" (Ps. 146:6). We believe in one Lord Jesus Christ, the Son of God, who became man for our salvation. And we believe in the Holy Spirit who foretold God's plan through the prophets: the coming of our beloved Lord Jesus Christ, his birth from the Virgin, his passion, his resurrection from the dead, his ascension into heaven, and his final coming from heaven in the glory of his Father.

The church, though spread throughout the whole world, lives as one house, and has received this preaching and this faith, and preserves it carefully. Having one soul and one heart, the church holds this faith, preaches and teaches it consistently with a single voice. For though there are different languages, there is one tradition.

The faith and the tradition of the churches founded in Germany are no different from those founded among the Spanish and the Celts, in the East, in Egypt, in Libya, and elsewhere in the Mediterranean world. Just as God's creature, the sun, is one and the same the world over, so also is the church's preaching one light that shines everywhere.

Now regarding teachers in the church, no preacher will utter anything different — for no one is above the Master — nor will he diminish what has been handed down. Since our faith is everywhere the same, it is impossible to add to or take away from.

Irenaeus

✦ 236 ✦

UNITY AND COMMUNITY IN PRAYER

They all joined together constantly in prayer, along with the women and Mary the mother of Jesus, and with his brothers. (Acts 1:14)

The Teacher of Peace and Master of Unity did not want us to pray by ourselves all the time, and thus pray only for ourselves. We do not say, "My Father, who art in heaven," or, "Give me this day my daily bread," nor does someone ask that only her own debt be forgiven her, nor does she request that she alone not be led into temptation and alone delivered from evil. Our prayer is public and common, and when we pray, we pray not for one person but for the whole church, since we, the whole people, are one body.

The God of Peace and the Master of Concord willed that we should pray for every believer, just as Christ himself carried every believer on the cross. The three children observed this law when they were thrown into the fiery furnace, praying with one voice and with one heart. Our divine Scripture teaches us how such people prayed, giving us an example to follow in our own prayers, so that we may become like them: "Then these three sang a hymn as if with one mouth, and blessed the Lord" [possibly referencing Azar. 1:1]. They spoke as if with one mouth, even though Christ had not yet taught them how to pray.

We find the apostles and disciples praying this way as well, after the ascension of the Lord. The urgency and unanimity of their prayers showed that God, "who makes the inhabitants of a house be of one mind" (Acts 4:32), allows those whose prayer is unanimous into his eternal home.

Cyprian of Carthage

✣ 237 ✣

UNLOCKING THE DOORS
OF HEAVEN

*Brothers and sisters, we do not want you to be uninformed about those
who sleep in death, so that you do not grieve like the rest of mankind,
who have no hope. For we believe that Jesus died and rose again, and so
we believe that God will bring with Jesus those who have fallen asleep
in him. (1 Thessalonians 4:13–14)*

Christ is risen! He has burst open the gates of hell and let the
dead go free; he has renewed the earth through the members
of his church now born again in baptism, and has made it blossom
again with men and women brought back to life. His Holy Spirit
has unlocked the doors of heaven, which stand wide open to receive
those who rise up from the earth. Because of Christ's resurrection
the thief ascends to paradise, the bodies of the blessed enter the holy
city, and the dead are restored to the company of the living. There is
an upward movement in the whole of creation, each element raising
itself to something higher. We see hell restoring its victims to the
upper regions, earth sending its buried dead to heaven, and heaven
presenting the new arrivals to the Lord. In one and the same movement, our Savior's passion raises people from the depths, lifts them
up from the earth, and sets them in the heights.

Christ is risen. His rising brings life to the dead, forgiveness to
sinners, and glory to the saints. And so David the prophet summons
all creation to join in celebrating the Easter festival: "Rejoice and be
glad," he cries, "on this day which the LORD has made" (Ps. 118:24).

Maximus of Turin

✤ 238 ✤

THE RIGHT PRIORITIES

*Believers in humble circumstances ought to take pride in their high
position. But the rich should take pride in their humiliation —
since they will pass away like a wild flower. (James 1:9 – 10)*

Lord God, look with patience on people, as you have in the past,
and how fastidiously they follow the conventional rules of letters and grammar — which are only invented and passed on by
other people — but neglect the eternal rules of everlasting salvation
received from you! Men and women are so wrongly focused that if
a teacher of language mispronounced a word, for instance saying
"uman" instead of "human," other people would be more offended
at this error than if the same person, being a human being, should
hate another human being!

How wrong it is for us to think that our enemies could be more
destructive to us than our own hatred of our enemies would be to
ourselves — and how wrong for us to believe that we could physi-
cally destroy our persecutor more easily than our own hatred would
spiritually destroy us.

Truthfully there is no grammar more natural to us than the
words we write in our minds, and what we speak to others in our
minds, we would not wish upon ourselves. Mysterious God, who
dwells on high in silence, the only great thing there is — how amazing that you punish those with ugly desires with blindness! For
instance, when a vain person seeking recognition for eloquence
stands before a human judge and wild crowds, and slanders his or
her opponent with fierce hatred, the slanderer takes great care not
to accidentally make a grammatical error, but is blind and careless
about cutting an innocent person off from society!

Augustine

✦ 239 ✦

THE DARK NIGHT OF THE SOUL (I)

My God, my God, why have you forsaken me? Why are you so far from saving me, so far from my cries of anguish? (Psalm 22:1)

The blessed David recognizes that sometimes it is to our advantage to be deserted by God, since we see him praying not that God might not absolutely forsake him (since he was aware that this would have been harmful to himself and to God's plan of redemption), but instead that it would be partial and temporary, as he said, "Do not utterly forsake me" (Ps. 119:8).

It is as if he means to say, "I know that you forsake your followers for their advantage, in order to fortify them, since we could not be tempted by the devil if we were not at least a little forsaken by you. So I do not ask that you would never forsake me, because I know that it is good for me to feel my weakness and say, 'It is good for me that you have brought me low' (Ps. 119:71). I also would have no opportunity to fight temptation if your divine shield always protected me. For the devil will not dare to attack me while I am supported by your defense, since he is always bringing this complaint and objection against you and your servants: 'Does Job serve God for nothing? Have you not made a fence around him and his house and all that he has?' (Job 1:9–10). Instead, I ask that you would not forsake me too much." [Continued in next entry ...]

John Cassian

✦ 240 ✦

THE DARK NIGHT
OF THE SOUL (II)

You know that the testing of your faith produces perseverance. (James 1:3)

David continues: "And just as it is good for me that you sometimes forsake me a little, so that my love for you is built up, it is in fact dangerous if you allow me to be forsaken too much, in proportion to my faults and what I deserve. Nothing in our nature can resist temptation forever and stop us from giving in to the enemy's attack, unless you yourself, who know the strength of man and oversee his struggles, 'allow us not to be tempted above what we can handle, but provide a way of escape alongside the temptation, so that we may be able to bear it' (1 Cor. 10:13)."

We read about something like this in the book of Judges, when God mysteriously preserves Israel's enemies in order to test the chosen nation: "These are the nations, which the LORD left so that by them he might instruct Israel, that they might learn to fight with their enemies ... And the LORD left them so that he might try Israel by them, whether or not they would hear the commandments of the LORD, which he had commanded their fathers by the hand of Moses" (Judg. 3:1–4). God reserved this conflict for Israel not to interrupt their peace or to deliberately hurt them, but because he knew that if they felt continually oppressed by these other nations, Israel would continue to be aware of their need for the Lord's help. As a result they would persist in praising and praying to God and not grow careless and sinful through an easy life. For time and again, we see that when people face no adversity, they are ruined by negligence and prosperity.

John Cassian

✢ 241 ✢

THE COMPLETE IMAGE
OF OUR CREATOR

*For all of you who were baptized into Christ have clothed yourselves
with Christ. (Galatians 3:27)*

"The man made from the earth is the pattern of those who belong to the earth; the man from heaven is the pattern of those who belong to heaven" (1 Cor. 15:48). How is it that these men and women belong to heaven, even though they do not belong to heaven by birth — people who do not stay what they were by birth, but transform and remain what they have become by rebirth? The reason is that the heavenly Spirit, by the mysterious infusion of his light, gives fertility to the womb of the baptismal font. The Spirit brings forth men and women belonging to heaven whose earthly parents brought them forth as children of the earth and in a condition of corruption; he gives them the likeness of their Creator. Now that we are reborn, refashioned in the image of our Creator, we must fulfill what the Apostle commands: just as we used to wear the likeness of the man of earth, let us now wear the likeness of the man of heaven.

Now that we are reborn in the likeness of our Lord and have been adopted by God as his children, we should put on the complete image of our Creator to be wholly like him — not in the glory that only he possesses, but in innocence, simplicity, gentleness, patience, humility, mercy, harmony — those qualities he chose to have when he became one with us.

Peter Chrysologus

✦ 242 ✦

AS MUCH AS WE KNOW TO ASK FOR

You, God, are my God, earnestly I seek you; I thirst for you, my whole being longs for you, in a dry and parched land where there is no water.
(Psalm 63:1)

The one, true, and only life of happiness is to contemplate the Lord's graciousness forever, using our immortal and incorruptible body and spirit. Everything else is sought and requested for the sake of this one thing. Those who have this will have all that they want; in heaven, they will be unable to want, because they will be unable to possess anything undesirable.

In heaven is the fountain of life, for which we should thirst in prayer as long as we live, hoping while we do not yet see the object of our hope. Yet since this is a peace that surpasses all understanding, even when we ask for it in prayer we do not know how to pray properly. Obviously we do not know something if we cannot think of it as it really is; whatever comes to mind we reject as imperfect; we know that this is not what we are seeking, even though we have yet to see it for the first time.

So there is within us a kind of instructed ignorance, led by the Spirit of God who helps our weakness. The Spirit moves the saints to plead with sighs too deep for words, inspiring in them a desire for the great and as yet unknown reality that we patiently look forward to. How can words express what we desire when it remains unknown? If we were entirely ignorant of it we would not desire it, and we would not desire it with sighs and groans if we were able to see it.

Augustine

✤ 243 ✤

THE VEIL OF MODESTY

I also want the women to dress modestly, with decency and propriety, adorning themselves, not with elaborate hairstyles or gold or pearls or expensive clothes, but with good deeds, appropriate for women who profess to worship God. (1 Timothy 2:9–10)

Let our custom itself teach us: a woman covers her face with a veil so that in public her modesty may be safe. But if she covers herself with a veil in order to stop improper looking, how much more should she cover herself with the veil of modesty, so that even in public she has her own secret place?

Even if your eyes have fallen upon another person, at least do not let internal passion follow. To have seen is not a sin, but you must be careful that seeing does not become the source of sin. The bodily eyes can see while the eyes of the heart remain closed; maintain modesty of mind.

We have a Lord who is both strict and indulgent. The prophet said, "Do not look upon the beauty of a woman who is all harlot" [possibly synopsis of Prov. 5]. But the Lord said, "Whoever looks on a woman to lust after her has committed adultery with her already in his heart" (Matt. 5:28). He does not say, "Whoever looks has committed adultery," but "Whoever looks on her to lust after her." He did not condemn the look, but the inward lust. We will see with our eyes whatever appears in front of us, but if we pay no attention to this with our mind, the sight also fades away, so that in reality we see more with the mind than with the body.

Ambrose

✤ 244 ✤

A LAMB SLAIN

They will wage war against the Lamb, but the Lamb will triumph over them because he is Lord of lords and King of kings—and with him will be his called, chosen and faithful followers. (Revelation 17:14)

There was much proclaimed by the prophets about the mystery of the Passover: that mystery is Christ, and to him be glory forever and ever. Amen.

For the sake of suffering humanity he came down from heaven to earth, clothed himself in humanity in the Virgin's womb, and was born a man. Then having a body capable of suffering, he took the pain of fallen humanity upon himself; he triumphed over the diseases of soul and body that were its cause, and by his Spirit, which was incapable of dying, he dealt humanity's destroyer, death, a fatal blow.

He was led forth like a lamb; he was slaughtered like a sheep. He ransomed us from our servitude to the world, as he had ransomed Israel from the hand of Egypt; he freed us from our slavery to the devil, as he had freed Israel from the hand of Pharaoh. He sealed our souls with his own Spirit, and the members of our body with his own blood.

He is the one who covered death with shame and cast the devil into mourning, as Moses cast Pharaoh into mourning. He is the one that struck sin and robbed iniquity of its offspring, as Moses robbed the Egyptians of their offspring. He is the one who brought us out of slavery into freedom, out of darkness into light, out of death into life, out of tyranny into an eternal kingdom; who made us a new priesthood, a people chosen to be his own forever. He is the Passover that is our salvation.

Melito of Sardis

❖ 245 ❖

THE SHEEP IMITATE
THE SHEPHERD

"Because you have scattered my flock and driven them away and have
not bestowed care on them, I will bestow punishment on you for the evil
you have done," declares the LORD. (Jeremiah 23:2)

Even a strong sheep, if he sees his shepherd living wickedly, will
turn his eyes from the Lord's laws and begin to say in his heart:
"If my pastor lives like that, why should I not live like him?" The
wicked shepherd has killed the strong sheep. And if he can kill the
strong one, what does he do to the rest?

My advice is from the Scriptures: even if the sheep have life and
are strong in the Word of the Lord, and if they hold fast to what
they have heard from their Lord, the sheep ought to "Do what they
say but not what they do" (Matt. 23:3). Nonetheless, as far as the
shepherd is concerned, if he lives a wicked life in front of the people
he kills the sheep under his care. Let such a shepherd not deceive
himself because his sheep is not dead, for though it still lives, he is
a murderer—just as when the lustful man looks on a woman with
desire, even though she is chaste, he has committed adultery. For
the Lord said plainly: "Whoever has looked upon a woman with
desire has already committed adultery with her in his heart" (Matt.
5:28). He has not entered her bedroom, yet he has ravished her
within the bedroom of his heart.

Therefore you are a killer if you live wickedly in front of those
you care for. Whoever imitates him, dies; whoever does not, has
life. But as for him, he kills both of them.

Augustine

✤ 246 ✤

THE HONORS GIVEN TO MAN

"How will this be," Mary asked the angel, "since I am a virgin?"
(Luke 1:34)

A virgin conceived, bore a son, but remained a virgin. This is no everyday occurrence, but a sign; God's power is the only cause, and not nature. It is a special event and shares nothing with other events; it is divine, not human. Christ's birth was not necessary, but an expression of omnipotence, a sacrament of holiness for the redemption of men. The one who formed man out of pure clay made a man again, this time born from a pure body. The hand that touched clay to make our flesh condescended to assume a body for our salvation. Our Creator residing in a creature gives man dignity without bringing dishonor to God.

So why do you count yourself worthless in your own eyes when you are so precious to God? Why give yourself dishonor when you are honored by him? Why do you ask how you were created and not want to know why you were created? Was not the entire visible universe made as a home for you? It was for you that the light cut through the overshadowing darkness, and for your sake that the night and day were measured and the heavens decorated with the varied brilliance of the sun, the moon, and the stars. The earth was adorned with flowers, groves, and fruit, and a stunning variety of lovely living things was created in the air, the fields, and the seas for you, so that sad solitude might not destroy your joy in God's new creation.

Peter Chrysologus

✢ 247 ✢

KNOCK AT THE DOOR OF SCRIPTURE

They are more precious than gold, than much pure gold; they are sweeter than honey, than honey from the honeycomb. (Psalm 19:10)

Scripture sets our mind on the brilliant, gold-gleaming back of the divine Dove (Ps. 68:13), whose bright wings lift us to the only begotten Son, tender of his spiritual vineyard, who in turn brings us to the Father of Lights (Jas. 1:17).

But do not knock without care; rather, knock with zeal every day! Do not grow weary of knocking, for the door is promised to open to us. If you do not understand on the first or second reading, do not grow weary, but instead persist, talk about the text, and ask questions of it. For as Moses says, "Ask your Father and he will show you, and ask your elders and they will tell you" (Deut. 32:7). For "not every man has that knowledge" (1 Cor. 8:7).

Draw from the fountain in the eternal garden and from purest waters pouring from eternal life (John 4:14). Indulge and revel in this garden, for the Scriptures possess inexhaustible grace.

And if anything comes to you from outside sources, if it is profitable then use it. Be like experienced coin collectors, heaping up pure gold and throwing out the fake. Keep the wise and useful parts of the pagan world, but let them keep their absurd gods and strange myths, for Christ is sure to prevail over them and their false gods.

John of Damascus

❖ 248 ❖

THOUGHTS, WORDS, AND DEEDS

We demolish arguments and every pretension that sets itself up against the knowledge of God, and we take captive every thought to make it obedient to Christ. (2 Corinthians 10:5)

Having been found worthy of the name of Christ, what must we do? Each of us must examine his thoughts, words, and deeds to see whether they are directed toward Christ or away from him. We do this in various ways. Our deeds or thoughts or words are not in harmony with Christ if they come from passion. This is the mark of the enemy, who smears the pearl of the heart with the slime of passion, marring or even destroying the luster of the precious stone.

On the other hand, if they are untainted by every passionate inclination, they are directed toward Christ, the author and source of peace. He is like a pure stream. If you draw from him the thoughts in your mind and the inclinations of your heart, you will show a likeness to Christ, your source and origin, as the gleaming water in a jar resembles the flowing water from which it was obtained.

For the purity of Christ and the purity shown in our hearts are identical. Christ's purity, however, is the fountainhead; ours has its source in him and flows out of him. Our life is stamped with the beauty of his thought. The inner and the outer person are harmonized in a kind of music. The mind of Christ is the controlling influence that inspires us to moderation and goodness in our behavior. As I see it, Christian perfection is this: since we share the titles that are given to Christ, we conform to their meaning in our minds, our prayers, and our way of life.

Gregory of Nyssa

✣ 249 ✣

STAND FIRM AND PROSPER

Dear friends, although I was very eager to write to you about the salvation we share, I felt compelled to write and urge you to contend for the faith that was once for all entrusted to God's holy people. (Jude 1:3)

Let Christ's goodness be your model, for if he ever imitated our behavior, we would be truly lost. Now that we are his disciples we should lead Christian lives. Throw out the leaven that is old and sour, and pick up the new leaven, which is Jesus Christ. Be preserved by the salt of Christ so that you do not decay, since you will be judged by your fragrance. It is ridiculous to talk of Jesus Christ and to practice Judaism at the same time. For Christianity did not base its faith on Judaism, but Judaism on Christianity, and all believing nations are brought together under Christ.

The next warning I give as a precaution, not because I think you believe this: do not fall into the trap of false doctrine. Be convinced of the birth and passion and resurrection that took place at the time of Pontius Pilate. These things were truly and certainly done by Jesus Christ, our hope. I pray that none of you would be turned aside.

Do your utmost to stand firm in the precepts of the Lord and the apostles, so that "you may prosper in all that you do" (Deut. 29:9) in the flesh and in the spirit, in faith and love, in the Son and the Father and the Spirit, at the beginning and at the end, together with your elder and clergy and deacons. Submit to the elder and to one another, just as Jesus Christ submitted to the Father, and the apostles submitted to Christ and to the Father, so that there may be complete unity in flesh and spirit.

Ignatius of Antioch

❖ 250 ❖

HOLY LIVING, HOLY DYING

When he opened the fifth seal, I saw under the altar the souls of those who had been slain because of the word of God and the testimony they had maintained. (Revelation 6:9)

In the Psalms, where the Holy Spirit speaks to us and counsels us, it is written: "Precious in the sight of God is the death of his holy ones" (Ps. 116:15). He calls this death "precious" because the martyr courageously pays in his or her own blood for God's reward of immortality.

Christ was there, happily fighting alongside and conquering through his servants. He protects our faith and gives strength to believers in proportion to the trust that each person places in him. Christ was there to wage his own battle; he rallied the soldiers who fought for his name; he made them spirited and strong. He who conquered death once for all for us, now continually conquers in us.

How blessed is our church! Honored and illuminated by God, and encouraged by the glorious blood of martyrs! In earlier times it shone white with the good deeds of our brothers and sisters, and now it is adorned with the red blood of martyrs. It is dressed in both lilies and roses. Each of us should strive for the maximum glory that God has chosen us for, whether the pure white crown of a holy life or the royal red crown of martyrdom.

Cyprian of Carthage

✣ 251 ✣

HUMAN GLORY IS FLEETING

He destroys both the blameless and the wicked. (Job 9:22)

I want creation to penetrate you with so much admiration that everywhere, wherever you may be, the smallest plant may remind you of the Creator. If you see the grass of the fields, think of human nature, and remember the comparison of wise Isaiah: "All flesh is grass, and all its beauty is as the flower of the field" (Isa. 40:6). Truly the rapid flow of life, the short gratification that an instant of earthly happiness gives a man, wonderfully suits the comparison of the prophet.

Today a man is vigorous in body, fattened by luxury, and in the prime of life, with a handsome face, strong and powerful and energetic; tomorrow he will be an object of pity, withered by age and exhausted by sickness.

Another man shines in all the splendor of a huge fortune, and a multitude of flatterers surround him, an escort of false friends trail behind his generosity; a crowd of kinsfolk, but no true kin; a swarm of servants crowd after him to feed him and satisfy his needs. And in his comings and goings this innumerable throng, which he drags after him, excites the envy of whomever he meets. On top of fortune may be added political power, the government of a province, or the command of armies; underlings to fill his subjects with awe, to beat, rob, banish, and imprison them — all he needs to strike terror into everyone he rules.

And what then? One night, a fever, a heart malady, or an inflammation of the lungs snatches this man away from the midst of humankind, stripped in a moment of all his stage props, and all his "glory" is proved a mere dream. Therefore the prophet has compared human glory to the weakest flower.

Basil the Great

⊹ 252 ⊹

HAD THERE BEEN NO CROSS

For Christ did not send me to baptize, but to preach the gospel — not with wisdom and eloquence, lest the cross of Christ be emptied of its power.
(1 Corinthians 1:17)

We are celebrating the feast of the cross, which drove away darkness and brought in the light. As we remember the cross, we are lifted up with the crucified Christ, leaving the world and its sins behind us so that we may gain the things above. The cross is a possession so great and outstanding that whoever receives it has won a treasure. It is right to call this treasure the fairest and costliest of all gifts, for on it and through it and for its sake the riches of salvation that had been lost were restored to us.

Had there been no cross, Christ could not have been crucified. Had there been no cross, Life itself could not have been nailed to the tree. And if Life had not been nailed to it, there would be no streams of immortality pouring from Christ's side, blood and water for the world's cleansing. The legal bond of our sin would not have been canceled, we would not have attained our freedom, we would not have enjoyed the fruit of the tree of life, and the gates of paradise would not stand open. Had there been no cross, death would not have been trodden underfoot, nor hell robbed of its quarry.

Andrew of Crete

✣ 253 ✣

THE MANIFOLD CREATION
OF GOD

He makes clouds rise from the ends of the earth; he sends lightning with
the rain and brings out the wind from his storehouses. (Psalm 135:7)

Consider God's works! The reliable rotation of the seasons and the changes in temperature; the consistent march of the stars; the well-ordered course of days and nights and months and years; the various beauties of seeds and plants and fruits; and the diverse species of four-legged animals and birds and reptiles and fish in sea and river.

Or consider the instinct given these animals to have offspring, not for their own profit, but for human use; and the providence through which God provides nourishment for all creatures; or that he has ordained all things to be subject to humankind.

Consider too the flowing of sweet springs and rushing rivers, and the seasonable supply of dews and showers and rains; the manifold movement of the heavenly bodies, the morning star rising and announcing the sun's rising; and the constellations of Pleiades and Orion and Arcturus; and the orbit of the other stars that circle through the heavens, all of which God in his manifold wisdom has given unique names. He is God, who alone made light out of darkness and brought forth light from his creations and collected the waters in the storehouses of the deep.

He is God, who cracks the sky with his thunder to terrify and foretells the peal of the thunder by the lightning, so that no one faints from the sudden shock; and who wrangles the violence of the lightning as it flashes out of heaven, so that it does not consume the earth; for, if the lightning were allowed all its power, it would burn up the earth; and if the thunder were allowed all its power, it would overthrow all of humanity's works.

Theophilus of Antioch

✢ 254 ✢

HE MUST INCREASE

*This is love: not that we loved God, but that he loved us and sent his
Son as an atoning sacrifice for our sins. (1 John 4:10)*

Those who are in love with themselves are unable to love God. Those who love God give themselves up for the sake of the immeasurable blessings of divine love. These people never seek their own glory but only the glory of God. If people love themselves they seek their own glory, but those who love God love the glory of their Creator.

Anyone moved by the love of God can be recognized by the way he constantly strives to glorify him by fulfilling his commandments and delighting in his own submission. It is right for God to receive glory because of his great majesty; we become friends of God by doing what is right for us, which is submitting ourselves to him. By doing this we will rejoice in his glory as John the Baptist did, and we will never stop repeating, "His fame must increase, but mine must diminish" (John 3:30).

Anyone who loves God in the depths of her heart has already been loved by him. In fact, the intensity of a person's love for God depends upon how aware she is of God's love for her. When she is keenly aware of God's love, then she longs to be enlightened by the divine light, and this longing is so intense that it seems to penetrate her very bones. She loses all consciousness of herself and is entirely transformed by the love of God.

Diadochus of Photice

✤ 255 ✤

JOB PREFIGURES CHRIST (I)

In the land of Uz there lived a man whose name was Job. This man was
blameless and upright; he feared God and shunned evil. (Job 1:1)

My beloved brothers and sisters, the story of Job prefigures that of Christ. We understand it this way, and we can see the truth of this by detailed comparison.

Job was called a righteous man by God; and God is righteousness itself, the fountain of righteousness from which the blessed drink. Of him it was said: "The sun of righteousness shall rise for you" (Mal. 4:2)

Job was called truthful; and the Lord is truly Truth itself, for as he says in the Gospel, "I am the way and the truth" (John 14:6).

Job was rich; and what could be richer than the Lord? For all the rich are his slaves, the whole world and all that exists is his, as David said in the Psalms: "The earth is the LORD's and the fullness thereof, the world and all who live in it" (Ps. 24:1).

The devil tempted Job three times; and three times, according to the Gospel, he tried to tempt the Lord.

Everything that Job had, he lost; and for love of us the Lord forgot all his heavenly blessings and made himself poor, that we might be rich.

Job was disfigured with boils; and the Lord, taking on human flesh, was fouled with the sins of all mankind. [Continued in next entry ...]

Zeno of Verona

✦ 256 ✦

JOB PREFIGURES CHRIST (II)

As you know, we count as blessed those who have persevered. You have heard of Job's perseverance and have seen what the Lord finally brought about. The Lord is full of compassion and mercy. (James 5:11)

The devil, raging, destroyed Job's sons; and the Lord's sons, the prophets, were killed by the people of the Pharisees in their madness.

Job's own wife urged him to sin; and the synagogue, the bride of God, tried to compel the Lord to follow the corrupt behavior of the elders.

Job's friends, it is said, insulted him; and the Lord was insulted by his own priests — his own worshipers.

Job sits on a dunghill full of worms; and the Lord lived in a real dunghill, that is, this world, surrounded by people seething with every vice and every crime: true worms.

Job received back his health and his riches; and the Lord, rising, did not only regain health but granted immortality to those who believed in him and took back dominion over all of nature. For as he himself bears witness, "All things have been given to me by my Father" (Matt. 11:27).

Job begot new sons to replace the ones who had died; the Lord, to replace the prophets, begot his holy sons, the apostles.

Job went to his rest in blessedness and peace; but the Lord remains blessed in all eternity: before time, and from the beginning of time, and to the end of all ages.

Zeno of Verona

✧ 257 ✧

LET THIS AFFLICTION PASS

*Therefore, in order to keep me from becoming conceited, I was given a
thorn in my flesh, a messenger of Satan, to torment me.*
(2 Corinthians 12:7)

Three times Paul asked the Lord to take the thorn in his side away from him, which showed that even Paul did not know what to pray for. But finally he heard the Lord's answer, which explained why it was not expedient for his prayer to be granted: "My grace is sufficient for you, for power shines forth more perfectly in weakness" (2 Cor. 12:9).

We do not know whether our afflictions will bring good or ill, so we do not know what is right to pray for; but because it is difficult, weak as we are, we do what every human would do, and we pray that it may be taken away from us. However, we owe God at least this much faith: if he does not take it away, we must not imagine that we are forgotten, but should look forward to greater blessings in its place. In this way, "power shines forth more perfectly in weakness." These words are written to prevent us from being dejected and distrustful of God's mercy toward us if our prayer is not granted. God knows that we often ask for something that would bring us greater affliction or completely ruin us through the corrupting influence of prosperity. In these cases we do not know what is right to ask for in prayer.

Therefore, if something happens that we did not pray for, we must have no doubt that God wants what is better than what we wanted ourselves. Our great Mediator gave us an example of this. After he had said, "Father, if it is possible, let this cup be taken away from me," he immediately added, "Yet not what I will, but what you will, Father" (Matt. 26:39).

Augustine

✢ 258 ✢

EASTER POEM (I)

"Who will roll the stone away from the entrance of the tomb?"
(Mark 16:3)

Restore the promised pledge, I pray you, O power
benign!
The third day has returned; arise, my buried one;
It is not fitting that your limbs should lie in the lowly
sepulcher,
Nor that worthless stones should press that which is the
ransom of the world.
It is unworthy that a stone should shut in with a confining
rock,
And cover him in whose fist all things are enclosed.
Take away the linen clothes, I pray; leave the napkins in the
tomb:
You are sufficient for us, and without you there is nothing.
Release the chained ghosts of the infernal prison,
And recall to the upper regions whatever sinks to the lowest
depths.
Give back your face, that the world may see the light;
Give back the day which flees from us at your death.
But returning, O holy conqueror! You did altogether fill
the heaven!
Hell lies depressed, nor retains its rights.
The ruler of the lower regions,
Insatiably opening his hollow jaws,
Who has always been a spoiler,
Becomes a prey to you.
[Continued in next entry . . .]

Venantius Fortunatus

✛ 259 ✛

EASTER POEM (II)

Death and Hades gave up the dead that were in them. (Revelation 20:13)

You rescue innumerable people from the prison of death,
And they follow in freedom to the place where their
leader approaches.
The fierce monster in alarm vomits forth
The multitude whom he had swallowed up,
And the Lamb withdraws the sheep from the jaw of the wolf.
Hence re-seeking the tomb from the lower regions, having
resumed your flesh,
As a warrior you carry back ample trophies to the heavens.
A host, clad in white, comes forth from the bright waves,
And cleanse their old fault in a new stream.
Drawing those who wander in Gentile error to better things,
That a beast of prey may not carry them away,
He guards the fold of God.
Those whom guilty Eve had before infected, he now
restores,
Fed with abundant milk at the bosom of the church.
About to remain with you through an age with the return
of a hundredfold,
You fill the barns with the produce of an abundant harvest.
May this people, free from stain, be strengthened in your
arms,
And may you bear to the stars a pure pledge to God.

Venantius Fortunatus

✤ 260 ✤

EFFECTIVE PRAYER

As he was going into a village, ten men who had leprosy met him. They stood at a distance and called out in a loud voice, "Jesus, Master, have pity on us!" (Luke 17:12–13)

"Offer God a sacrifice of praise and fulfill your vows to the Most High" (Ps. 50:14). If you praise God you offer your vow and fulfill the promise you have made. So the Samaritan leper, healed by the Lord's word of command, gained greater credit than the other nine; he alone returned to Christ, praising God and giving thanks. Jesus said of him: "There was no one to come back and thank God except this foreigner" (Luke 17:18). He tells him: "Stand up and go on your way, for your faith has made you whole" (Luke 17:19).

The Lord Jesus, in his divine wisdom, taught you about the goodness of the Father, who always gives good things, so that you might ask for good things from Goodness itself. He urges you to pray earnestly and frequently, not babbling long prayers, but praying often and with perseverance. Lengthy prayers are filled with empty words, and if you neglect prayer you become indifferent to it.

Christ urges you, when you ask forgiveness for yourself, to be especially generous to others, so that your actions may commend your prayer. The Apostle too teaches you how to pray; you must avoid anger and contentiousness, so that your prayer may be serene and wholesome.

Ambrose

✢ 261 ✢

EVERYONE CAN HELP (I)

But a poor widow came and put in two very small copper coins, worth only a few cents. Calling his disciples to him, Jesus said, "Truly I tell you, this poor widow has put more into the treasury than all the others."
(Mark 12:42–43)

There is nothing colder than a Christian who does not seek to help others.

You cannot plead poverty here; the widow putting in her two small coins testifies against you. Peter said, "I have no silver and gold" (Acts 3:6). Paul was so poor that he was often hungry and went without food.

You cannot plead humble birth, for they were all of humble stock. You cannot offer the excuse of lack of education, for they were uneducated. You cannot plead poor health, for Timothy had poor health and was frequently ill.

Everyone can help their neighbor as long as they are willing to do what they can. Trees that do not bear fruit can be strong and tall and upstanding but give us nothing for nourishment. We would prefer a garden of fruit-bearing trees — pomegranates and olives — for they provide us with life.

People who only think of their own concerns are like fruitless trees. In fact, they are even worse, since the trees are at least useful for building or protection, whereas the selfish are only fit for punishment. The foolish virgins were like this: chaste, beautiful, and self-controlled, but they did nothing for anyone — so they are consumed in the fire (Matt. 25:1–12). People who refuse to give Christ food are like this. [Continued in next entry …]

John Chrysostom

⁂ 262 ⁂

EVERYONE CAN HELP (II)

Then he will say to those on his left, "Depart from me, you who are
cursed, into the eternal fire prepared for the devil and his angels.
For I was hungry and you gave me nothing to eat, I was thirsty
and you gave me nothing to drink." (Matthew 25:41–42)

Notice that none of [the judged in Matthew 25] is accused of personal sins. They are not accused of committing fornication or perjury or any other sin, but only of not helping anybody else. The man who buried the talent was like this (Matt. 25:14–30). His life was blameless, but he was of no service to others.

How can a person like this be a Christian? If yeast did not make the whole dough rise, is it really yeast? Or if perfume failed to fill the room with its fragrance, would we call it perfume?

Do not say, "It is impossible for me to influence others." If you are a Christian, it is impossible for this not to happen. Things in nature have inherent qualities specific to them, and likewise with Christians, for influencing others is part of the nature of a Christian.

Do not insult God. If you say that the sun cannot shine, you have insulted him. If you say that a Christian cannot help others, you have insulted God and called him a liar. It is easier for the sun not to shine or give warmth than it is for a Christian not to shed God's light. It is easier for light to be darkness than for this to happen.

So do not say that it is impossible! The opposite is impossible. Do not insult God. The light of a Christian cannot escape notice. A lamp as bright as this cannot be hidden.

John Chrysostom

❖ 263 ❖

OUTDO ONE ANOTHER IN SERVICE

Now that I, your Lord and Teacher, have washed your feet,
you also should wash one another's feet. (John 13:14)

A person who openly despises the honors of this world and rejects all earthly glory must also practice self-denial. Self-denial means that you never seek your own will but God's, using God's will as a sure guide; it also means possessing nothing apart from what is held in common. In this way it will be easier for you to carry out your elder's commands promptly, with joy and hope; this is required of Christ's servants, who have been redeemed for service to their brothers and sisters. This is what the Lord means when he says, "Whoever wishes to be first and great among you must be the last of all and a servant to all" (Mark 9:35).

Our service to humankind must be given freely. We must be subject to everyone and serve our brothers as if we were paying off a debt. Moreover, those who are in charge should work harder than the others and conduct themselves with greater submission than those that are under them. Their lives should be a visible example of what service means, and they should remember that those who are committed to their trust are given to them by God.

Those who are in a position of authority must look after their brothers and sisters as dutiful teachers look after young children given to them by their parents. If brothers and sisters and elders have this loving relationship, then brothers and sisters will be happy to obey whatever is commanded, while elders will be delighted to lead their brothers and sisters to perfection. If you try to outdo one another in showing respect, your life on earth will be like that of the angels.

Gregory of Nyssa

✦ 264 ✦

PRAY FROM THE HEART

These people come near to me with their mouth and honor me with their lips, but their hearts are far from me. Their worship of me is based on merely human rules they have been taught. (Isaiah 29:13)

In the first book of the Kings, Hannah, who is a type of the church, observes that she prays to God not with loud petitions, but silently and modestly within the recesses of her heart. Her prayer was hidden but her faith was revealed. She spoke not with her voice, but with her heart, because she knew that that is how God hears, and she received what she sought because she asked for it with belief. The divine Scripture asserts this when it says, "She spoke in her heart, and her lips moved, but her voice was not audible; and God listened to her" (1 Sam. 1:13, 19). Likewise we read in the Psalms, "Speak in your hearts and in your beds, and be pierced" (Ps. 4:4).

Brothers and sisters, the worshiper should remember how the tax collector prayed next to the Pharisee in the temple: not with his eyes boldly raised up to heaven, nor with hands held up in pride, but beating his breast and confessing his sins, imploring the help of the divine mercy. While the Pharisee was pleased with himself and confident of his innocence (yet no one is innocent), it was the tax collector who deserved to be sanctified, because he prayed humbly and confessed his sins to God, who pardons the humble (Luke 18:9–14).

Cyprian of Carthage

✢ 265 ✣

BEING MADE MERCIFUL BY MERCY

But we know that when Christ appears, we shall be like him,
for we shall see him as he is. (1 John 3:2)

Just as concern for one's neighbor is part of our love of God, so too the virtue of mercy is part of the desire for righteousness, as it is said: "Blessed are the merciful, for God will be merciful to them" (Matt. 5:7).

Remember, Christian, the surpassing worth of the wisdom that is yours. Bear in mind the kind of school in which you are to learn your skills, and the rewards to which you are called. Mercy itself wishes you to be merciful, righteousness itself wishes you to be righteous, so that the Creator may shine forth in his creature and the image of God may be reflected in the mirror of the human heart as it imitates his qualities. The faith of those who live their faith is a serene faith. What you long for will be given you; what you love will be yours forever.

Since it is by giving alms that everything is pure for you, you will also receive that blessing that is promised next by the Lord: "Blessed are the pure of heart, for they shall see God" (Matt. 5:8). What a great and happy reward! What mind can conceive, what words can express the great happiness of seeing God? Yet human nature will achieve this when it has been transformed so that it sees the godhead no longer in a mirror or obscurely, but face-to-face—the godhead that no person has been able to see. In the inexpressible joy of this eternal vision, human nature will possess what no eye has seen nor ear heard, and what no heart has ever conceived.

Leo the Great

✦ 266 ✦

EXPECTATION OF ADOPTION

For in this hope we were saved. But hope that is seen is no hope at all.
Who hopes for what they already have? (Romans 8:24)

One who has the Spirit of God becomes a child of God, so much so that the Holy Spirit bears witness to our spirit that we are sons of God. This is the witness of the Holy Spirit: he cries out in our hearts, "Abba, Father" (Gal. 4:6), as we read in the letter to the Galatians.

To encourage us in suffering, Paul says that all our sufferings are small in comparison with the wonderful reward that will be revealed in us (Rom. 8:18); we truly do not deserve the blessings that are to come. We shall be restored to the likeness of God and made worthy of seeing him face-to-face.

He emphasizes the greatness of this future revelation by adding that creation also looks forward to the revealing of the sons and daughters of God (Rom. 8:19). Creation is at present condemned to frustration, not of its own choice, and lives in hope. Its hope is in Christ, as it awaits the grace of his ministry. It hopes that it will share in the glorious freedom of the children of God and be freed from its bondage to corruption.

At present, however, while the revelation is delayed, all creation groans as it looks forward to the glory of adoption and redemption; it is already in labor with the spirit of salvation and is anxious to be freed from its subjection to frustration.

The meaning is clear: those who have the firstfruits of the Spirit are groaning in expectation of their adoption as children. But this adoption is of the whole body of creation, when it will itself be a child of God and see the divine goodness face-to-face.

Ambrose

⊰ 267 ⊱

PURSUING THE LOST

Therefore the people wander like sheep oppressed for lack of a shepherd.
(Zechariah 10:2)

The shepherd seeks out the straying sheep, but because they have wandered and are lost they think that they are not ours. "Why do you want us? Why do you seek us?" they ask, as if their straying and being lost were not the very reason for our seeking them out! "If I am straying," the sheep says, "if I am lost, why do you want me?" You are straying, that is why I wish to recall you. You have been lost — I wish to find you. "But I wish to stray," it says, "I wish to be lost."

So you wish to stray and be lost? Thank the Lord that I do not also wish this! Clearly I am unwelcome with you. But I listen to the Apostle who says, "Preach the word; insist upon it, welcome and unwelcome" (2 Tim. 4:2). Of course we are welcome by those who desire it, and unwelcome by those who do not. However unwelcome I might be, I dare to say, "You wish to stray and to be lost, but I do not want this." For I fear one greater than you who does not wish this.

I will recall the straying; I will seek the lost. Whether they wish it or not, I shall do it. And if the brambles of the forests tear at me as I pursue, I shall force myself through the tightest thickets, and I shall cut down all hedges. As far as the God whom I fear grants me the strength, I shall search everywhere. I shall recall the straying; I shall seek after those on the verge of being lost. If you do not want me to suffer, do not stray and become lost! It is trying enough that I lament your straying and loss.

Augustine

✢ 268 ✢

CONSOLATION AND RESURRECTION

Jesus Christ ... will transform our lowly bodies so that they will be like his glorious body. (Philippians 3:20–21)

After preaching the blessings of poverty, the Lord went on to say: "Blessed are they who mourn, for they shall be comforted" (Matt. 5:4). But the mourning for which he promises eternal consolation, dearly beloved, has nothing to do with ordinary worldly distress; for the tears which have their origin in the sorrow common to all humankind do not make anyone blessed. It is more than that—religious grief mourns for sin, one's own or another's; it does not lament because of what happens as a result of God's justice, but because of what is done by human malice. Indeed, we should lament the wrongdoers more than their victims, for their wickedness plunges the sinners into punishment, whereas endurance can raise the just persons to glory.

Next the Lord says: "Blessed are the meek, for they shall inherit the earth" (Matt. 5:5). To the meek and gentle, the lowly and the humble, and to all who are ready to endure any injury, he promises that they will possess the earth. And this inheritance is not small or insignificant, as though it were distinct from our heavenly dwelling; for we know that the kingdom of heaven is also the inheritance of the meek, and the additional gifts given to the gentle are their new bodies. Through the merit of their humility their bodies will be transformed by a joyous resurrection and clothed in the glory of immortality. No longer opposed in any way to their spirits, their bodies will remain in perfect harmony and unity with the will of the soul. Then, indeed, the outer person will be the peaceful and unblemished possession of the inner person.

Leo the Great

✣ 269 ✣

CHRIST IN THE PSALMS

*I will proclaim the LORD's decree: He said to me, "You are my son;
today I have become your father." (Psalm 2:7)*

If someone wants to study the deeds of our ancestors and imitate the best of them, she can find a single psalm that contains the whole of their history, a complete treasury of past memories in just one short reading.

If someone wants to study the law and learn about the power behind the law (it is the bond of love, "for whoever loves his neighbor has fulfilled the law" [Rom. 13:8]), let her read in the Psalms how love led one man to undergo great dangers to wipe out the shame of his entire people. This triumph of virtue recounted in the Psalms will lead her to recognize the great things that love can do.

And as for the power of prophecy—what can I say? Other prophets spoke in riddles. To the Psalmist alone, it seems, God promised openly and clearly that the Lord Jesus would be born of his seed: "I promise that your own son will succeed you on the throne" (Ps. 132:11).

Thus in the book of Psalms, Jesus is not only born for us: he also accepts his saving passion, he dies, he rises from the dead, he ascends into heaven, he sits at the Father's right hand. The Psalmist announced what no other prophet had dared to say, the full story of Christ, that which was later preached by the Lord himself in the Gospel.

Ambrose

✢ 270 ✢

PEACE BY RECONCILIATION

For he himself is our peace, who has made the two groups one and has destroyed the barrier, the dividing wall of hostility. (Ephesians 2:14)

Since we think of Christ as our peace, we can only call ourselves true Christians if our lives express Christ by our own peace. As the Apostle says, "He has put enmity to death" (Eph. 2:16). We must never allow hatred to be rekindled in us in any way but must declare that it is absolutely dead. God gloriously destroyed enmity in order to save us; we should not risk the life of our souls by being resentful or by bearing grudges. We must not awaken that enmity or call it back to life by our sin, for it is better off dead.

No, since we possess Christ who is peace, we must put an end to hatred and live as he lived. He broke down the separating wall, united what was divided, and established peace by reconciling in his person those who disagreed. In the same way, we must be reconciled not only with those who attack us from outside, but also with whatever disturbs our soul's peace; then our flesh will no longer be opposed to the spirit, nor the spirit to the flesh. Once we subject the thinking of the flesh to God's law, we will be re-created as a unified person at peace. Having become one instead of two, we shall have peace within ourselves.

Peace is defined as harmony among those who are divided. Therefore, when we end the civil war within our nature and cultivate peace within ourselves, we become peace. By this peace we demonstrate that our name of "Christian" is authentic and appropriate.

Gregory of Nyssa

✣ 271 ✣

THE POWER
OF THE ASCENSION

When the proconsul saw what had happened, he believed,
for he was amazed at the teaching about the Lord. (Acts 13:12)

At Easter, beloved brothers and sisters, it was the Lord's resurrection that was the cause of our joy; our present rejoicing is on account of his ascension into heaven. With all due solemnity we are commemorating that day on which our poor human nature was carried up, in Christ, above all the hosts of heaven, above all the ranks of angels, beyond the highest heavenly powers to the very throne of God the Father. It is upon these divine acts in the plan of redemption that we have been firmly established, so that the grace of God may be multiplied when, in spite of the risen and glorious Christ being withdrawn from men's sight, faith does not fail, hope is not shaken, charity does not grow cold.

Our faith is nobler and stronger because, instead of seeing, our believing hearts are enlightened by heaven to accept this doctrine. This faith was increased by the Lord's ascension and strengthened by the gift of the Spirit; it would remain unshaken by chains and imprisonment, exile and hunger, fire and ferocious beasts, and the most refined tortures ever devised by brutal persecutors. Throughout the world women no less than men, tender girls as well as boys, have given their life's blood in the struggle for this faith. It is a faith that has driven out devils, healed the sick, and raised the dead.

Leo the Great

❧ 272 ❧

PARADISE IS OUR COUNTRY

After this I looked, and there before me was a great multitude that no one could count, from every nation, tribe, people and language, standing before the throne and before the Lamb. They were wearing white robes and were holding palm branches in their hands. (Revelation 7:9)

We ought never to forget that we have renounced the world. We are living here now as aliens and only for a time. When the day of our homecoming puts an end to our exile, frees us from the bonds of the world, and restores us to paradise and the kingdom, we should welcome it. What man, stationed in a foreign land, would not want to return to his own country as soon as possible? Paradise is our country, and a great crowd of our loved ones awaits us there; countless parents, siblings, and children long for us to join them. Though assured of their own salvation, they are still concerned about ours. What joy we will share when we see one another and embrace! The delight of that heavenly kingdom where there is no fear of death! The supreme and endless bliss of everlasting life!

The glorious band of apostles is there, with the joyful assembly of prophets, and the innumerable host of martyrs who are crowned for their glorious victory in combat and death. The triumphant virgins are there, who subdued their passions by the strength of chastity. There the merciful are rewarded, who served justice by providing for the poor. In obedience to the Lord, they turned their earthly goods into heavenly treasure.

Dear brothers and sisters, let us yearn to join them as soon as possible. Pray that God sees our desire and Christ sees our faithful commitment, for the more fervently we long for him, the greater will our reward be.

Cyprian of Carthage

⊹ 273 ⊹

LIKE GOLD
IN THE FURNACE

*"Look," he said, "I see heaven open and the Son of Man standing
at the right hand of God." (Acts 7:56)*

Looking up to heaven, Polycarp [Bishop of Smyrna] said, "Lord, almighty God, Father of your beloved and blessed Son Jesus Christ, through whom we have come to the knowledge of yourself; God of angels, of powers, of all creation, of all the race of saints who live in your sight, I bless you for judging me worthy of this day, this hour, so that in the company of the martyrs I may share the cup of Christ, your Anointed One, and so rise again to eternal life in soul and body, immortal through the power of the Holy Spirit. May I be received among the martyrs in your presence today as a rich and pleasing sacrifice. God of truth, stranger to falsehood, you have prepared this and revealed it to me and now you have fulfilled your promise.

"I praise you for all things, I bless you, I glorify you through the eternal priest of heaven, Jesus Christ, your beloved Son. Through him be glory to you, together with him and the Holy Spirit, now and forever. Amen."

When he had said "Amen" and finished the prayer, the officials lit the pyre. But when a great flame burst out, those of us privileged to see it witnessed a strange and wonderful thing. Indeed, we have been spared in order to tell the story to others. Like a ship's sail swelling in the wind, the flame became as it were a dome encircling the martyr's body. Surrounded by the fire, his body was like bread that is baked, or gold and silver white-hot in a furnace, not like flesh that has been burnt. The fragrance that came to us was so sweet that it was like burning incense or some other costly and sweet-smelling spice.

from *The Martyrdom of Polycarp*

✤ 274 ✤

GIVE AS GOD GAVE TO YOU

Each of you should give what you have decided in your heart to give,
not reluctantly or under compulsion, for God loves a cheerful giver.
(2 Corinthians 9:7)

Even better is what the Lord says in another place, "Give to every one that asks you" (Luke 6:30). This is truly how much God delights in giving. Even holier would be not to wait to be asked, but to find out who is in need and give before they ask.

And to think that God appoints such a reward simply for giving—an eternal home! What an excellent trade! What a divine gift! You purchase immortality with money; you receive an everlasting mansion in heaven by giving finite and corruptible things. If you are wise, rich soul, you will shop at this market! If necessary sail round the whole world. Deal with whatever perils and toils you have to in order to purchase the heavenly kingdom.

Why do gold and jewels excite you so much? Why would you desire a house that stands only temporarily and is consumed by a fire, eroded by time, destroyed by an earthquake, or knocked over by a tyrant? You ought to aspire to live in heaven and reign with God. Let Christ receive a little from you here, and there he will make you a son or daughter and heir. Ask so that you may receive. Hurry and strive. Fear that he might disgrace you, for he is not commanded to receive, but you are commanded to give.

The Lord did not mean, "Give, or do good, or help only once," but really meant, "Become friends with me." And a friend proves his friendship not by a single gift, but by lifelong intimacy. Remember this, because you are not saved through the faith, hope, or love of a single day, but "he that endures to the end shall be saved" (Matt. 10:22).

Clement of Alexandria

⊹ 275 ⊹

THE GOOD SHEPHERD'S EXAMPLE

Suppose one of you has a hundred sheep and loses one of them.
Doesn't he leave the ninety-nine in the open country and go after
the lost sheep until he finds it? And when he finds it, he joyfully
puts it on his shoulders. (Luke 15:4–5)

In the Scripture, in the form of a parable, we see a shepherd who had a hundred sheep. When one of them was separated from the flock and lost its way, the shepherd did not remain with the sheep who kept together at pasture. No, he went off to look for the stray. He crossed many valleys and thickets, he climbed great and towering mountains, he spent much time and labor in wandering through solitary places until at last he found his sheep.

When he found it, he did not punish it; he did not strike it with a rod to drive it back but gently placed it on his own shoulders and carried it back to the flock. He took greater joy in this one sheep, lost and found, than in all the others.

Let us look more closely at the hidden meaning of this parable. The sheep is more than a sheep, the shepherd more than a shepherd. They are signs pointing to holy truths. They teach us that we should not consider any person as lost or beyond hope; we should not abandon them when they are in danger, but quickly come to their help. When they stray from the right path and wander, we must lead them back and rejoice at their return, welcoming them back into the company of those who lead good and holy lives.

Asterius of Amasea

✛ 276 ✛

THE REJECTED
PASSOVER LAMB

Worthy is the Lamb, who was slain! (Revelation 5:12)

It is he who endured every kind of suffering in everyone who fore-shadowed him. In Abel he was slain, in Isaac bound, in Jacob exiled, in Joseph sold, in Moses exposed to die. He was sacrificed in the Passover lamb, persecuted in David, dishonored in the prophets.

It is he who was made man from the Virgin, he who was hung on the tree; it is he who was buried in the earth, raised from the dead, and taken up to the heights of heaven. He is the mute lamb, the slain lamb born of Mary, the fair ewe. He was seized from the flock, dragged off to be slaughtered, sacrificed in the evening, and buried at night. On the tree no bone of his was broken; in the earth his body knew no decay. He is the one who rose from the dead and who raises man from the depths of the tomb.

It is he who was murdered. And where was he murdered? In the very center of Jerusalem! Why? Because he had healed their lame, and had cleansed their lepers, and had guided their blind with light, and had raised up their dead. For this reason he suffered. Some-where it has been written in the Law and Prophets, "They paid me back evil for good, and my soul with barrenness" (Ps. 35:12), "plotting evil against me" (Ps. 35:4), saying, "Let us bind this just man because he is troublesome to us" (Isa. 3:10).

Why, Israel did you do this strange injustice? You dishonored the one who had honored you. You held in contempt the one who held you in esteem. You denied the one who publicly acknowledged you. You renounced the one who proclaimed you his own. You killed the one who made you alive.

Melito of Sardis

⤞ 277 ⤝

ALLELUIA TO THE FAITHFUL GOD

*But the Lord is faithful, and he will strengthen you
and protect you from the evil one. (2 Thessalonians 3:3)*

Let us sing alleluia here on earth, while we still live in anxiety, so that we may sing it one day in heaven in security. Why do we now live in anxiety? Can you expect me not to feel anxious when I read, "Is not man's life on earth a time of trial?" (Job 7:1). Can you expect me not to feel anxious when these words still ring in my ears: "Watch and pray that you will not be put to the test" (Mark 14:38)? Every day we make out petitions, every day we sin. Do you want me to feel secure when I ask pardon for my sins daily and request help in hardships? Because of my past sins I pray for forgiveness, and because of the dangers before me I pray, "Deliver us from evil" (Matt. 6:13). Regardless, brothers and sisters, while we are still in the midst of this evil, let us sing alleluia to the good God who delivers us from evil.

"God is faithful," says Holy Scripture, "and he will not allow you to be tried beyond your strength" (1 Cor. 10:13). So let us sing alleluia, even here on earth. Man is still a debtor, but God is faithful. Whatever the trial, he will see you through it safely, and so enable you to endure. You have entered upon a time of trial but you will come to no harm—God's help will bring you through it safely. You are like a piece of pottery, shaped by teaching, fired by tribulation. Therefore when you are put into the oven, keep your thoughts on the time when you will be taken out again; for God is faithful, and "he will guard both your going in and your coming out" (Ps. 121:8).

Augustine

✦ 278 ✦

KINSHIP WITH GOD

But whoever is united with the Lord is one with him in spirit.
(1 Corinthians 6:17)

The Lord calls himself the vine and those united to him branches in order to teach us how much we benefit from our union with him, and how important it is for us to remain in his love. By receiving the Holy Spirit, who is the bond of union between us and Christ, those who are joined to him share in his nature, as branches do to a vine.

The prophet Isaiah calls Christ the foundation (Isa. 28:16), because it is upon him that we as living and spiritual stones are built into a holy priesthood, a dwelling place for God. This temple can be built upon nothing but Christ. Christ teaches the same truth by calling himself the vine (John 15:1), since the vine is the parent of its branches and provides their nourishment.

From Christ and in Christ, we have been reborn through the Spirit in order to bear the fruit of life — not the fruit of our old, sinful life but the fruit of a new life founded upon our faith in him and our love for him. Like branches growing from a vine, we now draw our life from Christ, and we cling to his holy commandments in order to preserve this life. We safeguard the blessing of our noble birth and are careful not to grieve the Holy Spirit, who lives in us and makes us aware of God's presence in us.

Just as the vine gives its own natural properties to each of its branches, Christ gives us kinship with himself and the Father through the Spirit's indwelling, who effects their union by giving them faith and obedience.

Cyril of Alexandria

✢ 279 ✢

CHRIST IS
THE LIGHT OF DAY

God is light; in him there is no darkness at all. (1 John 1:5)

The light of Christ is an endless day that knows no night. Christ is this day, says the Apostle; such is the meaning of his words: "Night is almost over; day is at hand" (Rom. 13:12). He tells us that night is almost over, not that it is about to fall. By this we are meant to understand that the coming of Christ's light puts Satan's darkness to flight, leaving no place for any shadow of sin. His everlasting radiance dispels the dark clouds of the past and checks the hidden growth of vice. And as in heaven no night can follow day, so no sin can overshadow the justice of Christ. The celestial day is perpetually bright and shining with brilliant light; clouds can never darken its skies. In the same way, the light of Christ is eternally glowing with luminous radiance and can never be extinguished by the darkness of sin. This is why John the Evangelist says: "The light shines in the darkness, and the darkness has never been able to overpower it" (John 1:5).

And so, my brothers and sisters, each of us ought surely to rejoice on this holy day. Let none of you, conscious of your sinfulness, withdraw from our common celebration, nor let any be kept away from our public prayer by the burden of guilt. Sinners you may indeed be, but you must not imagine that the Lord does not pardon on this day that is so highly privileged; for if a thief could receive the grace of paradise, how could a Christian be refused forgiveness?

Maximus of Turin

✢ 280 ✢

CLEAN MY LIPS

For I am a man of unclean lips, and I live among a people
of unclean lips. (Isaiah 6:5)

Now I must believe the Prophet Isaiah's confession, which he makes before declaring the word of the Lord: "Woe is me, my heart is smitten, for I, a man of unclean lips, and living in the midst of a people of unclean lips, have seen the LORD of Sabbath" (Isa. 6:5). Now if Isaiah, who looked upon the Lord of Sabbath, said, "Woe is me," what shall I say of myself, who is also "a man of unclean lips"? How can I speak of things that are fearful to me when David prays that a guard may be set over his mouth regarding things he knows about (Ps. 39:1–2; 141:3–4)? I wish that one of the seraphim would bring a burning coal from the heavenly altar to me also, take it in the tongs of the two testaments, and purge my unclean lips with its fire (Isa. 6:6–7)!

However, while the seraph came down in a vision to the prophet, you Lord have come to us in the flesh in revelation of the mystery. So I ask you, Lord, and not any deputy or messenger, to mercifully cleanse my conscience from secret sins, so that I might be made clean through faith and sing in the words of David: "I will make music to you upon a harp, God of Israel, my lips shall rejoice in all my song to you, and so shall my soul, which you have redeemed" (Ps. 71:22–23).

Ambrose

✤ 281 ✤

EMPOWER OUR EVANGELISM (I)

*Then Philip began with that very passage of Scripture
and told him the good news about Jesus. (Acts 8:35)*

I am well aware, God and Father, that in my life I owe you a particular duty. It is to make my every thought and word speak of you.

In fact, you have blessed me with this gift of speech, and it can yield no greater return than to be at your service. Its purpose is to make you known as Father, the Father of the only begotten God, and to preach this to the world that does not know you and to the heretics who refuse to believe in you.

My preaching is only of limited value in this endeavor. For the rest, I need to pray for the gift of your help and your mercy. As we spread our sails of trusting faith and public confession before you, fill them with the breath of your Spirit, to drive us on as we begin this course of proclaiming your truth. We have been promised, and he who made the promise is trustworthy: "Ask, and it will be given to you; seek, and you will find; knock, and it will be opened to you" (Matt. 7:7).

Yes, in our poverty we will pray for our needs. We will study the sayings of your prophets and apostles with tireless attention, and knock for admittance wherever the gift of understanding is safely kept. Let it be your will, Lord, to grant our petitions, to be present when we seek you, and to open when we knock. [Continued in next entry ...]

Hilary of Poitiers

✤ 282 ✤

EMPOWER OUR EVANGELISM (II)

The Lord opened her heart to respond to Paul's message. (Acts 16:14)

There is something in our nature that makes us dull. In our attempts to comprehend your truth we are bound by our ignorance and the weakness of our minds. Yet we are able to understand divine ideas by earnest attention to your teaching and by obedience to the faith that goes beyond mere human apprehension.

So we trust in you to inspire the beginnings of this ambitious venture, to strengthen its progress, and to call us into a partnership in the Spirit with the prophets and the apostles. To that end, help us grasp precisely what they meant to say, taking each word in its real and authentic sense. For we are about to declare what they have already declared as part of the mystery of revelation: that you are the eternal God, the Father of the eternal, only begotten God; that you are one and not born from another; and that the Lord Jesus is also one, born of you from all eternity. We must not proclaim that there is more than one God; we must not deny that Christ is begotten of you who are the one God; and we must not assert that he is something besides the true God, born of you, who are truly God the Father.

Bless us with the meaning of the words of Scripture and the light to understand it, with reverence for the doctrine and confidence in its truth. Grant that we may express what we believe. Through the prophets and apostles we know about you, the one God and Father, and the one Lord Jesus Christ. May we have the grace, in the face of heretics who deny you, to honor you as God, who is not alone, and to proclaim this as truth.

Hilary of Poitiers

✛ 283 ✛

THE SON AND THE FATHER

I have revealed you to those whom you gave me out of the world.
They were yours; you gave them to me and they have obeyed your word.
(John 17:6)

No one can know the Father apart from God's Word—that is, unless the Son reveals him—and no one can know the Son unless the Father wills it. Accordingly, the Son fulfills the Father's good pleasure: the Father sends, the Son is sent, and he comes to us.

The Father is beyond our sight and comprehension; but he is known by the Word, who tells us of the Father who is himself beyond all telling. Likewise, only the Father has knowledge of his Word. And the Lord Jesus has revealed both himself and his Father. Therefore, the Son reveals knowledge of the Father by his revelation of himself. Knowledge of the Father consists in the self-revelation of the Son, for everything is revealed through the Word.

The Father's purpose in revealing the Son was to make himself known to all of us, and thereby to welcome believers into eternal rest, establish them in justice, and preserve them from death. To believe in him means to do his will.

Through creation itself the Word reveals God the Creator. Through the world he reveals the Lord who made the world. Through all that is fashioned he reveals the craftsman who fashioned it all. Through himself the Word reveals the Father, who begot him as Son. All the Scriptures speak of these things.

Irenaeus

❖ 284 ❖

AGNES, VIRGIN MARTYR

*I praise you, Father, Lord of heaven and earth, because you have
hidden these things from the wise and learned, and revealed them
to little children. (Matthew 11:25)*

Today is the birthday of a virgin; let us imitate her purity. It is
the birthday of a martyr; let us offer ourselves in sacrifice. It is
the birthday of Saint Agnes, who suffered martyrdom at the age of
twelve. The cruelty that killed her demonstrates, against its intention, the power of faith in someone so young to bear witness to it.

There was little space in that small body for a wound. Though
she could hardly receive the blow, she could rise superior to it. Girls
of her age cannot even bear the sight of their parents' frowns, and if
pricked by a needle they weep! Yet she shows no fear of the blood-
stained hands of her executioners.

The crowd of witnesses cries, but she sheds no tears herself. The
crowds marvel at her recklessness in throwing away her life unlived,
though she carries herself as if she had already lived life to the full.
All are amazed that one so young can give her testimony to God, by
which she convinces others. What is beyond the power of nature,
they argue, must come from its Creator.

Promises were made to win her, and influential men desired her
in marriage! But she answered, "You do wrong to my Spouse in
thinking that anyone else will please me. I will be his who first chose
me for himself. Executioner, why do you delay?" She stood still,
prayed, and offered her neck.

You could see fear in the eyes of the executioner, as if he were
the one condemned; his right hand trembled, his face grew pale as
he saw the girl's peril, while she had no fear for herself. One victim,
but a double martyrdom, to modesty and to faith. Agnes preserved
her virginity and gained a martyr's crown.

Ambrose

✦ 285 ✦

PRAYING THE
LORD'S PRAYER (I)

And when you pray, do not keep on babbling like pagans, for they think
they will be heard because of their many words. (Matthew 6:7)

When we say, "Hallowed be your name" (Matt. 6:9), we are reminding ourselves to desire that his name, which is always holy, should also be considered holy among people. It should not be held in contempt. But this is a help for people, not for God.

And as for our saying, "Your kingdom come" (10), it will surely come whether we will it or not. But we are stirring up our desires for the kingdom, so that it will come to us and we can be worthy of reigning there.

When we say, "Your will be done on earth as it is in heaven" (10), we are asking him to make us obedient, so that his will may be done in us as it is done in heaven by his angels.

When we say, "Give us this day our daily bread" (11), we are asking to be provided for in this world. Here we ask for whatever is sufficient for our lives, and we use the word "bread" to stand for everything. We are also asking for the sacrament of the faithful, which is taken in this world for everlasting happiness in the next.

When we say, "Forgive us our trespasses as we forgive those who trespass against us" (12), we are reminding ourselves of our need to be forgiven, and what we must do to be worthy of forgiveness. [Continued in next entry ...]

Augustine

✢ 286 ✢

PRAYING THE LORD'S PRAYER (II)

*Do not be like them, for your Father knows what you need
before you ask him. (Matthew 6:8)*

When we say, "Lead us not into temptation" (Matt. 6:13), we are reminding ourselves that we are continually in need of his help, and asking that it may not depart from us; otherwise we could be seduced and give in to some temptation, or despair over our weakness and yield to it.

When we say, "Deliver us from evil" (13), we are reminding ourselves of the fact that we do not yet enjoy the state of blessedness in which we will suffer no evil. This is the final petition contained in the Lord's Prayer, and it has a wide application. In this petition Christians can utter their cries of sorrow, in it they can shed their tears, and with it they can begin, continue, and conclude their prayers, regardless of the distress they are presently experiencing. Yes, this prayer is a treasure, and contains many truths that are good to remember.

However else we sometimes choose to pray — with words that help us focus on the state of our heart or that help intensify our passion for the Lord — we say nothing that is not already contained in the Lord's Prayer in some way, provided of course we are praying in a correct and proper way. But if anyone does say something that is incompatible with this Gospel prayer, the person is praying in the flesh, even if he or she is not exactly sinning. Then again, I do not know how this could be called anything but sinful, since those who are born again through the Spirit ought to pray only in the Spirit.

Augustine

❖ 287 ❖

RESTORE HIS IMAGE WITH LOVE

If you love me, keep my commands. (John 14:15)

It is a glorious privilege that God has granted humanity his image and likeness. Our likeness to God gives us high dignity, if we preserve it.

We will be like God if we practice the virtues that God has given us through obedience to the commandments. The first command is "to love our Lord with our whole heart because he loved us first" (Matt. 22:37; 1 John 4:19), even before our existence. Loving God renews his image in us. Anyone who loves God keeps his commandments, and he tells us, "This is my command, that you love each other as I also have loved you" (John 15:12).

True love is shown not merely "in word, but in deed and in truth" (1 John 3:18). So we must reflect a pure and holy image back to God, for his image is holy: "Be holy, for I am holy" (Lev. 11:44; 1 Pet. 1:16). We must restore his image with love, for he is love: "God is love" (1 John 4:8). Our image must depict God, for someone malicious and fickle would display the image of a despot.

Let Christ paint his image in us with his words: "My peace I give you, my peace I leave with you" (John 14:27). But we must practice it to benefit from it. This peace is valuable and therefore fragile, and can be broken by insensitive talk that injures our brothers and sisters. We like nothing better than minding the business of others, carelessly making comments and criticizing people behind their backs. So if you cannot say truthfully that "The LORD has given me a discerning tongue, that I may support the weary with a word" (Isa. 50:4), you should keep silent. Anything you say should promote peace.

Columbanus

✤ 288 ✤

REIGNING WITH HIM

Then the end will come, when he hands over the kingdom to God the
Father after he has destroyed all dominion, authority and power.
(1 Corinthians 15:24)

The Our Father continues: "Your kingdom come" (Matt. 6:10). We ask that the kingdom of God may appear to us, just as we ask that his name may be sanctified in us. For God is always reigning, and his kingdom has always existed and will never end. We are praying that our kingdom would come, the kingdom that was acquired by the blood and passion of Christ, which has been promised to us by God; and that we, who started off as his subjects in this world, may reign with Christ when he reigns in the world to come, as he himself promised when he said, "Come, you whom my Father has blessed, take up the kingdom which has been prepared for you from the beginning of the world" (Matt. 25:34).

But it may be, dear brothers and sisters, that Christ himself is the kingdom of God and that we ask daily for his return. Since he is himself our resurrection, since in him we rise again, and since it is in him that we will reign, then the kingdom of God may be understood to be Christ himself. It is right to ask for the coming of the kingdom of God, the heavenly kingdom, for there is also an earthly kingdom, and if you have already renounced the present kingdom you are greater than any of its principalities or powers.

Cyprian of Carthage

✦ 289 ✦

STOKE YOUR DESIRE IN PRAYER

Let your gentleness be evident to all. The Lord is near. Do not be
anxious about anything, but in every situation, by prayer and petition,
with thanksgiving, present your requests to God. (Philippians 4:5–6)

Let us always desire the happy life from the Lord God and always pray for it. It is for this very reason we turn our mind to the task of prayer at appointed hours, since that desire grows lukewarm from our involvement in other concerns and occupations. We remind ourselves through the words of prayer to focus our attention on the object of our desire; otherwise, the lukewarm desire may grow cold altogether and may be totally extinguished unless it is repeatedly stirred into flame.

Since this is the case, it is often good to pray for a long time when there is the opportunity — as long as it does not keep us from performing other good actions or obligations we may have. But even during these duties, we must always pray with that desire. To pray for a longer time does not mean to pray by artificially adding words, as some people suppose. Lengthy talk is one thing; a prayerful disposition that lasts a long time is another. Even the Lord himself spent the night in prayer and prayed at great length. Was he not giving us an example by this? In time, he prays when it is appropriate; and in eternity, he hears our prayers with the Father.

Augustine

✢ 290 ✢

WE STRUGGLE IN THE SAME CONFLICT

Three times I was beaten with rods, once I was pelted with stones, three times I was shipwrecked, I spent a night and a day in the open sea.
(2 Corinthians 11:25)

Let us not dwell on ancient examples, but consider the most recent spiritual heroes. Let us take the noble examples in our own generation. The greatest and most righteous pillars of the church have been persecuted and put to death through envy and jealousy. Look at the lives and deaths of the illustrious apostles. Peter endured not one or two but numerous tortures, inflicted on him by unrighteous envy; when he had finally suffered martyrdom, he departed to the place of glory prepared for him. Because of envy, Paul also received the reward for patient endurance, but only after being thrown into captivity seven times, compelled to flee, and stoned. After preaching in both the east and west and having taught righteousness to the whole world, he gained an illustrious reputation because of his faith; and having come to the far western border, he suffered martyrdom under the rulers. In this way he was removed from the world and went into the holy place, having proved himself a striking example of patience.

We write these things to you, beloved, not merely to admonish you to do your duty, but also to remind ourselves. For we are struggling in the same arena, and the same conflict is assigned to both of us. So let us give up vain and fruitless pursuits and adopt the glorious and worthy rule of our holy calling. Let us attend to what is good, pleasing, and acceptable in the sight of the one who formed us.

Clement of Rome

✦ 291 ✦

A SHEPHERD'S SILENCE

The harvest is plentiful, but the workers are few. Ask the Lord of the harvest, therefore, to send out workers into his harvest field. (Luke 10:2)

Listen to what the Lord says as he sends preachers out. Our heart is heavy over the scarcity of laborers for the harvest, for there are many to hear the good news but only a few to preach it. Look and see how full of pastors the world is, but in God's harvest a laborer is rare; for though we have accepted the office, we do not fulfill its demands.

Brothers and sisters, consider Jesus' command: "Pray earnestly to the Lord of the harvest to send out laborers into his harvest" (Luke 10:2). Pray for us so that we may have the strength to work on your behalf, that our voices may not grow weary from exhortation, and that we might never be silent about the Gospel. I ask this because so often a preacher's own sins prevent him from preaching, and other times the Spirit removes his preaching because of the sins of the assembly.

With reference to the former situation, the Psalmist says, "But God asks the sinner: Why do you recite my commandments?" (Ps. 50:16). And with reference to the latter, the Lord tells Ezekiel, "I will make your tongue stick to the roof of your mouth, so that you shall be silent and unable to rebuke them, for they are a rebellious house" (Ezek. 3:26).

He clearly means this: the word of preaching will be taken away from you because the deeds of these people irritate him, and they are unworthy to hear the truth. We cannot be sure whose sinfulness is the cause but can be certain that the shepherd's silence will always harm his flock and usually himself too.

Gregory the Great

✤ 292 ✤

REVERSING THE CURSE

Cursed is everyone who is hung on a pole. (Galatians 3:13)

Of his own free will Jesus ran to meet those sufferings that were foretold in the Scriptures concerning him.

He allowed himself to be slapped, spat upon, insulted, tortured, scourged, and finally crucified. He accepted two robbers as his companions in punishment, on his right and on his left. He endured being judged with murderers and criminals. He drank the vinegar and the bitter wine yielded by the unfaithful vineyard of Israel. He submitted to being crowned with thorns instead of with vine twigs and grapes; he was ridiculed with the purple cloak, holes were dug in his hands and his feet, and at last he was carried to the grave.

All this he endured in working out our salvation. Because those who were enslaved to sin were liable to the penalties of sin, he himself underwent the punishment of sinners, despite being exempt from sin and walking in the path of perfect righteousness.

By drinking the vinegar he took on himself the degradation humanity had suffered and in the same act gave us the grace to better our condition. By the purple robe he signified his kingship, by the reed he hinted at the weakness and rottenness of the devil's power. By taking the slap in the face and suffering the violence and punishment that were due to us, he proclaimed our freedom.

His side was pierced as Adam's was; yet what came forth was not a woman who was tricked into being the death-bearer, but a fountain of life that regenerates the world by its two streams: the one to renew us in the baptismal font and clothe us with the garment of immortality, the other to feed us, the reborn, at the table of God, just as babies are nourished with milk.

Theodoret of Cyrus

⚜ 293 ⚜

DON'T HIDE THE LAMP

You are the light of the world. A town built on a hill cannot be hidden.
(Matthew 5:14)

The Lord called his disciples the salt of the earth because they seasoned the hearts of people with heavenly wisdom. He calls them the light of the world as well because they have been enlightened by him, who is the true and everlasting light, and have themselves become a light in the darkness.

It is right for him to call his disciples the light of the world since he is the Sun of Justice. Through them, as through the sun's shining rays, he has shone the light of the knowledge of himself upon the entire world. By manifesting the light of truth, his disciples have dispelled the darkness of ignorance from the hearts of men and women.

Saint John also asserts in his letter, "God is light" (1 John 1:5), and whoever abides in God is in the light just as God himself is in the light. Therefore, because we rejoice in having been freed from the darkness of error, we should always walk in the light as children of light. This is why the Apostle says, "Among them you shine as lights in the world, holding fast to the word of life" (Phil. 2:15–16).

Consequently, the brilliant lamp that was lit for our salvation should always shine in us. And that lamp is the heavenly commandment and spiritual grace, to which David referred: "Your law is a lamp to my feet and a light to my path" (Ps. 119:105).

Therefore, we must not hide this lamp of law and faith. Rather, we must set it up in the church, as on a lampstand, for the salvation of many, so that we may enjoy the light of truth itself and all believers may be enlightened.

Chromatius

◦ 294 ◦

THE INNER BEAUTY
OF VIRGINS

*And just as we have borne the image of the earthly man, so shall we
bear the image of the heavenly man. (1 Corinthians 15:49)*

Now I wish to address the order of virgins. Because their way of
life is more praiseworthy, our concern for them must be greater.
If we compare the church to a tree, then they are its blossom. Virgins display the beauty of God's grace; they are the image of God
that reflects the holiness of the Lord; they are the more illustrious
members of Christ's flock. They are the glory of mother church and
manifest her fruitfulness. The more numerous her virgins, the greater
her joy is.

It is not from a rash impulse or misplaced fear that virgins
pursue the path of salvation and keep the Lord's life-giving commandments. By renouncing the pleasures of the flesh, they have
dedicated themselves to Christ and made their bodies holy to God,
with their minds set on finishing their task and winning their prize.
They should not adorn themselves or aim to please anyone but the
Lord, from whom they hope to be rewarded for their chastity.

Virgins, persevere in the way of life you have begun, and remain
now what you will be in heaven. You will receive a glorious prize
for your virtue, a most excellent reward for your chastity. You have
already begun to be what we will all be in the future. You already
possess, here in this world, the glory of the resurrection. You pass
through this world without the world's infection. If you persevere in
chastity and virginity, you are equal to God's angels. Just keep your
profession of virginity strong and invulnerable. You began your way
of life courageously, so continue without faltering. Decorate yourself
not with jewelry or attractive clothing, but with right conduct.

Cyprian of Carthage

✤ 295 ✤

THE GROWTH
OF TRUE DOCTRINE (I)

God sent his Son, born of a woman, born under the law. (Galatians 4:4)

Should there not be development of religion in the church of Christ? Certainly, there should be development and on the largest scale.

Who can be such an enemy to people, so full of hate for God, that he or she would try to prevent it? But it must truly be development of the faith, not alteration of the faith. Development means that a thing expands to be itself, while alteration means that a thing is changed from one thing into another.

Therefore the understanding, knowledge, and wisdom of one and all, of individuals as well as the whole church, ought to make great and vigorous progress with the passing of the ages and the centuries—but only along its own line of development, that is, with the same doctrine, the same meaning, and the same importance. The religion of souls should grow in the same manner in which our bodies grow. Though bodies develop their component parts with the passing of the years, they always remain what they were. There is a great difference between the flower of childhood and the maturity of age, but those who become old are the same people who were once young. Though the appearance of an individual may change, it is one and the same nature, one and the same person. The tiny fingers of infants and the grown fingers of young people are still the same fingers. Adults have the same number of limbs as children. Whatever develops at a later age was already present in seminal form; there is nothing new in old age that was not already latent in childhood. [Continued in next entry ...]

Vincent of Lerins

⁍ 296 ⁌

THE GROWTH
OF TRUE DOCTRINE (II)

*He made known to us the mystery of his will according to his good
pleasure, which he purposed in Christ, to be put into effect when the
times reach their fulfillment—to bring unity to all things in heaven
and on earth under Christ. (Ephesians 1:9–10)*

There is no doubt, then, that the legitimate and correct rule of
development, the established and wonderful order of growth,
is this: the parts of the body that the Creator wisely fashions in the
earlier years are brought to completion in the fullness of years.

If, however, the human form were to turn into some shape that
did not belong to its nature, or if something were added to the sum of
its members or subtracted from it, the whole body would necessarily
perish, or become grotesque, or at least crippled. In the same way,
the doctrine of the Christian religion should properly follow these
laws of development, that is, by becoming firmer over the years, more
complete in the course of time, more exalted as it advances in age.

In ancient times our ancestors sowed the good seed in the harvest field of the church. It would be very wrong and unfitting if we,
their descendants, were to reap, not the genuine wheat of truth, but
the intrusive growth of error.

On the contrary, what is right and fitting is this: there should
be no inconsistency between first and last, but we should reap true
doctrine from the growth of true teaching. This way, in the course
of time, when what was first sown yields its fruit, it may flourish
and be tended in our day.

Vincent of Lerins

✛ 297 ✛

THE BENEFIT
OF BEING MOCKED

That is why, for Christ's sake, I delight in weaknesses, in insults,
in hardships, in persecutions, in difficulties. For when I am weak,
then I am strong. (2 Corinthians 12:10)

A vain person is often distracted by superficial happiness when other people compliment what she does. So she gives up her own personal choices in order to be at the mercy of whatever others tell her. In this way she is satisfied not with actual blessedness, but with being called blessed. She is so eager for praise that she gives up real holiness and so is severed from God by her attempt to appear commendable.

However, sometimes a person truly strives for righteousness but is ridiculed by people. He does what is admirable but is mocked. He might have been drawn out by human praise, but he returns to himself when repelled by their abuse. Finding no resting place without, he cleaves more intensely to God within. All his hope is fixed on his Creator, and amid all the ridicule and abuse he takes comfort from the Lord alone. Someone afflicted in this way grows closer to God the more he or she turns away from human popularity. The afflicted pours him or herself out in prayer to penetrate what is within, and is refined into a more perfect purity.

In this context, the words from Scripture apply: "Whoever is mocked by his friend, as I am, shall call upon God, and he shall hear him" (Job 12:4). At the same time that the wicked insult the just, they direct the just to God who is the witness of their actions. The soul afflicted in this way strengthens itself by prayer; it is united to God who listens from on high precisely because his or her soul is cut off from the praise of people.

Gregory the Great

✛ 298 ✛

SOW ALL YOU CAN TO REAP BLESSINGS

Whoever sows to please their flesh, from the flesh will reap destruction;
whoever sows to please the Spirit, from the Spirit will reap eternal life.
Let us not become weary in doing good, for at the proper time we will
reap a harvest if we do not give up. (Galatians 6:8–9)

Men and women! Be like the earth. Bear fruit like her and do not produce less than what mere inanimate matter can achieve! The earth bears crops not for its own benefit, but for yours. You, on the other hand, when you give to the poor, are bearing fruit that you will gather for yourself, since the reward for good deeds goes to those who perform them. If you give to a hungry man, you receive back what you have given with interest. Just as the wheat that falls on the ground benefits the one who sowed it, so too does the bread given to a hungry man profit you in the world to come. So be mindful of sowing this heavenly seed; as Scripture says, "Sow integrity for yourselves" (Hos. 10:12).

Look at how people throw away their wealth for a moment's glory, for the shouts and praise of crowds in the theater, at sporting events, and at contests in the arena. How can you get that sort of glory for yourself if you hold on to your money or spend it miserly? God will give his approval; the angels will praise you; everyone who has ever lived will call you blessed. You will receive eternal glory and the crown of righteousness as a prize for generously giving of your wealth — wealth that in any case cannot last and must decay!

Basil the Great

✛ 299 ✛

THE CHARIOT OF CHRIST

Since the children have flesh and blood, he too shared in their humanity
so that by his death he might break the power of him who holds the
power of death — that is, the devil — and free those who all their lives
were held in slavery by their fear of death. (Hebrews 2:14 – 15)

Death trampled our Lord underfoot, but he in turn treated death as a highway for his own feet. He submitted to it and endured it willingly, because by doing this he was able to destroy death in spite of itself. Death had its way when our Lord went out from Jerusalem carrying his cross; but when from the cross he summoned the dead from the underworld, death was powerless to prevent it.

Death killed the body that he had assumed, but that same body was the weapon with which he conquered death. Concealed beneath the cloak of his manhood, his divinity was challenged to a duel by death; but by killing our Lord, death was itself destroyed. It was able to kill a natural human life but was itself killed by the divine life of Christ.

Death could not devour our Lord, nor could hell swallow him up, unless he possessed a body, so he came to earth in search of a chariot to ride into the underworld. This chariot was the body that he received from the Virgin. With it he invaded death's fortress, broke open its vault, and plundered all its treasure.

Ephrem the Syrian

✢ 300 ✢

FASTING AND ALMSGIVING

Jesus looked at him and loved him. "One thing you lack," he said. "Go, sell everything you have and give to the poor, and you will have treasure in heaven. Then come, follow me." (Mark 10:21)

Dear friends, what the Christian should be doing at all times should be done especially now with even greater care and devotion, so that the Lenten fast directed by the apostles may be fulfilled not simply by abstinence from food, but moreover by the renunciation of sin.

There is no better companion practice to holy and spiritual fasting than almsgiving. This merciful virtue includes many excellent works of devotion, so that the good intentions of all the faithful may be of equal value, even where their means are not. The love we ought to have for God and people is a love that frees us from idleness and overcomes any obstacles that get in the way of our good intentions. The angels sang, "Glory to God in the highest, and peace to his people on earth" (Luke 2:14). The person who shows love and compassion to those in any kind of affliction is blessed not only with the virtue of good will, but also with the gift of peace.

The works of mercy are innumerable. Their very variety brings this advantage to those who are true Christians, that with almsgiving not only the rich and affluent but also those of average means and the poor are able to play their part. Those who are unequal in their capacity to give can be equal in the love and generosity within their hearts.

Leo the Great

✛ 301 ✛

DOCTRINES MIXED WITH MELODIES

My soul is weary with sorrow; strengthen me according to your word.
(Psalm 119:28)

All Scripture is inspired by God and is useful, composed by the Spirit so that we may select the remedy for our own condition, as if in a general hospital for souls. For it says, "healing will make the greatest sin cease" (Eccl. 10:4).

Now, the prophets teach one thing, historians another, the law something else, and the proverbs something different still. But the book of Psalms has taken what is profitable from all of them. It foretells coming events; it recalls history; it lays out laws for life; it suggests what must be done; it is the common treasury of good doctrine, providing what is suitable for everyone. It cures the old wounds of souls, and to new ones it brings speedy improvement; it treats the diseased and preserves the unharmed. Overall it disarms the passions, which otherwise wield power over souls, doing this with persuasion and sweetness which produce sound thoughts.

When the Holy Spirit saw that virtue was difficult for us, and that we neglected holy living because of our inclination toward pleasure, what did he do? He mingled the doctrines with delightful melodies, so that we would receive the benefit of divine wisdom through soft and pleasing sounds, just as wise doctors do who smear the cup of medicine with honey. Therefore, he devised these harmonious melodies for us to sing and, while singing, to be trained in goodness. For while it is difficult to hold in our mind an apostolic or prophetic message, we easily chant the words of the Psalms, even in the home and around in the marketplace. They can even sooth our wrath and lull us to sleep through their sweet melodies.

Basil the Great

✛ 302 ✛

NO PLACE WITHOUT HIS PRESENCE

And a voice from heaven said, "This is my Son, whom I love;
with him I am well pleased." (Matthew 3:17)

We should be amazed that Jesus came to be baptized by John. To think of Christ, the infinite river that gladdens the city of God, being bathed in a poor little stream on the earth — the Son of God, the unfathomable fountainhead that gives life to all people, being immersed in the shallow waters of this decaying world! The filler of creation, leaving no place without his presence — incomprehensible to the angels and hidden from human sight — came to be baptized because it was his will.

The loving Father begets the beloved, and eternal light generates light eternal. In his divine nature he is the Father's only Son, though he was known as the son of Joseph. Though hungry himself, he feeds thousands; though weary, he refreshes those who labor. He has no place to lay his head yet holds all creation in his hand. By the passion inflicted on him by others, he frees us from the passions we inflicted on ourselves; by getting struck in the face he gives the world its freedom; by being pierced in the side he heals the wound of Adam.

So this is my message to the world: let the people from all nations come and receive the immortality that flows from baptism. This is the water of the Spirit, the water that flows through paradise, makes the earth fertile, gives growth to plants, and creates living things. This is the water by which a person is born again and lives a new life, the water in which even Christ was baptized, the water into which the Holy Spirit descended in the form of a dove.

Hippolytus

✣ 303 ✣

FROM THE LIFE
OF SAINT ANTONY (I)

They sold property and possessions to give to anyone who had need.
(Acts 2:45)

[Antony the Great was a prominent ascetic monk who helped spread monasticism] When Antony was about eighteen or twenty years old, his parents died, leaving him with an only sister. He cared for her as she was very young and also looked after their home.

Not six months after his parents' death, as he was on his way to church for his usual visit, he began to think of how the apostles had left everything and followed the Savior, and also of those mentioned in the book of Acts who had sold their possessions and gave the apostles the money for distribution to the needy. He reflected too on the great hope stored up in heaven for saints such as these. This was all in his mind when, entering the church just as the Gospel was being read, he heard the Lord's words to the rich man: "If you want to be perfect, go and sell all you have and give the money to the poor — you will have riches in heaven. Then come and follow me" (Matt. 19:21).

It seemed to Antony that it was God who had brought the saints to his mind, and that the words of the Gospel had been spoken directly to him. Immediately he left the church and gave away all the property he had inherited to the villagers, about two hundred acres of very beautiful and fertile land, so that it would cause no distraction to his sister and himself. He sold all his other possessions as well, giving to the poor the considerable sum of money he collected. However, in order to care for his sister he retained a few things. [Continued in next entry ...]

Athanasius

✤ 304 ✤

FROM THE LIFE OF SAINT ANTONY (II)

See how the flowers of the field grow. They do not labor or spin.
Yet I tell you that not even Solomon in all his splendor was dressed
like one of these. (Matthew 6:28–29)

The next time he went to church he heard the Lord say in the Gospel, "Do not be anxious about tomorrow" (Matt. 6:34). Without a moment's hesitation he went out and gave the poor all that he had left. He placed his sister in the care of some well-known and trustworthy virgins and arranged for her to be brought up in the convent. Then he gave himself up to the ascetic life, not far from his own home. He kept a careful watch over himself and practiced great austerity. He did manual work because he had heard the words, "If anyone will not work, do not let him eat" (2 Thess. 3:10). He spent some of his earnings on bread and he gave the rest to the poor.

Having learned that we should always be praying, even when we are by ourselves, he prayed without ceasing. He was so attentive when Scripture was read that nothing escaped him, and since he retained all he heard, his memory served him in place of books.

Seeing the kind of life he lived, the villagers and all the good men he knew called him the friend of God, and they loved him as both son and brother.

Athanasius

✣ 305 ✣

INCREASING JOY
IN THE LORD

*On that day they will say to Jerusalem, "Do not fear, Zion; do not let
your hands hang limp. The LORD your God is with you, the Mighty
Warrior who saves. He will take great delight in you; in his love he will
no longer rebuke you, but will rejoice over you with singing."
(Zephaniah 3:16–17)*

Dear brothers and sisters, God's love is calling us to the joys of
eternal happiness for the salvation of our souls. You have just
listened to the reading from the Apostle in which he says, "Rejoice
in the Lord always" (Phil. 4:4). The "joys" of this world lead to
eternal misery, but the joys willed for us by the Lord are enduring
and everlasting if we persevere. The Apostle therefore says, "Again
I say: rejoice" (Phil. 4:4).

He urges us to find ever-increasing joy in God and in keeping
his commandments. The more we give ourselves to God by obeying
his commands, the greater our happiness in the life to come will be,
and the greater the glory that we will share in the presence of God.

"The Lord is near; have no anxiety" (Phil. 4:5–6). The Lord is
always near to all who call upon his help with sincerity, true faith,
sure hope, and perfect love. He knows what you need, even before
you ask him. He is always ready to come to the aid of his faithful
servants, whatever their need. There is no reason for us to worry
when evils threaten us; we must remember that God is very near to
us always as our protector. "But in every prayer and supplication
let your petitions be made known to God, with thanksgiving" (Phil.
4:6). In time of trouble we must not grumble or be downhearted;
God forbid! We must rather be patient and cheerful, "giving thanks
to God always in everything" (Eph. 5:20).

Ambrose

⊹ 306 ⊹

OUR MEASURE OF TEARS

How long, LORD? Will you forget me forever? How long will you hide your face from me?... But I trust in your unfailing love; my heart rejoices in your salvation. (Psalm 13:1, 5)

When they see that trials are coming, some people brace themselves more and are, so to speak, eager to drain the cup. The ordinary path of the faithful is not extravagant enough for them; they seek the glorious death of the martyrs. Others hear of the temptations to come, and when they do arrive—as arrive they must—they become weak and broken. But it is right for the Christian to shoulder his or her sufferings, and only the true Christian honors them properly.

Offer the bandage of consolation and bind up what has been broken. Say this: Do not be afraid. God, in whom you believe, does not abandon you in temptations. God is faithful. He does not allow you to be tempted beyond your strength. It is not I who says this, but the Apostle, and he says further: Are you willing to accept his trial, the trial of Christ who speaks in me? When you hear this you are hearing it from Christ himself, you are hearing it from the shepherd who gives pasture to Israel. The prophet said of him: "You will give us tears to drink in measure" (Ps. 80:5). The prophet's words "in measure" refer to what Paul says: "He does not allow you to be tempted beyond your strength" (1 Cor. 10:13). God rebukes but also encourages; he brings fear and he brings consolation; he strikes and he heals. Do not reject him.

Augustine

✤ 307 ✤

JESUS THE GOOD FARMER

Other seed fell among thorns, which grew up and choked the plants,
so that they did not bear grain. (Mark 4:7)

When a house has no master living in it, it becomes dark, vile, and contemptible, choked with filth and disgusting refuse. So too is a soul that has lost its Master, who once rejoiced there with his angels. This soul is darkened with sin, its desires are degraded, and it knows nothing but shame.

Woe to the path that is not walked on, for then it becomes the haunt of wild animals. Woe to the soul if the Lord does not walk within it to banish with his voice the spiritual beasts of sin. Woe to the soul without Christ as its true pilot; drifting in the darkness, beaten by the waves of passion, storm-tossed at the mercy of evil spirits, its end is destruction. Woe to the soul that does not have Christ to cultivate it with care to produce the good fruit of the Holy Spirit. Left to itself, it is choked with thorns and thistles. Woe to the soul that does not have Christ dwelling in it; deserted and foul with the filth of the passions, it becomes a haven for all the vices.

When a farmer prepares to till the soil he must put on clothing and use tools that are suitable. So Christ, our heavenly King, came to till the soil of mankind devastated by sin. He assumed a body and, using the cross as his ploughshare, cultivated the barren soul of humanity. He removed the thorns and thistles, which are the evil spirits and pulled up the weeds of sin. And when he had ploughed the soul with the wood of the cross, he planted in it a most lovely garden of the Spirit, which would produce for its Lord and God the sweetest and most pleasant fruit of every kind.

Macarius

✢ 308 ✢

IN BUT NOT OF
THE WORLD (I)

*For it is God's will that by doing good you should silence the ignorant
talk of foolish people. (1 Peter 2:15)*

Christians are indistinguishable from other people either by
nationality, language, or customs. They do not live in separate
cities or speak a strange dialect or follow some strange way of life.
Their teaching is not based upon the dreams of men. Unlike many
others, they do not follow a human doctrine. They follow the customs of their home city, whether dress, food, or manner of living.

Yet there is something extraordinary about their lives. They live
in their own countries as though they were only passing through.
They are upright citizens but are in a real sense aliens. Any country can be their homeland, but for them their homeland is a foreign
country. Like others, they marry and have children, but they do not
mistreat them. They share their meals but not their spouses. They
live in the flesh but are not ruled by the desires of the flesh. They pass
their days upon earth, but they are citizens of heaven. They obey the
laws of the state but live on a level that transcends the law.

Christians love all people, but all people persecute them. Condemned because they are not understood, they are put to death but
raised to life again. They live in poverty but enrich many; they are
totally destitute but possess an abundance of riches. They suffer
dishonor, but that is their glory. They are maligned but vindi-
cated. A blessing is their answer to abuse. For the good they do
they receive punishment from villains, but even then they rejoice,
as though receiving a gift. They are attacked by the Jews as aliens
and persecuted by the Greeks, yet no one can explain the reason for
this hatred. [Continued in next entry ...]

From *The Letter to Diognetus*

✢ 309 ✢

IN BUT NOT OF
THE WORLD (II)

An inheritance that can never perish, spoil or fade. This inheritance is
kept in heaven for you, who through faith are shielded by God's power
until the coming of the salvation that is ready to be revealed
in the last time. (1 Peter 1:4−5)

Generally speaking, we may say that the Christian is to the world what the soul is to the body. Just like the soul is present in every part of the body, while remaining distinct from it, Christians are found in all the cities of the world but cannot be identified with the world. As the visible body contains the invisible soul, so Christians are seen living in the world, but their religious life remains unseen. The body hates the soul and wars against it, not because of any injury the soul has caused it, but because the soul moderates the pleasures of the body. Similarly, the world hates the Christians not because they have done it any wrong, but because they are opposed to its depravity.

Christians love those who hate them, just as the soul loves the body and all its members despite the body's hatred. It is by the soul, enclosed within the body, that the body is held together, and similarly, it is by the Christians, detained in the world as in a prison, that the world is held together. The soul, though immortal, has a mortal dwelling place; and Christians also live for a time in the perishable world, while awaiting freedom from corruption and decay that will be theirs in heaven. As the soul benefits from the fasting of food and drink, so Christians flourish under persecution. All this is the Christians' holy and divinely ordained calling, from which they are not permitted to excuse themselves.

From *The Letter to Diognetus*

✣ 310 ✣

WORK AND REST TOGETHER

And let us consider how we may spur one another on toward love and good deeds, not giving up meeting together, as some are in the habit of doing, but encouraging one another. (Hebrews 10:24–25)

Avoid evil practices, and of course preach against them. Tell my sisters to love the Lord and be content with their husbands in the flesh and in the spirit; in the same way tell my brothers in Christ to love their wives as the Lord loves his church. If anyone can remain chaste in honor of the Savior's flesh, then let them do so without boasting. If they boast, they are lost, and if they are better than their pastor because of it, they are lost. Those who get married should be united with the pastor's approval, so that the marriage may follow God's will and not fleshly desires. Let everything be done for God's honor.

Listen to your pastor, that God may listen to you. My life is a sacrifice for those who are obedient to the pastor, the elders, and the deacons; I hope to share with them my reward. Work together in harmony: struggle together, run together, suffer together, rest together, rise together, as stewards, advisors, and servants of God. Seek to please your commander and benefactor, and never desert your company. Let your baptism be your armor, your faith your helmet, your charity your spear, your patience your uniform. Deposit good works so that you may withdraw well-earned savings. Be patient and gentle with one another, as God is with you. May I have joy in you forever!

Christians are not their own masters: their time is God's. This is God's work, and it will be yours as well when you have performed it. I have trust in the grace of God that you are ready to act generously when it comes to God's work.

Ignatius of Antioch

✦ 311 ✦

BY FAITH, THROUGH WISDOM

Blessed are the pure in heart, for they will see God. (Matthew 5:8)

So who is God? God is the Father, Son, and Holy Spirit; he is one God. Do not ask to know more of God. If you want to see into the depths of God, you must know the depths of the natural world, for knowledge of the Trinity is compared to knowledge of the sea: "And the great depths, who shall fathom them?" (Job 11:7). Just as the depths of the sea are invisible to the human eye, so too the godhead of the Trinity is beyond human sense and understanding. I submit, therefore, that if people want to know what they should believe, they should not think that they will understand better through arguments than through belief; if they do that, they will be further from the wisdom of God than they were before.

If you seek the highest knowledge of God, do not search through words and arguments but through perfect and right action. Forget the tongue with its godless theories and supposals, but take up faith, which flows out of a pure and simple heart. How can you find something beyond the world if you seek it by means of an argument? But if you seek it by faith, you will find knowledge of God through the gate of wisdom. Wisdom is in a certain sense attained when you believe in the invisible without first demanding to understand it. You must believe in God as he is, that is, invisible—and then perhaps with your pure heart you will be able to see him.

Columbanus

✤ 312 ✤

THE PATH OF HUMILITY

All of you, clothe yourselves with humility toward one another, because,
"God opposes the proud but shows favor to the humble." (1 Peter 5:5)

Christ, the spotless lamb, became the sacrificial victim, led to the slaughter for the sheep that were blemished — as if we were merely blemished and not entirely corrupt! Such is the grace we have received! Let us live worthily of that great grace and not show contempt for it. So powerful is the Godly physician that he has healed all our sins! If we choose to be sick again, we will not only harm ourselves, but show ingratitude to the physician as well.

So let us follow the paths that Christ has revealed to us, above all the path of humility, which he himself became for us. He showed us the path by his teachings, and he himself followed it by his suffering on our behalf. In order to die for us — because as God he could not die — "the Word became flesh and dwelt among us" (John 1:14). The immortal one took on mortality to die for us, and then died for us to destroy our own death. This is what the Lord did, and this is the gift he granted to us. The mighty one was brought low, the lowly one was murdered, and after he was killed, he rose again and was exalted. For he did not intend to leave us dead in hell, but to honor those who rise with him at the resurrection of the dead, believers that he has already honored by justifying them through their faith.

Yes, he gave us the path of humility. If we keep to it we shall confess our belief in the Lord and have good reason to sing: "We shall praise you, God, we shall praise you and call upon your name" (Ps. 86:12).

Augustine

⤜ 313 ⤛

GAINING THE RICHES OF DIVINITY

The Word became flesh and made his dwelling among us. We have seen his glory, the glory of the one and only Son, who came from the Father, full of grace and truth. (John 1:14)

The very Son of God, older than the ages, the invisible, the incomprehensible, the incorporeal, the beginning of beginning, the light of light, the fountain of life and immortality, the image of the archetype, the immovable seal, the perfect likeness, the definition and Word of the Father: he is the one who comes to us, his own image, and takes our nature for the good of our nature and unites himself to an intelligent soul for the good of his soul, to purify man by manhood. He takes to himself all that is human, except for sin. He was conceived by the Virgin Mary, whose body and soul were prepared by the Spirit; his birth had to be treated with honor, and virginity received a new honor. He comes to us as God, in the human nature he has taken: one being, made of two contrary elements, flesh and spirit. Spirit gave divinity, and flesh received it.

He who makes rich is made poor; he takes on the poverty of my flesh, that I may gain the riches of his divinity. He who is full is made empty; he is emptied of his glory for a brief time, that I may share in his fullness. Can you understand the wealth of his goodness? What is this mystery that surrounds me? I received the likeness of God but failed to preserve it. He takes on my flesh to bring salvation to the image, immortality to the flesh. He enters into a second union with us, a union far more wonderful than the first.

Gregory of Nazianzus

✤ 314 ✤

THE DIGNITY OF VIRGINITY

These are those who did not defile themselves with women, for they
remained virgins. They follow the Lamb wherever he goes.
(Revelation 14:4)

So what did the Lord, who is the Truth and the Light, take in his
hand when he came down from heaven? He took flesh from a
virgin and kept his virginity, so that we might endeavor to honor
virginity, if we wished to pursue the likeness of God and Christ. For
the likeness of God is the avoiding of corruption.

Further, just like he was chief Shepherd and chief Prophet of the
church, so also did he become chief Virgin when he became incarnate, as John shows us in the book of Revelation, telling us that the
Lord is leader of the choir of virgins. And note how very great in the
sight of God is the dignity of virginity: "These were redeemed from
among men, being the firstfruits to God and to the Lamb. And in
their mouth no lie was found: for they are blameless" (Rev. 14:4–5).
He adds, "and they follow the Lamb wherever he goes." And by this
he clearly intends to teach us that the number of virgins was, from
the beginning, restricted to a certain number, namely a hundred and
forty four thousand, while the multitude of the other saints is innumerable. Thus virginity is a calling of high and special honor.

Methodius

⤞ 315 ⤝

UNSHAKEN COURAGE

Therefore, "they are before the throne of God and serve him day and
night in his temple; and he who sits on the throne will shelter them
with his presence. 'Never again will they hunger; never again will they
thirst. The sun will not beat down on them,' nor any scorching heat."
(Revelation 7:15–16)

"The sufferings of this present time are not to be compared with the glory that is to be revealed in us" (Rom. 8:18). Who would not wholeheartedly strive after such glory, to become a friend of God and immediately rejoice with Christ, to receive heavenly rewards after earth's torment and suffering? Soldiers of this world take pride in triumphantly returning to their home country after they have defeated the enemy. How much greater is the glory in returning triumphantly to heaven after conquering the devil? The presumptuous accuser is ousted and the trophies of victory are returned to heaven, the place from which Adam was cast out for his sin.

We offer the Lord a most acceptable gift: our uncorrupted faith, the unshaken courage of our spirit, and the glorious pride of our dedication. We accompany him when he comes to take vengeance on his enemies; we sit at the side of his judgment seat, share in his inheritance, have an equal footing with the angels, and enjoy the possession of a heavenly kingdom together with the patriarchs, apostles, and prophets. What persecution can defeat such thoughts? What torture can overwhelm them?

Cyprian of Carthage

⁘ 316 ⁘

WEAK GUARDIANS OF THE VINEYARD

When he saw the crowds, he had compassion on them, because they were harassed and helpless, like sheep without a shepherd. (Matthew 9:36)

There is something else about the life of the shepherds, dear brothers, that discourages me greatly. But so that I do not seem unjust, I accuse myself of the same thing, although I fall into it unwillingly, compelled by the urgency of these dangerous times. I am talking about our absorption in external affairs; we accept the duties of this office but attend to things besides our duties. We abandon the ministry of preaching and, in my opinion, are called bishops to our detriment because we fail to practice the appropriate virtues while retaining the honorable office. When those who have been entrusted to our care abandon God, we are silent. They fall into sin, and we fail to rebuke them.

But how can we correct someone else when we are neglecting ourselves? We are wrapped up in worldly concerns, and the more we devote ourselves to superficial things, the more insensitive we become to spiritual things.

It is therefore accurate for the church to say of its own weak shepherds, "They made me keeper of the vineyards, but my own vineyard I have not kept" (Song 1:6). We are made guards of the vineyards but do not guard our own, for we get involved in irrelevant pursuits and neglect the performance of our ministry.

Gregory the Great

✦ 317 ✦

THE SUFFICIENT ATONEMENT

"What do you think, Simon?" he asked. "From whom do the kings of the earth collect duty and taxes—from their own children or from others?" "From others," Peter answered. "Then the children are exempt," Jesus said to him. (Matthew 17:25–26)

Christ is free from all sin and does not pay the price of his own redemption. His blood could pay the ransom for all the sins of the whole world. The one who has no debt to pay for himself is the right person to set others free.

It is not only that Christ has no ransom to pay or atonement to make for his own sins; his words mean that other individuals do not need to make atonement for themselves, for Christ is the atonement for all and the redemption for all.

Is any normal person's blood precious enough to pay for his or her own redemption, seeing that it was Christ who shed his blood for the redemption of all? Is anyone's blood comparable to Christ's? Is anyone great enough to make self-atonement over and above the atonement that Christ has offered in himself, Christ who alone has reconciled the world to God by his blood? What greater victim, what more excellent sacrifice, what better advocate can there be than he who became the propitiation for the sins of all, and gave his life for us as our redemption?

We do not need, then, to look for an atonement or redemption made by each individual, because the price paid for all is the blood of Christ—the blood by which Christ has redeemed us, through which he alone has reconciled us to the Father. He has labored even to the end, shouldering our burdens himself. "Come to me," he says, "all you that labor, and I will refresh you" (Matt. 11:28).

Ambrose

✛ 318 ✛

REMEMBER YOUR DIGNITY

If we claim to have fellowship with him and yet walk in the darkness,
we lie and do not live out the truth. (1 John 1:6)

Dearly beloved, today our Savior is born; let us rejoice. Sadness should have no place on the birthday of life. The fear of death has been swallowed up; life brings us joy with the promise of eternal happiness.

No one is shut out from this joy; all share the same reason for rejoicing. Our Lord, victor over sin and death, finding no person free from sin, came to free us all. Let the saints rejoice as they see the palm of victory. Let the sinners be glad as they receive the offer of forgiveness. Let the pagans take courage as they are summoned to life.

In the fullness of time, chosen in the unfathomable depths of God's wisdom, the Son of God took for himself our common humanity in order to reconcile it with its Creator. He came to overthrow the devil, the origin of death, in that very nature by which the devil had overthrown mankind.

Christian, remember your dignity, and now that you share in God's own nature, do not return to your former base condition by sinning. Bear in mind who your head is and of whose body you are a member. Do not forget that you have been rescued from the power of darkness and brought into the light of God's kingdom.

Leo the Great

✢ 319 ✢

THE PASTOR'S PRAYER

God, whom I serve in my spirit in preaching the gospel of his Son, is my
witness how constantly I remember you in my prayers at all times; and
I pray that now at last by God's will the way may be opened for me to
come to you. I long to see you so that I may impart to you some spiritual
gift to make you strong. (Romans 1:9–11)

Now you have called me, Lord, by the hand of your bishop to minister to your people. I do not know why you have done so, for you alone know that. Lord, lighten the heavy burden of the sins through which I have seriously transgressed. Purify my mind and heart. Like a shining lamp, lead me along the straight path. When I open my mouth, tell me what I should say. By the fiery tongue of your Spirit make my own tongue ready. Stay with me always and keep me in your sight.

Lead me to pastures, Lord, and graze there with me. Do not let my heart lean either to the right or to the left, but let your good Spirit guide me along the straight path. Whatever I do, let it be in accordance with your will, now until the end.

And you, church, are a most excellent assembly, the noble summit of perfect purity, whose assistance comes from God. You, in whom God lives, receive now from us an exposition of the faith that is free from error, to strengthen the church, just as our fathers handed it down to us.

John of Damascus

⊹ 320 ⊹

OUR DEBT TO THE LORD

I will fulfill my vows to the LORD in the presence of all his people.
(Psalm 116:14)

For while we were dead, our Lord Jesus Christ restored us to life again, and how he did it is even more amazing than the fact itself: despite his divine state, he did not cling to his equality with God, but emptied himself to assume the condition of a slave (Phil. 2:6–7).

He bore our weaknesses and endured our sorrows. He was wounded for our sake so that by his wounds we might be healed. He redeemed us from the curse by becoming a curse for our sake, and he submitted to the most shameful death in order to raise us to the life of glory. But he was not satisfied with merely giving us life again; he also shared with us the dignity of his divine nature and prepared a place of eternal rest for us, with joys beyond human imagination.

How then shall we repay the Lord for all his goodness to us? He is so good that he asks for nothing except our love — that is the only payment he desires. To speak personally, after reflecting on all these blessings, the notion of ceasing to love God causes dread and numbness in me. I bring shame upon Christ by not remembering his grace and being preoccupied with trivialities.

Basil the Great

✢ 321 ✢

THE CORNERSTONE
OF THE TEMPLE

Unless the LORD builds the house, the builders labor in vain. Unless the
LORD watches over the city, the guards stand watch in vain.
(Psalm 127:1)

This is the house and temple of God, full of his doctrine and his power, a dwelling place holy enough to house the heart of God. The same inspired author is speaking of this with the words, "Your temple is holy, marvelous in its goodness" (Ps. 65:4). The holiness, justice, and self-restraint of men and women constitute God's temple.

Such a temple must be built by God; if it were constructed by human effort, it would not last. It is not held together by worldly teachings, nor is it protected by our own vain efforts or anxious concerns. We must build it and protect it in a different way. It cannot have its foundation on dirt or sand that is unstable and treacherous. Its foundation must be rooted in the prophets and apostles.

It must be built up from living stones, held together by a cornerstone; it will grow with ever-increasing unity into perfect harmony with Christ; its beauty and its charm are the adornment given to it by supernatural grace.

Such a house built by God will not collapse. Through the efforts of each believer this house will grow into many houses, and the blessed and spacious city of God will be raised up.

Hilary of Poitiers

✤ 322 ✤

ADVENT: PROMISE AND FULFILLMENT (I)

All this took place to fulfill what the Lord had said through the prophet:
"The virgin will conceive and give birth to a son, and they will call him
Immanuel" (which means "God with us"). (Matthew 1:22–23)

God established a time for his promises and a time for their fulfillment. The time for promises was in the time of the prophets, until John the Baptist; from John until the end is the time of fulfillment.

God, who is faithful, put himself in our debt, not by receiving anything from us, but by promising so much. But a promise from his mouth was not sufficient for him; he chose to commit himself in writing as well, as if making a contract of his promises. He produced an account of the promises and their fulfillment, so that we could read and see how he delivers on his promises. And so the time of the prophets was, as we have often said, the foretelling of the promises.

He promised eternal salvation, everlasting happiness with the angels, an immortal inheritance, endless glory, the joyful vision of his face, his holy dwelling in heaven, and no more fear of dying after the resurrection. This is his final promise, the goal of all our striving. When we reach it, we shall ask for nothing more. But regarding how we are to arrive at our final goal, he has also revealed, by promise and prophecy. [Continued in next entry . . .]

Augustine

ADVENT: PROMISE AND FULFILLMENT (II)

"But this has all taken place that the writings of the prophets might be fulfilled." Then all the disciples deserted him and fled. (Matthew 26:56)

He has promised humans divinity, mortals immortality, sinners justification, and the utterly poor a rising to glory.

But because all of God's promises seemed impossible to people — equality with the angels in exchange for death, corruption, poverty, weakness, dust, and ashes — God not only made a written contract with people to win their belief, but established a mediator of his good faith, not a prince or angel or archangel, but his only Son. Through his Son's leading he would give us the way to the goal he has promised.

God was not satisfied with giving us his Son to be merely our guide; he made him the way itself, that we might travel with him as leader and by him as the way.

Therefore, it was decided that the only Son of God was to come among us, to take our nature and be born an infant in this nature. He was to die, to rise again, to ascend into heaven, to sit at the right hand of the Father, and after that to come again and fulfill his promises among the nations — to fulfill now what was decreed from the beginning — to separate those deserving his anger from those deserving his mercy, to execute his threats against the wicked, and to reward the just with the promised salvation.

In his wisdom, therefore, God ordained that all of this be prophesied, foretold, and impressed upon us as an event in the future, so that we might wait for it in faith and not be overcome by sudden or dreadful events.

Augustine

✛ 324 ✛

LET YOUR HEART
BE AN ALTAR

*Therefore, when Christ came into the world, he said: "Sacrifice and
offering you did not desire, but a body you prepared for me."*
(Hebrews 10:5)

The Apostle says, "I appeal to you by the mercy of God to present your bodies as a living sacrifice" (Rom. 12:1). Brothers and sisters, this sacrifice follows the pattern of Christ's sacrifice, in which he gave his body as a living offering for the life of the world. He really made his body a living sacrifice, because though he was killed, he continues to live. In this transaction death receives its ransom, but the victim remains alive. Death itself suffers the punishment. This is why death is actually a birth for the martyrs, and their end a beginning. Their execution is the door to life, and as their light is extinguished on earth, they are lit with brilliance in heaven.

Paul says, "I appeal to you by the mercy of God to present your bodies as a sacrifice, living and holy" (Rom. 12:1). We are each called to be both a sacrifice to God and his priest. Do not cast aside what divine authority gives to you. Put on the garment of holiness, equip yourself with the belt of chastity. Let Christ be your helmet, let the cross on your forehead be your unfailing protection. Your breastplate should be the knowledge of God that he himself has given you. Continually burn the sweet-smelling incense of prayer. Take up the sword of the Spirit. Let your heart be an altar. Then, with full confidence in God, present your body for sacrifice. God desires not death, but faith; God thirsts not for blood, but for self-surrender; God is appeased not by slaughter, but by the offering of your free will.

Peter Chrysologus

⋆⊱ 325 ⊰⋆

DEALING WITH SPIRITUAL DEPRESSION (I)

Why, LORD, do you reject me and hide your face from me? (Psalm 88:14)

We asked this wise Daniel [a monk interviewed by John] why we were sometimes filled with hearty gladness, felt an inexpressible delight and the holiest feelings, and spoke prayers easily, even in our sleep; and on the other hand why we were sometimes suddenly filled with grief, weighed down by depression for no reason, and our prayers would become difficult and confused, almost as if we were intoxicated. We further asked why, while in this miserable condition, our mind was unable to get back to its former calmness, since the harder it would try to focus on God, the more violently it would be carried away by distracted thoughts without any spiritual fruit — like a sleep so powerful that not even desire for heaven or fear of hell could snap us out of it.

To this he replied: "The elders have given a threefold account of the mental gloom of which you speak. It comes from either our own carelessness, from the devil's abuse, or from the Lord's permission. Regarding our own carelessness, clearly we sometimes act carelessly and become lazy with spiritual things and cause the soil of our own hearts to produce thorns and thistles, which make us powerless over prayer or meditation or anything spiritually edifying. Regarding the devil's assaults, oftentimes we actually have good intentions, but the enemy creeps into our hearts and draws us away from holy things, without our knowledge and against our will." [Continued in next entry ...]

John Cassian

✛ 326 ✛

DEALING WITH SPIRITUAL DEPRESSION (II)

Do not hide your face from your servant; answer me quickly, for I am in trouble. Come near and rescue me; deliver me because of my foes.
(Psalm 69:17–18)

He continued: "As for God's permitting of this state of mind, there are two reasons. First, by being shut off from the Lord for a short time, and seeing with humble eyes how weak our own heart is, we might not be so prideful about our own holiness or purity. Further, by being shown that we cannot recover our former happiness through our own efforts, we might also learn that our previous joy was God's gift and not the result of anything inherent to us, and that we must seek it again from his grace and enlightenment.

"The second reason for God's allowing this to happen is this: to expose to ourselves our perseverance and endurance in the face of trouble, and to train us in purposeful and passionate prayers for the Holy Spirit's return to us. It also convinces us to carefully preserve and firmly hold on to the joy of purity and other spiritual fruits, even more than we did before, for we tend to be careless about things we think can be easily replaced."

John Cassian

❧ 327 ❧

RICH IN GRACE

They recognized him as the same man who used to sit begging at the
temple gate called Beautiful, and they were filled with wonder
and amazement at what had happened to him. (Acts 3:10)

Therefore, when the apostle Peter was on his way up to the temple and was asked for alms by the lame man, he replied, "Silver and gold I have not; but what I have I give you. In the name of Jesus Christ of Nazareth, arise and walk" (Acts 3:6). What is more sublime than this humility? And what could be richer than this poverty? Though Peter cannot assist with money, he can confer the gift of a restored nature. With a word Peter brought healing to the man who had been lame from birth; he could not give a coin with Caesar's image, but he could refashion the image of Jesus in this man.

And by the riches of this treasure, not only did he help the man who recovered the power to walk, but also five thousand others who believed the preaching of the apostle because of this miraculous cure. Thus Peter, who in his poverty had no money to give to the beggar, bestowed such a bounty of divine grace that in restoring to health the feet of one man, he healed the hearts of many thousands of believers. He had found all of them lame; but he made them leap for joy in Christ.

Leo the Great

⊁ 328 ⊰•

HE COMMANDED ALL THESE THINGS

The earth is the LORD's, and everything in it, the world, and all who
live in it; for he founded it on the seas and established it on the waters.
(Psalm 24:1–2)

The heavens are in motion by his direction, and they are peacefully subjected to him. Day and night fulfill the course he has established without interfering with each other. The sun, the moon, and the choirs of stars revolve in harmony at his command in their appointed paths without deviation. By his will the earth blossoms in the proper seasons and produces abundant food for men and animals and all living things, without reluctance and without any violation of what he has arranged.

Beyond this, unexplored regions of the sea and inexpressible realms of space are subject to his laws. The mass of the boundless sea, joined together by his Word in a single expanse, does not overflow its prescribed limits but flows as he commands it. For he said, "Thus far you will come, and your waves will stop here" (Job 38:11). The ocean, impassable for men, and the worlds beyond it are governed by the same edicts of the Lord.

The seasons follow one another in harmony. The winds from the four quarters blow in their seasons without the least deviation. And the flowing springs, created for our health and enjoyment, unfailingly offer their breasts to sustain human life. The tiniest of living creatures meet together in harmony and peace. The great Creator and Lord of the universe commanded all these things to be established in peace and harmony, out of his goodness to all, and in overflowing mercy to us especially, who seek refuge in our Lord Jesus Christ. To him be glory and majesty forever and ever. Amen.

Clement of Rome

✦ 329 ✦

MINISTRY AND MISSION

For God did not send his Son into the world to condemn the world,
but to save the world through him. (John 3:17)

Our Lord Jesus Christ appointed his apostles to be guides and teachers of the world and stewards of his divine mysteries. He asked them to shine out like lamps to cast their light not only on the Jews, but on every country under the sun and on people settled in distant lands. These holy men became the pillars of truth, and Jesus said that he was "sending them just as the Father had sent him" (John 17:18).

These words make clear the dignity of the apostolate and the glory of the power given to them, but they also give them a hint about the methods they are to adopt in their apostolic mission. For if Christ sent out his intimate disciples this way, just as the Father had sent him, then it was necessary for their own mission that they understood exactly why the Father had sent the Son. So Christ interpreted his mission for them, one time saying, "I have come to call not the righteous but sinners to repentance" (Luke 5:32).

From what he said they could see that it was their vocation to call sinners to repentance, to heal those who were sick whether in body or spirit, to seek in all things to do not their own will but the will of him who sent them, and as far as possible to save the world by their teaching.

And we find his holy disciples striving for these ends. We need only to look at the Acts of the Apostles or Paul's epistles to see them on this mission.

Cyril of Alexandria

⊹ 330 ⊹

THE PLAN OF SALVATION

*Has any god ever tried to take for himself one nation out of another
nation, by testings, by signs and wonders, by war, by a mighty hand
and an outstretched arm, or by great and awesome deeds, like all the
things the LORD your God did for you in Egypt before your very eyes?
(Deuteronomy 4:34)*

From the beginning God created man out of his own generosity.
He chose the patriarchs to give them salvation. He took his
people in hand, teaching them, unteachable as they were, to follow
him. He gave them prophets, acquainting humanity with his Spirit
and showing them communion with God on earth. He who stands
in need of no one gave communion with himself to those who need
him. Like an architect he outlined the plan of salvation to those
who sought to please him. By his own hand he gave food in Egypt
to those who did not see him. To those who were restless in the
desert he gave a law perfectly suited to them. To those who entered
the land of prosperity he gave a worthy inheritance. He killed the
fattened calf for those who turned to him as Father, and clothed
them with the finest garments. In so many ways he was training the
human race to take part in the harmonious song of salvation.

For this reason John in the book of Revelation says, "His voice
was as the voice of many waters" (Rev. 1:15). The Spirit of God is
indeed a multitude of waters, for the Father is rich and great. As the
Word passed among all these people he provided generous gifts of
help for those who were obedient to him, by drawing up a law that
was suitable and fitting for every circumstance.

Irenaeus

⤞ 331 ⤝

SEEKING EACH OTHER'S WELFARE

A new command I give you: Love one another. As I have loved you,
so you must love one another. (John 13:34)

This is the kind of love that renews us. When we love as he loved us we become new men, heirs of the new covenant, and singers of the new song.

This love gathers together a new people into one body, from the entire human race throughout the world, to be the bride of God's only Son. The church is the bride of whom it is asked in the Song of Songs, "Who is this who comes clothed in white?" (Song 6:10). Her garments are white because she has been made new, and the source of her renewal is this new commandment.

And so all her members make each other's welfare their common care. When one member suffers, all the members suffer with him, and if one member is glorified all the rest rejoice.

They love one another as God loves them so that they may be brothers and sisters of his only Son. He will lead them to the only satisfying goal, where all their desires will be fulfilled. For when God is all in all, there will be nothing left to desire.

This love is the gift of the Lord, who said, "As I have loved you, you also must love one another" (John 13:34). By loving us, then, he enabled us to love each other. By loving us himself, our mighty head has linked us all together as members of his own body, bound to one another by the tender bond of love.

Augustine

✦ 332 ✦

THE GIFT OF AFFLICTION

Oh, how I wish that God would speak, that he would open his lips
against you and disclose to you the secrets of wisdom, for true wisdom
has two sides. Know this: God has even forgotten some of your sin.
(Job 11:5–6)

When our desire for good things becomes disproportionate and sinful, peace with God is restored to us when those things are turned into punishments and become evil for us. It is through sin that we become opposed to God; therefore, it is right that we should return to his peace by way of punishments. This way, when every created thing is turned into a source of pain for us, the mind is chastened and humbled and can return to a renewed peace with its Creator.

We ought to observe how Job skillfully responds to his wife's arguments. It is a great comfort in times of tribulation if we recall the gifts our Creator has given us. Overwhelming sorrow will never break us if we quickly call to mind the gifts that have sustained us. For it is written, "On the day of prosperity do not forget affliction, and on the day of affliction do not forget prosperity" (Sir. 11:23). For if anyone receives God's gifts but forgets their affliction, they can fall through their own complacency. On the other hand, when someone is bruised by life's pain but is not consoled by recalling the blessings they have received, they are hopeless.

So both attitudes should be united so that one can support the other: the memory of gifts can soothe the pain of the affliction, and the fear of affliction can temper the joy of the gift.

Gregory the Great

✦ 333 ✦

DIFFERENT KINDS OF MERCY

For the LORD your God is a merciful God; he will not abandon
or destroy you or forget the covenant with your ancestors,
which he confirmed to them by oath. (Deuteronomy 4:31)

"Blessed are the merciful, for they shall receive mercy" (Matt. 5:7). Brothers and sisters, the thought of mercy is sweet, but mercy itself is even sweeter. All people hope for it, but unfortunately not all people deserve it. For while all of us wish to receive it, only a few are willing to give it.

How can we ask for something that we refuse to give to someone else? If we expect to receive any mercy in heaven, we should give mercy on earth. We all desire to receive mercy! Let us serve Lady Mercy now, and she will serve us in the world to come. Of course there is mercy in heaven, but the road to heaven is paved with our merciful acts on earth. As Scripture says: "LORD, your mercy is in heaven" (Ps. 36:5).

Similarly, there is both an earthly and a heavenly mercy, that is to say, a human and a divine mercy. Human mercy has compassion on the hardships of the poor. Divine mercy grants forgiveness of sins. The mercies we give here on earth will be returned to us in our homeland. God feels the cold and hunger in all the world's poor, as he once said: "What you have done to the least of my brothers you have done to me" (Matt. 25:40). God, who bestows his mercies on us in heaven, wishes the earth to be full of mercy as well.

Caesarius of Arles

✤ 334 ✤

AUGUSTINE'S MOMENT OF CONVERSION (I)

How long, LORD? Will you forget me forever? How long will you hide your face from me? How long must I wrestle with my thoughts and day after day have sorrow in my heart? (Psalm 13:1–2)

A profound reflection formed in the secret depths of my soul, bringing all my misery before the sight of my heart, and a storm arose in my mind, accompanied by a mighty shower of tears. To let my tears fall as they wanted I ran away from Alypius [friend of Augustine], because it seemed more appropriate to weep in solitude. So I went far enough away that I could not even sense his presence.

That is how it happened, and he knew something was wrong, because I must have choked on my tears when I spoke to him, just before I ran off. He remained where we had been sitting, completely astonished.

I flung myself down under a fig tree, gave myself over to my tears, and the streams of my eyes gushed out, an acceptable sacrifice to you (1 Pet. 2:5). And there I spoke to you, not in these very words but to this effect, for I spoke much: "But you, LORD, how long? How long, LORD? Will you be angry forever? Oh, do not hold our past iniquities against us!" For I felt that I was enslaved by them. I sent up these sorrowful cries: "How long, how long? Tomorrow, or the next day? Why not now? Why does my uncleanness not end at this very moment?" [Continued in next entry . . .]

Augustine

⊹ 335 ⊹

AUGUSTINE'S MOMENT OF CONVERSION (II)

From infancy you have known the Holy Scriptures, which are able
to make you wise for salvation through faith in Christ Jesus.
(2 Timothy 3:15)

As I was saying these things and weeping with the most bitter remorse in my heart, I suddenly heard the voice of a child coming from a neighboring house, chanting and repeating the words, "Take up and read; take up and read." Immediately my face changed, and I asked myself if the words were part of a song or child's game, since I could not recall ever having heard them.

So, restraining my tears, I rose up, believing it to be a command to me from heaven to open the book and read the first chapter to which I turned. For I had heard the story of Antony [a prominent monk who helped spread monasticism, who by chance came in while the gospel was being read, and received the admonition as if it were addressed directly to him: "Go and sell what you have, and give to the poor, and you shall have treasure in heaven; and come and follow me" (Matt. 19:21). And by this miracle he was immediately converted to you.

So quickly I returned to the place where Alypius was sitting, for I had left my volume of the New Testament there when I ran off. I grabbed and opened the book and in silence read the paragraph on which my eyes first fell: "Not in rioting and drunkenness, not in sexual immorality and pleasure-seeking, not in strife and envying; but put on the Lord Jesus Christ, and make no provision for the flesh, to fulfill its lusts" (Rom. 13:13–14). I read no further when instantly, just as the sentence ended, when something like a light of security pierced my heart, and the gloom of doubt vanished. [Continued in next entry ...]

Augustine

✤ 336 ✤

AUGUSTINE'S MOMENT OF CONVERSION (III)

Who are you to judge someone else's servant? To their own master, servants stand or fall. And they will stand, for the Lord is able to make them stand. (Romans 14:4)

So I closed the book and held the page with my finger, and with a peaceful face told Alypius of my experience. He asked to look at what I had read. I showed him, and he read even further in the book, where the Apostle writes, "He that is weak in the faith, receive" (Rom. 14:1). He applied this to himself and told me as much. He was strengthened by this admonition, and with resolve and purpose, and without delay, he joined me in faith, which very much reflects his character (which is much different than mine, but for the better).

Then we went in to see my mother. We told her we were converted, and she rejoiced. We related the details of the story, and she leapt for joy, celebrating your triumph and blessing you, who are able to do abundantly more than all we ask or think (Eph. 3:20). She realized that you had given me more than what she used to ask for in her sad and pitiful prayers. You converted me so thoroughly that from that point on I neither looked for a wife, nor any of this world's other hopes, and adopted that rule of faith that my mother had seen me embracing in a vision you showed her so many years before. And you turned her grief into a gladness more plentiful, precious, and holy than the gladness she formerly desired—which was having grandchildren through me!

Augustine

⊹ 337 ⊹

GOD'S MYSTERIOUS DEPTH

Oh, the depth of the riches of the wisdom and knowledge of God!
How unsearchable his judgments, and his paths beyond tracing out!
(Romans 11:33)

God is everywhere. He is immeasurably vast but everywhere close at hand, as he himself bears witness: "I am a God close at hand, and not a God who is distant" (Jer. 23:23). The God we are seeking is not far away, because he is within us, if we have deserved his Spirit. He lives in us as the soul lives in the body, but only if we are his healthy limbs and not dead in our sin. Then he really lives within us, as he has said: "And I will live in them and walk among them" (2 Cor. 6:16). If we are worthy of his presence in us, then he gives us life that is true and makes us his living limbs. As Saint Paul says, "In him we live and move and have our being" (Acts 17:28).

Given his indescribable and incomprehensible essence, who can explore the Most High? Who can examine the depths of God? Who will say that he knows the infinite God who fills all things and surrounds all things, who pervades all things and transcends all things, who takes possession of all things but is not himself possessed by anything? The infinite God whom no one has seen as he is?

No one can begin to penetrate the secrets of God, what he is, how he is, who he is. These things cannot be described, examined, or explored. I say very simply, but very strongly, believe that God is as he was, and will be as he has always been, for he cannot be changed.

Columbanus

✤ 338 ✤

THE SUPERIOR PASSOVER

*The blood will be a sign for you on the houses where you are, and when
I see the blood, I will pass over you. No destructive plague will touch
you when I strike Egypt. (Exodus 12:13)*

The Passover we celebrate brings salvation to the whole human race beginning with the first man, who together with all the others is saved and given life.

In an imperfect and transitory way, the types and images of the past prefigured the perfect and eternal reality that has now been revealed. The presence of the real thing makes the symbol obsolete: when the king appears in person no one pays reverence to his statue.

How far the symbol falls short of the reality is seen from the fact that the symbolic Passover celebrated the brief life of the Jews' firstborn, whereas the real Passover celebrates the eternal life of all humankind. It is a small gain to escape death for a short time, only to die soon afterward; it is a very different thing to escape death altogether as we do through the sacrifice of Christ, our Passover.

Correctly understood, its very name shows why this is our greatest feast. It is called the Passover because, when he was striking down the firstborn, the destroying angel passed over the houses of the Hebrews, but it is even more true to say that he passes over us, for he does so once and for all when we are raised up by Christ to eternal life.

Pseudo-Chrysostom

✢ 339 ✢

THE TRIUMPHAL CHRIST

If God is for us, who can be against us? He who did not spare his own
Son, but gave him up for us all—how will he not also, along with him,
graciously give us all things? Who will bring any charge against those
whom God has chosen? Who shall separate us from the love of Christ?
Shall trouble or hardship or persecution or famine or nakedness or
danger or sword? (Romans 8:31–33, 35)

The Lord, though he was God, became man. He suffered for the sake of those who suffer, he was bound for those in bonds, condemned for the guilty, buried for those who lie in the grave; but he rose from the dead and cried aloud: " 'Who will contend with me? Let him confront me' (Isa. 50:8). I have freed the condemned, brought the dead back to life, raised people from their graves. Who has anything to say against me? I," he said, "am the Christ; I have destroyed death, triumphed over the enemy, trampled hell under-foot, bound the strong one, and taken people up to the heights of heaven: I am the Christ.

"Come, then, all you nations of the earth, receive forgiveness for the sins that defile you. I am your forgiveness. I am the Passover that brings salvation. I am the lamb who was sacrificed for you. I am your ransom, your life, your resurrection, your light. I am your salvation and your King. I will bring you to the heights of heaven. With my own right hand I will raise you up, and I will show you the eternal Father."

Melito of Sardis

✦ 340 ✦

THE RICHNESS
OF THE PSALMS

Let the message of Christ dwell among you richly as you teach and admonish one another with all wisdom through psalms, hymns, and songs from the Spirit, singing to God with gratitude in your hearts.
(Colossians 3:16)

Although the whole of Scripture breathes God's grace upon us, this is especially true of the most delightful book, the book of the Psalms. Moses, when he told of the deeds of the patriarchs, did so in a plain and unadorned style. But when he had miraculously led the people of Israel across the Red Sea, and when he had seen King Pharaoh with all his army drowned, he transcended his own normal style and sang a song of triumph to the Lord — just as through the miracle Moses' powers were transcended by God's. Miriam the prophetess herself took up a timbrel and led the others in the refrain: "Sing to the LORD: he has covered himself in glory, horse and rider he has thrown into the sea" (Ex. 15:21).

History instructs us, the law teaches us, prophecy foretells, rebukes condemn us, wisdom persuades us; but the book of Psalms goes further than all of these. It is medicine for our spiritual health. When we read it we find a medicine to cure the wounds caused by any of our passions. Whoever studies it deeply will find it to be like a gymnasium for their soul, where the different psalms are like different exercises set out before them. In that gymnasium, in that stadium of virtue, they can choose the exercises that will best train them to win the victor's crown.

Ambrose

⊹ 341 ⊹

THE PATH TO PEACE

When they hurled their insults at him, he did not retaliate;
when he suffered, he made no threats. Instead, he entrusted himself
to him who judges justly. (1 Peter 2:23)

Why is it that sometimes we can hear nasty words but be unaffected by them, as if we had not heard them, but sometimes we become disturbed as soon as we hear such words? What is the cause of this inconsistency? I believe it all comes from our state of mind at the time.

If someone is engaged in prayer or contemplation, he can easily take an insult from his brother and be unmoved by it. Or perhaps his love for his brother is strong enough that he is unfazed by it — love bears all things with patience (1 Cor. 13:7).

On the other hand, it is possible for someone to be troubled by her sister's words, either because she is not in a good frame of mind or because she hates her sister. There are a great number of other reasons as well. But the reason for all disturbance, at its roots, is that no one finds fault with himself or herself. This is the reason why we become angry and upset, why we sometimes have no peace in our soul. We should not be surprised, because holy people have already taught us that this is the path to peace.

We see that this is true in so many other people, yet out of laziness we stick to our own path, thinking we will one day attain peace, even when we are irritated by everything and cannot accept any blame ourselves.

This is the way things are. We could have innumerable other virtues, but if we have left the path of self-accusation we will never have peace. We will be afflicted by others or we will be an affliction to them, and all our efforts will be wasted.

Dorotheus of Gaza

✦ 342 ✦

THE MERCY OF CHRIST

For all have sinned and fall short of the glory of God, and all are
justified freely by his grace through the redemption that came
by Christ Jesus. (Romans 3:23–24)

For "we have been saved by his grace," says the Apostle, "and not by our works, so that no one may boast; for it is by his grace that we have been saved" (Eph. 2:8–9). It is not as if we showed God a good life first, and afterward God showed his love and esteem for us from heaven, saying, "Let us come to the aid of these people because they are living a good life." No, our life was displeasing to him. He will, therefore, condemn what we have done, but he will save what he himself has done in us.

We were not good, but God had pity on us and sent his Son to die, not for good men and women but for bad ones, not for the just but for the wicked. Yes, "Christ died for the ungodly" (Rom. 5:6). Notice what is written next: "One will hardly die for a righteous man, though perhaps for a good man one will dare even to die" (Rom. 5:7). Perhaps someone can be found who will dare to die for a good person; but for the unjust person, for the wicked person, the sinner, who would be willing to die — except Christ alone who is so just that he justifies even the unjust?

And so, my brothers and sisters, we had no good works, for all our works were evil. But although humanity's actions were thoroughly ugly, God in his mercy did not abandon the human race. He sent his Son to redeem us, not with gold or silver but at the price of his blood poured out for us.

Augustine

✢ 343 ✢

A RIVER OF SPIRITUAL GIFTS

But whoever drinks the water I give them will never thirst.
Indeed, the water I give them will become in them a spring
of water welling up to eternal life. (John 4:14)

The river of God is brimming with water; that is to say, we are inundated by the gifts of the Holy Spirit, and from him the river of God pours into us like a full flood.

We also have food prepared for us. And who is this food? He is the one who prepares us for life with God, for by receiving his holy body we receive a place in the communion of his holy body. This is what is meant by the words of the psalm, "You have provided their food, for this is your way of preparing them" (Ps. 65:9). For in addition to refreshing us now, this food also prepares us for the life to come.

We who have been reborn through the sacrament of baptism experience intense joy when we feel the first stirrings of the Holy Spirit within us. We begin to have an insight into the mysteries of faith. We are able to prophesy and to speak with wisdom. We become steadfast in hope and receive the gift of healing. Demons are made subject to our authority. These gifts enter us like a gentle rain, and once they have done so, little by little, they bring forth fruit in abundance.

Hilary of Poitiers

✢ 344 ✢

LOVE AND OBEDIENCE

Dear friends, let us love one another, for love comes from God.
Everyone who loves has been born of God and knows God. (1 John 4:7)

Charity is a right attitude of mind that prefers nothing to the knowledge of God. If a person possesses any strong attachment to the things of this earth, he or she cannot possess true charity. For anyone who really loves God prefers to know and experience God rather than his creatures. The whole frame and longing of a person's mind is always directed toward him.

For God is far superior to all his creation, since everything that exists has been made by God and for him. And so, in deserting God, who is beyond compare, for the inferior works of creation, a person shows that he or she values God, the author of creation, less than creation itself.

The Lord himself reminds us: "Whoever loves me will keep my commandments. And this is my commandment: that you love one another" (John 14:21; 15:12). So the woman who does not love her neighbor does not obey God's command. But one who does not obey his command cannot love God. A woman is blessed if she can love all people equally. Moreover, if she truly loves God, she must love her neighbor absolutely. Such a woman cannot hoard her wealth. Rather, like God himself, she generously gives from her own resources to each person according to his or her needs.

Since she imitates God's generosity, the only distinction she draws is the person's need. She does not distinguish between a good person and a bad one, a just person and one who is unjust. Her own good will, however, will make her prefer the person who strives after virtue to the one who is depraved.

Maximus the Confessor

✤ 345 ✤

THE TWO COMINGS
OF CHRIST (I)

*I say this because many deceivers, who do not acknowledge Jesus Christ
as coming in the flesh, have gone out into the world. Any such person is
the deceiver and the antichrist. (2 John 1:7)*

We do not preach only one coming of Christ, but two, the second more glorious than the first. The first coming was marked by patience; the second will bring the crown of a divine kingdom.

In general, whatever relates to our Lord Jesus Christ has two aspects. There is a begetting from God in eternity, and a birth from a virgin in the fullness of time. There is a hidden coming, like that of dew on a fleece, and a coming before all eyes, still in the future.

At the first coming he was wrapped in swaddling clothes in a manger. At his second coming he will be clothed in light as in a garment. In the first coming he suffered the cross, enduring the shame; in the second coming he will be in glory, escorted by an army of angels.

We look beyond the first coming and await the second. At the first coming we said, "Blessed is he who comes in the name of the Lord" (Mark 11:9). At the second we shall say it again; we shall go out with the angels to meet the Lord and cry out in adoration, "Blessed is he who comes in the name of the Lord!"

The Savior will not come to be judged this time, but to judge those who judged him. At his own judgment he was silent; at his second coming he will address those who crucified him and will remind them: "You did these things, and I was silent" (Ps. 50:21). [Continued in next entry ...]

Cyril of Jerusalem

✢ 346 ✢

THE TWO COMINGS
OF CHRIST (II)

*"Look, he is coming with the clouds," and "every eye will see him,
even those who pierced him"; and all peoples on earth "will mourn
because of him." (Revelation 1:7)*

His first coming was to fulfill his plan of love and to teach people by gentle persuasion. Upon the second coming, people will be subjects of his kingdom, whether they like it or not. The prophet Malachi speaks of the two comings. One is spoken of here: "And the LORD whom you seek will come suddenly to his temple" (Mal. 3:1). He says of another coming: "Look, the LORD Almighty will come, and who can endure the day of his entry, or who can stand in his sight? Because he comes like a refiner's fire, a fuller's soap, and he will sit refining and cleansing" (Mal. 3:2–3).

These two comings are also referred to by Paul in writing to Titus: "The grace of God the Savior has appeared to all men, instructing us to put aside impiety and worldly desires and live self-controlled, upright, and godly lives in this present age, waiting for the joyful hope, the appearance of the glory of our great God and Savior, Jesus Christ" (Titus 2:11–13). Notice how he speaks of a first coming for which he gives thanks, and a second for which we still wait.

That is why the faith we profess has been handed on to you in the words of the [Niceno-Constantinopolitan] Creed: "He ascended into heaven, and is seated at the right hand of the Father, and he will come again in glory to judge the living and the dead, and his kingdom will have no end."

Our Lord Jesus Christ will therefore come from heaven. He will come at the end of the world, in glory, at the last day. For there will be an end to this world, and the created world will be made new.

Cyril of Jerusalem

❖ 347 ❖

RESTORING UNITY

You are still worldly. For since there is jealousy and quarreling among
you, are you not worldly? Are you not acting like mere humans?
(1 Corinthians 3:3)

[From a letter to the church at Corinth:] Why are there strife and schisms and even war among you? Do we not possess the same Spirit of grace and the same calling in Christ? Why do we rip apart and divide the body of Christ? Why do we harm our own body? How can we reach such insanity that we forget that we are members of one another? Your fighting has led many astray, made many doubt, made many despair, and has brought grief upon everyone. And still your dispute continues.

Pick up the letter of the apostle Paul. What did he write to you at the beginning of his ministry? Even then you had developed factions. So Paul, inspired by the Holy Spirit, wrote to you about himself and Cephas and Apollos, and instructed you in the ignorance of factions.

We should put an end to this division immediately. Let us fall down before our master and beg his mercy with our tears. Then he will be reconciled to us and restore us to the practice of brotherly love. This is the gate of justice that leads to life, as it is written: "Open to me the gates of justice. When I have entered there, I shall praise the LORD" (Ps. 118:19). Of the many gates that stand open, the gate of justice is the gateway of Christ.

Whoever enters this gate is blessed, pursuing holiness and justice, performing their tasks without discord. People may be faithful; they may have the power to prophesy; they may be a fair judge of words and pure in their actions. But the greater they are, the more humbly they ought to act, and the more they should be concerned for the common good rather than their own interests.

Clement of Rome

✦ 348 ✦

INSTRUCTION AND BEAUTY

I will sing praise to you with the lyre, Holy One of Israel. My lips will
shout for joy when I sing praise to you—I whom you have delivered.
(Psalm 71:22–23)

What is more pleasing than a psalm? David expresses it well: "Praise the LORD, for a song of praise is good: let there be praise of our God with gladness and grace" (Ps. 147:1). Yes, a psalm is a blessing on the lips of the people, a hymn in praise of God, the assembly's homage to God, a shout of approval, a word that speaks for all, the voice of the church, a confession of faith in song. It is the voice of complete assent, the joy of freedom, a cry of happiness, the echo of gladness. It soothes the temper, distracts from worry, and lightens the burden of sorrow. It is a source of security at night, and a lesson in wisdom by day. It is a shield when we are afraid, a celebration of holiness, a vision of serenity, a promise of peace and harmony. It is like a lyre, producing a harmony from a blend of notes. Day begins with the music of a psalm. Day closes with the recitation of a psalm.

In a psalm, there is instruction alongside beauty. We sing for pleasure. We learn for our profit. What human experience is not explored in a reading of the Psalms? I come across the words, "A song for the beloved" (Ps. 45), and I burn with desire for God's love. I go through God's revelation in all its beauty, the hints of the resurrection, the gifts of his promises. I learn to avoid sin. I discover the joy in repenting for my sins and feel no shame in my former guilt.

Ambrose

✢ 349 ✢

AMASSING IMPERISHABLE RICHES

You make known to me the path of life; you will fill me with joy in your presence, with eternal pleasures at your right hand. (Psalm 16:11)

The good and chaste soul is so happy to be filled with God that it desires to take delight in nothing else. For what the Lord says is very true: "Where your treasure is, there also will your heart be" (Luke 12:34). What is a person's treasure except the heaping up of profits and the fruit of his or her toil? "For whatever a man sows, this too will he reap" (Gal. 6:7), and each person's gain matches their toil; and where delight and enjoyment are found, there the heart's desire is attached. Now there are many kinds of wealth and a variety of reasons to rejoice; every person's treasure is that which he or she desires. If it is based on earthly ambitions, its acquisition makes people not blessed, but wretched.

But those who enjoy the things that are above and eternal, rather than earthly and perishable, possess an incorruptible, hidden store of which the prophet speaks: "Our treasure and salvation have come, wisdom and instruction and piety from the LORD: these are the treasures of justice" (Isa. 33:6). Through these, with the help of God's grace, even earthly possessions are transformed into heavenly blessings. It is a fact that many people use their wealth as a tool of devotion. By distributing their excess to support the poor, they are amassing imperishable riches, so what they have wisely given away cannot be subject to loss. They have properly placed those riches where their heart is; it is a most blessed thing to work to increase the heart's riches rather than to fear that they may pass away.

Leo the Great

⫸ 350 ⫷

THE VOICE
AND THE LORD

John replied in the words of Isaiah the prophet, "I am the voice of one
calling in the wilderness, 'Make straight the way for the Lord.'"
(John 1:23)

John is the voice, but the Lord is the Word who was "in the beginning" (John 1:1). John is the voice that lasts for a time; Christ is the Word from the beginning who lives forever.

Take away the word, the meaning, and what can the voice do? Where there is no understanding, there is only a meaningless sound. The voice without the word strikes the ear but does not build up the heart.

However, let us observe what happens when we seek to build up each other's hearts. When I think about what I am going to say, the word or message is already in my heart. When I want to speak to you, I look for a way to share with your heart what is already in mine.

I find that I can use my voice to speak to you, to put the word from my heart into yours. The sound of my voice brings the meaning of the word to you and then disappears. The word is now in your heart as well as in mine, my voice having carried it.

When you finally have the word, does not the sound seem to say, "The Word ought to grow, and I should diminish" (John 3:30)? The voice completed its duty in making the word known, and has gone away, as though it were saying, "My joy is complete" (John 3:29). So let us acknowledge the voice but hold on to the Word conceived inwardly in our hearts.

Augustine

✤ 351 ✤

TRIUMPHING IN ADVERSITY

*But even if I am being poured out like a drink offering on the sacrifice
and service coming from your faith, I am glad and rejoice with all of you.
(Philippians 2:17)*

Paul, more than anyone else, has shown us what humanity really is, and how it is possible for people to be noble, and of what virtues they are capable. Each day Paul aimed higher; each day he rose with greater passion and faced the dangers that threatened him with new eagerness. He summed up his attitude in the words, "I forget what is behind me and push on to what lies ahead" (Phil. 3:13). When he saw that his death was imminent, he told others to share his joy: "Rejoice and be glad with me!" (Phil. 2:18). And when he endured danger, injustice, and abuse, he said, "I am content with weakness, mistreatment, and persecution" (2 Cor. 12:10). He called these things the weapons of righteousness, which means he profited immensely from them.

Even among the traps that had been laid for him by his enemies, his joyful heart transformed every attack into a victory. He was constantly beaten, abused, and cursed, and yet boasted of it as though he were celebrating a triumph and receiving trophies, and thanked God through it all: "Thanks be to God who is always victorious in us!" (1 Cor. 15:57).

He was happier about the shameful abuse he received for preaching the Gospel than we are for any kind of honor. He was more eager for death than we are for life; more passionate for poverty than we are for wealth; more zealous for toil than we are for the rest after toil. The only thing he wanted was to please God. The one thing he feared, even dreaded, was to offend Christ. He could not be swayed by anything else.

John Chrysostom

❖ 352 ❖

THE WHOLE BODY WORKS IN HARMONY (I)

After he had provided purification for sins, he sat down at the right hand of the Majesty in heaven. So he became as much superior to the angels as the name he has inherited is superior to theirs. (Hebrews 1:3–4)

Beloved, Jesus Christ is our salvation. He is the high priest through whom we present our offerings and the helper who supports us in our weakness. Through him our gaze penetrates through to heaven, and we see, as in a mirror, the most holy face of God. Through Christ the eyes of our hearts are opened, and our weak and clouded understanding reaches up toward the light. Through him God willed that we should taste eternal knowledge, for Christ is the radiance of God's glory and is as superior to the angels as his name is superior to theirs.

Therefore let us do battle under his faultless command with all our strength. Think of the men serving under our military commanders. They are so well disciplined! How readily and submissively they carry out orders! Not everyone can be a prefect, a tribune, a centurion [ranks in the Roman army], or a captain of fifty, but each man in his own rank executes the orders of the emperor and his commanding officers.

The great cannot exist without the humble, and the humble cannot exist without the great. The well-being of the whole depends on the harmonious cooperation of the parts. Take our own body for example: the head is helpless without the feet, and the feet can do nothing without the head. Even our least important members are useful and necessary to the whole body, and all work together for its well-being in harmonious subordination. [Continued in next entry ...]

Clement of Rome

✢ 353 ✢

THE WHOLE BODY WORKS IN HARMONY (II)

But God has put the body together, giving greater honor to the parts that lacked it, so that there should be no division in the body, but that its parts should have equal concern for each other. If one part suffers, every part suffers with it; if one part is honored, every part rejoices with it. (1 Corinthians 12:24–26)

Let us preserve the unity of the body that we form in Jesus Christ, and let everyone defer to their neighbor according to their particular gifts. Let the strong care for the weak, and the weak respect the strong. Let the wealthy assist the poor, and the poor thank God for giving them someone to meet their needs. The wise should not tout their wisdom through speeches but by good works; the humble should not proclaim their own humility, but leave others to do it; the chaste should not boast of their self-control, but acknowledge the one who gives them the strength to tame their desires.

Think, my brothers and sisters, of how we first came into being, of what we were at the first moment of our existence. Think of the darkness out of which our Creator made us, and the grave from which he brought us into his world where he had gifts prepared for us even before we were born. All this we owe to him, and for everything we must give him thanks. To him be glory forever and ever. Amen.

Clement of Rome

✤ 354 ✤

OUR FATHER'S INDULGENCE

This, then, is how you should pray: "Our Father in heaven,
hallowed be your name." (Matthew 6:9)

We should not only notice that we are to call him "Father" who is in heaven, but we add to that and say "our Father," meaning the Father of those who believe—the Father of those who have begun to be children of God, having been sanctified and regenerated by the birth of spiritual grace.

How great is the Lord's indulgence! How great is his condescension, and how abundant his goodness toward us! For he wishes that we pray in his sight by calling him Father and calling ourselves sons and daughters of God, even though we know Christ is the Son of God. This is a name that none of us would dare to call ourselves unless he himself had commanded us to pray this way.

Therefore, beloved brothers and sisters, we ought to remember that when we call God "our Father" we should act as God's children, so that as much as we find pleasure in considering God as our Father, he might also find pleasure in us as his children. Let us speak as true temples of God, so that it might be obvious to the world that God dwells in us. Let our actions be in accordance with the Spirit, so that we who have begun to be citizens of heaven might do only heavenly things from now into eternity.

Cyprian of Carthage

✥ 355 ✥

GENTLENESS IS THE LOVELIEST VIRTUE

I had been like a gentle lamb led to the slaughter. (Jeremiah 11:19)

If the highest goal of virtue is the betterment of the most people, gentleness is the loveliest of all, which does not hurt even those it condemns, and makes those it condemns worthy of forgiveness. Moreover, it is the only virtue that has led to the growth of the church, which the Lord established at the price of his own blood, embodying the gentleness of heaven. Seeking the redemption of all, he speaks in a gentle voice that people's ears can endure, under which their hearts do not sink, nor their spirits tremble.

If you endeavor to improve the faults of human weakness, you should bear this weakness on your own shoulders and let it weigh upon you. For we read in the Gospel that the shepherd carried the weary sheep and did not cast it off (Luke 15:5). And Solomon says, "Do not be overly righteous" (Eccl. 7:16), for restraint should soften righteousness. For how can people whom you despise, who think that they will be an object of contempt and not of compassion, feel safe to seek healing from you, their physician?

The Lord Jesus had compassion on us in order to call us to himself and not frighten us away. He came in meekness and humility, and so he said, "Come to me, all you that labor and are heavy laden, and I will refresh you" (Matt. 11:28). So the Lord gives rest and does not shut out nor cast off and rightly chose disciples that would interpret his will, which is to gather together and not drive away the people of God.

Ambrose

✤ 356 ✤

THE ACCOMPLISHMENTS OF THE CROSS

Jesus said, "Father, forgive them, for they do not know what they are doing." And they divided up his clothes by casting lots. (Luke 23:34)

True reverence for the Lord's passion means fixing the eyes of our heart on Jesus crucified and recognizing in him our own humanity.

The earth — our earthly nature — should tremble at the suffering of its Redeemer. The rock — the hearts of unbelievers — should burst asunder. The dead, imprisoned in the tombs of their mortality, should come forth, the massive stones now ripped apart. Foreshadowings of the future resurrection should appear in the holy city, the church of God: what is to happen to our bodies should now take place in our hearts.

No one, however weak, is denied a share in the victory of the cross. No one is beyond the help of the prayer of Christ. His prayer brought benefit to the multitude that raged against him. How much more does it bring to those who turn to him in repentance?

Ignorance has been destroyed, obstinacy has been overcome. The sacred blood of Christ has quenched the flaming sword that barred access to the Tree of Life. The age-old night of sin has given way to the true light.

The Christian people are invited to share the riches of paradise. All who have been reborn have the way open before them to return to their native land, from which they had been exiled. It remains open unless they themselves close off the path, but even the faith of a thief was powerful enough to open it.

Leo the Great

✣ 357 ✣

TWO KINDS OF FAITH (I)

Therefore, since we have been justified through faith, we have peace
with God through our Lord Jesus Christ. (Romans 5:1)

The one word *faith* can have two meanings. One kind of faith concerns doctrines. It involves the soul's assent to and acceptance of some particular matter.

It also concerns the soul's good, according to the words of the Lord: "Whoever hears my voice and believes in him who sent me has eternal life, and will not come to be judged" (John 5:24). And again: "He who believes in the Son is not condemned, but has passed from death to life" (John 3:36).

How great is God's love for people! Some good men and women have been found pleasing to God because of years of work. What they achieved by working for many years at a task pleasing to God is freely given to you by Jesus in one short moment. For if you believe that Jesus Christ is Lord and that God raised him from the dead, you will be saved and taken up to paradise by him, just as he brought the thief there. Do not doubt that this is possible. After all, he saved the thief on the holy hill of Golgotha because of one hour's faith; will he not save you too since you have believed? [Continued in next entry ...]

Cyril of Jerusalem

✢ 358 ✢

TWO KINDS OF FAITH (II)

By faith in the name of Jesus, this man whom you see and know was
made strong. It is Jesus' name and the faith that comes through him
that has completely healed him, as you can all see. (Acts 3:16)

The other kind of faith is given by Christ by means of a special
grace. "To one wise sayings are given through the Spirit, to
another perceptive comments by the same Spirit, to another faith
by the same Spirit, to another gifts of healing" (1 Cor. 12:8 – 9).
Now this kind of faith, given by the Spirit as a special gift, is not
confined to doctrinal matters, for it produces effects beyond any
human capability. If a person who has this faith says to a mountain
" 'move from here to there,' it will move" (Matt. 17:20). For when
anybody says this in faith and believes it will happen and has no
hidden doubts, he or she receives that grace.

Jesus was speaking of this kind of faith when he said, "If you
have faith like a grain of mustard seed" (Matt. 17:20). The mustard
seed is small in size but it holds an explosive force; although it is
sown in a small hole, it produces great branches, and when it is
grown birds can nest there. In the same way faith produces great
effects in the soul instantaneously. When enlightened by faith, the
soul pictures God and sees him as clearly as any soul can. It views
earth from heaven, and even before the end of this world it sees the
judgment and the giving of promised rewards.

I pray that you would have the faith that is directed to God, so that
you may receive from him the faith that transcends human capacity.

Cyril of Jerusalem

✢ 359 ✢

INVINCIBLE FAITH

Women received back their dead, raised to life again. There were others who were tortured, refusing to be released so that they might gain an even better resurrection. Some faced jeers and flogging, and even chains and imprisonment. They were put to death by stoning; they were sawed in two; they were killed by the sword. (Hebrews 11:35–37)

[From a letter to martyrs and confessors:] Valiant brothers and sisters, what praises can I use to extol your brave hearts? And what words are good enough to celebrate your persevering faith? With what praises can I extol you, most valiant brothers and sisters? You were interrogated under cruel torture and held out until it ended in your glory; it was not you who yielded to the torments, but rather the torments that yielded to you! You were given no rest from the pain of those evil instruments, except your crowning death, which ended your pain. The butchery lasted longer not so that it would overthrow your firm faith, but rather that it might send you more quickly to the Lord.

The crowd marveled at Christ's heavenly battle. They saw his servants standing firm, free in speech, pure in heart, blessed with supernatural courage, naked and without any earthly weapons, but as believers equipped with the armor of faith. Tortured men and women stood more strongly than their torturers; whipped and bloody limbs triumphed over the clubs and claws that tore them.

Savage and prolonged beatings could not overcome their invincible faith. Enough blood flowed to quench the fire of persecution, a glorious river to cool the burning heat of hell. What a divine display it was, how sublime and magnificent! The sworn allegiance and loyalty of God's soldiers is a pleasing testimony to him!

Cyprian of Carthage

✤ 360 ✤

IGNORANCE OF OURSELVES

Who can discern their own errors? Forgive hidden faults. Keep your
servant also from willful sins; may they not rule over me!
(Psalm 19:12–13)

Now my sighs are evidence enough that I am displeased with myself, that you are my light and the source of my joy, and that you are loved and desired. I am thoroughly ashamed of myself; I have renounced myself and chosen you, knowing that I can please neither you nor myself unless you enable me to do so.

You, Lord, are my judge. Even though "no one knows a man's innermost self except the man's own spirit within him" (1 Cor. 2:11), there is something in a man that even his own spirit does not know. But you know all of him, for you have made him. As for me, I think nothing of myself in your sight, knowing that I am dust and ashes; but I know something of you that I do not know of myself.

True, "we see now indistinctly as in a mirror, but not yet face to face" (1 Cor. 13:12). Therefore, as long as I am in exile from you, I am more present to myself than to you. Yet I do know that you cannot be overcome, but do not know which temptations I can resist and which I cannot. Nevertheless, I have hope, because "you are faithful and do not allow us to be tempted beyond our endurance, but along with the temptation you give us the means to withstand it" (1 Cor. 10:13).

Therefore I confess what I know of myself, and also what I do not know. Any knowledge I have is because you have enlightened me, while the knowledge I do not have will be mine when I stand before your face, my darkness brightened as if by the noonday sun.

Augustine

⊰ 361 ⊱

A LIVING, LEAPING WATER

*Jesus answered her, "If you knew the gift of God and who it is
that asks you for a drink, you would have asked him
and he would have given you living water." (John 4:10)*

"The water I shall give him will become in him a fountain of living water, welling up into eternal life" (John 4:14). This is a new kind of water, a living, leaping water, welling up for those who are worthy. But why did Christ call the grace of the Spirit "water"? Because all things are dependent on water; plants and animals have their origin in water. Water comes down from skies as rain, and although it is always the same in itself, it produces many different effects, one in the palm tree, another in the vine, and so on throughout all of creation. It does not change itself for each different creature, but remains the same for each and feeds each in a different way.

It is the same for the Holy Spirit. His nature is always the same, simple and indivisible, but he apportions grace to each person according to his pleasure. Like a parched tree that produces buds when watered, the repentant soul bears the fruit of holiness when it receives the Holy Spirit. Although the Spirit never changes, the effects of his action are many and marvelous, as he works by the will of God and in the name of Christ.

Cyril of Jerusalem

✢ 362 ✢

BAPTISM CLEANSES
THE SOUL

In him you were also circumcised with a circumcision not performed by
human hands. Your whole self ruled by the flesh was put off when you
were circumcised by Christ. (Colossians 2:11)

To attain holiness, we must not only pattern our lives on Christ's by being gentle, humble, and patient, we must also imitate him in his death. Taking Christ for his model, Paul said that he wanted to become like him in his death in the hope that he too would be raised from death to life.

We imitate Christ's death by being buried with him in baptism. What does this kind of burial mean and what benefit do we derive from it? It means making a complete break with our former way of life, and our Lord himself said that this cannot be done unless a person is born again. In other words, we have to begin a new life, and we cannot do that until our previous life has been brought to an end. When runners reach the turning point on a racecourse, they have to pause briefly before they can go back in the opposite direction. In the same way, when we wish to reverse the direction of our lives, there must be a pause, or a death, to mark the end of one life and the beginning of another.

Our descent into hell takes place when we imitate the burial of Christ by our baptism. The bodies of the baptized are buried in the water, in a sense, as a symbol of their repentance of the sins of their unregenerate nature. Baptism cleanses the soul from the pollution of worldly thoughts and desires. The Psalmist says, "You will wash me and I will be whiter than snow" (Ps. 51:7). We receive this saving baptism only once because there was only one death and one resurrection for the salvation of the world, and baptism is its symbol.

Basil the Great

❖ 363 ❖

SALTED AND PRESERVED

Therefore go and make disciples of all nations. (Matthew 28:19)

Do not think that you are destined for easy struggles or unimportant tasks. "You are the salt of the earth" (Matt. 5:13), says Christ. What do these words imply? Did the disciples restore what had already turned rotten? Not at all. Salt cannot help what is already corrupted. That is not what they did. But Christ took something and renewed it, freed it from corruption, and then turned it over to them, which they then salted and preserved in the newness the Lord had bestowed. It took the power of Christ to free people from the corruption caused by sin; the apostles' task was to keep that corruption from returning through strenuous labor.

Have you noticed how, bit by bit, Christ shows them to be superior to the prophets? He says, "You will be teachers not just for Israel but for the whole world. Do not be surprised that I address you apart from the others and task you with such a dangerous enterprise. Think about the multitude of cities, peoples, and nations to which I will be sending you to govern. For this reason I need you to make others prudent, as well as being prudent yourselves. Unless you can do this, you will not even be able to sustain yourselves.

"If others lose their taste, then your ministry will help them regain it. But if you yourselves suffer that loss, you will drag others down with you. Therefore, your passion must grow as your responsibilities grow.

"Be prepared for curses and persecutions — they will not harm you and will be a testimony to your perseverance. But if fear stops you from demonstrating passion for the mission, your fate will be much worse, for everyone will speak evil of you and despise you. That is what being trampled by people's feet means."

Gregory of Nyssa

✦ 364 ✦

THE LANGUAGE
OF ALL NATIONS

*They saw what seemed to be tongues of fire that separated and came to
rest on each of them. All of them were filled with the Holy Spirit and
began to speak in other tongues as the Spirit enabled them. (Acts 2:3–4)*

The disciples spoke in the language of every nation. At Pentecost, God chose a particular sign to indicate the presence of the Holy Spirit: whoever had received the Spirit spoke in every kind of tongue. We must realize, dear brothers and sisters, that this is the same Holy Spirit who pours love into our hearts. It was love that was to bring the church of God together all over the world. And as individuals who received the Holy Spirit in those days spoke in all kinds of tongues, so today the church, united by the Holy Spirit, speaks in the language of every people.

Therefore if somebody should say to one of us, "If you have received the Holy Spirit, why do you not speak in tongues?" his or her reply should be, "I do indeed speak in the tongues of all people, because I am part of the body of Christ, which is the church, and she speaks all languages. What else did the presence of the Holy Spirit convey at Pentecost, except that God's church was to speak in the language of every people?"

So when the disciples were heard speaking in all kinds of languages, some people were not too wrong in saying, "They have been drinking too much new wine" (Acts 2:13). The truth is that the disciples had now become fresh wineskins, renewed and made holy by grace. The new wine of the Holy Spirit filled them, so that their fervor brimmed over and they spoke in manifold tongues. By this spectacular miracle they became a sign of the universal church, which embraces the language of every nation.

Sixth-Century African Writer

❖ 365 ❖

PARTICIPATING
IN THE DIVINE

*His divine power has given us everything we need for a godly life through
our knowledge of him who called us by his own glory and goodness.
Through these he has given us his very great and precious promises, so
that through them you may participate in the divine nature, having
escaped the corruption in the world caused by evil desires. (2 Peter 1:3–4)*

When we have come to know the true God, both our bodies and our souls will be immortal and incorruptible. We will enter the kingdom of heaven, because while we lived on earth we acknowledged heaven's King. As friends of God and coheirs with Christ, we will not be controlled by evil desires or tendencies, nor by any sickness of body or soul, for we will have become divine.

You may suffer evil as a person, and God allows it because of your humanity; however, God has promised you a share in every one of his attributes when you have been deified. The saying "Know yourself" therefore means that we should recognize and acknowledge the image in which God created us, for if we do this, we will in turn be recognized and acknowledged by our Maker.

So let us not be at war with ourselves, but change our way of life without delay. For Christ who "is God, exalted above all creation" (Ps. 83:18; Phil. 2:9–11), has taken away humanity's sin and refashioned our fallen nature. God proved his love for us in the beginning when he made man and woman in his image. If we obey his holy commands and learn to imitate his goodness, we shall be like him and he will honor us. God is not selfish, and has given us a share in his divinity for the sake of his own glory.

Hippolytus

✢ 366 ✢

THE TROPHY OF HIS VICTORY

Just as Moses lifted up the snake in the wilderness,
so the Son of Man must be lifted up. (John 3:14)

The cross is something wonderfully great and honorable. It is great because through it the many noble acts of Christ found their consummation—very many indeed, for both his miracles and his sufferings were fully rewarded with victory. The cross is honorable because it is both the sign of God's suffering and the trophy of his victory. It stands for his suffering because on it he freely suffered death. But it is also his trophy because it was the means by which the devil was wounded and death conquered; the barred gates of hell were smashed, and the cross became the one common salvation of the whole world.

The cross is called Christ's glory; it is saluted as his triumph. We recognize it as the cup he longed to drink and the climax of the sufferings he endured for our sake. Is the cross Christ's glory? Listen to his words: "Now is the Son of Man glorified, and in him God is glorified, and God will glorify him at once" (John 13:31–32). And again: "'Father, glorify your name.' Then a voice came from heaven: 'I have glorified it and will glorify it again'" (John 12:28). Here he speaks of the glory that the Father would bestow on him through the cross. And if you understand that the cross is Christ's triumph, hear what he himself also said: "When I am lifted up, then I will draw all men to myself" (John 12:32). Now you can see that the cross is Christ's glory and triumph.

Andrew of Crete

CHURCH FATHERS FEATURED IN *AWAKENING FAITH*

AMBROSE

Ambrose (c. 330–397) was bishop of Milan and a highly influential fourth-century theologian. He was an outspoken anti-Arian and had significant influence on the conversion of Augustine. He was first a lawyer and governor before being ordained bishop at the demand of the people of Milan. (See readings 17, 38, 46, 55, 101, 105, 114, 122, 134, 149, 159, 174, 204, 243, 260, 266, 269, 280, 284, 305, 317, 340, 348, and 355.)

ANASTASIUS OF ANTIOCH

Anastasius (d. 599) was bishop of Antioch twice, being deposed and exiled under Justin II and later reinstated with Gregory the Great's help. He was martyred by a Jewish mob. (See reading 86.)

ANASTASIUS OF SINAI

Anastasius Sinaita (fl. 7th century) was a prolific Greek writer and abbot of a monastery at Mount Sinai. He wrote a variety of Christian works including antiheresy treatises and ecclesial and pastoral instruction. The authorship of some of his work is still disputed. (See readings 224–25.)

ANDREW OF CRETE

Andrew (c. 650–c. 720) was a deacon at Hagia Sophia in Constantinople and later a metropolitan at Gortyna in Crete. Tradition says he was mute until he received his first communion at age seven. He is still well known for his hymns. (See readings 104, 252, and 366.)

ANTONY THE GREAT

Antony the Great (c. 251 – 356) was known as "the father of monasticism" and the most famous of the Desert Fathers from upper Egypt. We know of his ascetic life as a hermit from the biography *The Life of Antony* by Athanasius. He is known to have lived to be 105 years old. (The life of Antony the Great is discussed in readings 303 – 4.)

ASTERIUS OF AMASEA

Asterius (c. 350 – c. 410) was bishop of Amasea and a young contemporary of the Cappadocian Fathers. His sermons are notable for their value to anthropology, because they often discuss art and clothing. (See readings 88 and 275.)

ATHANASIUS

Athanasius (c. 296 – 373) was the bishop of Alexandria for over forty years but spent much of that time in exile for his commitment to orthodox Trinitarianism. He is known for his fight against Arianism, a heresy that held that Jesus was not fully God. (See readings 16, 32, 99, 145 – 46, 181, 206, and 303 – 4.)

AUGUSTINE

Augustine (354 – 430) was the bishop of Hippo in Algeria and a prolific theological and philosophical writer. He is best known for his *Confessions, City of God*, and *On the Trinity*. He had a dramatic conversion at age thirty-two and was outspoken against the Pelagian heresy. (See readings 9, 15, 37, 39, 43 – 44, 50, 53, 73 – 74, 83, 90, 94, 102 – 3, 123, 127, 137, 150, 152 – 53, 157 – 58, 166, 170 – 71, 197, 199, 208 – 9, 214, 223, 238, 242, 245, 257, 267, 277, 285 – 86, 289, 306, 312, 322 – 23, 331, 334 – 36, 342, 350, and 360.)

BARNABAS

Modern scholars believe that *The Epistle of Barnabas* was likely written around AD 130. It was traditionally thought to have been composed by the disciple Barnabas mentioned in Acts 11, though it is now attributed to Pseudo-Barnabas (Barnabas of Alexandria), a later Father. (See readings 33 and 58–59.)

BASIL THE GREAT

Basil (c. 329–379), one of the three Cappadocian Fathers, was a bishop in Asia Minor and defender of Nicene orthodoxy, especially against the Arian position. His famous work *On the Holy Spirit* defends the divinity of the third person of the Holy Trinity. (See readings 10, 26, 30, 62, 106, 251, 298, 301, 320, and 362.)

BEDE THE VENERABLE

Bede (c. 672–735) was an English monk from the ancient Kingdom of Northumbria, most famous for his *Ecclesiastical History of the English People*. He was sensitive to literary beauty and evinces a wide learning in his own writings. (See readings 18, 66, and 135.)

BENEDICT OF NURSIA

Benedict (c. 480–543) was a monk and abbot who established and led numerous monastic communities in Italy. His famous *Rule of Saint Benedict* outlined instructions for monks living in communal orders and struck a balance between private devotion and institutional function. He is known as the father of Western monasticism. (See reading 65.)

BONIFACE

Boniface (d. 754) was an English-born monk and missionary, also called the Apostle of the Germans. As archbishop over Germany he baptized thousands into the Roman church and was martyred in Frisia (northwest continental Europe) during his efforts to bring pagans to faith. (See readings 22–23.)

BRAULIO

Braulio (d. 651) was bishop of Saragossa in Hispania and friend and helper of Isidore of Seville. His collection of letters has aided scholars in constructing a history of Spain during the seventh century. (See reading 107.)

CAESARIUS OF ARLES

Caesarius (c. 468–542) was a bishop in Gaul for forty years and very involved in the political affairs of the state. He is known for his sermons, for presiding over the Council of Orange in 529, and for influencing the medieval notion of Christendom. (See readings 140–41, 187, and 333.)

CHROMATIUS

Chromatius (d. c. 406) was bishop of Aquileia (an ancient Roman city) and a productive exegete of Scripture, especially the New Testament. He corresponded with the better-known Ambrose and Jerome and was a staunch anti-Arian. (See reading 293.)

CLEMENT OF ALEXANDRIA

Clement (c. 150–c. 215) was a theologian and catechetical instructor at Alexandria in Egypt. He was a Christian convert familiar with Greek philosophy and wrote a number of works about the relationship between philosophy and faith. (See readings 54, 64, 81, and 274.)

CLEMENT OF ROME

Clement (fl. 96) was a bishop of Rome in the first century, possibly third or fourth after the apostle Peter. Almost nothing is known of his life except that he authored a letter to the church at Corinth, now known as *1 Clement*. It is one of the earliest noncanonical Christian writings. (See readings 4, 25, 67, 161, 165, 290, 328, 347, and 352–53.)

2 CLEMENT

The Second Epistle of Clement (c. 100–140) was likely not written by the author of *1 Clement*, though they were preserved together. It is the earliest complete Christian sermon from the Patristic era. (See reading 144.)

COLUMBANUS

Columbanus (543–615) was an Irish monk and missionary to mainland Europe, responsible for many conversions and forming a number of monasteries. His short *Monastic Rule* and various letters, sermons, and poems survive. (See readings 56, 61, 207, 287, 311, and 337.)

COMMODIANUS

Commodianus (fl. 250) was a Latin Christian poet, most likely a layman, whose geographical origin is uncertain. He wrote stylized acrostic essays on theology and faith. Though his theology is suspect in some places, his work is noteworthy for its imagery and employment of various poetic structures. (See readings 31.)

CYPRIAN OF CARTHAGE

Cyprian (d. 258) was made bishop of Carthage in Africa in 249, when he was probably middle-aged and a relatively new Christian. He was involved in the Novatian controversy and wrote on church unity. He was beheaded in Carthage under the persecution of Emperor Valerian. (The life of Cyprian of Carthage is discussed in readings 193–195; for his writings, see readings 5, 21, 36, 51, 110, 164, 180, 222, 236, 250, 264, 272, 288, 294, 315, 354, and 359.)

CYRIL OF ALEXANDRIA

Cyril (c. 376–444) was patriarch of Alexandria and a central figure in the First Council of Ephesus (431) and in combating the Nestorian heresy. He composed many worthy theological and exegetical works. His reputation is tarnished because of his possible involvement in the murder of a renowned Alexandrian neo-Platonist. (See readings 131, 278, and 329.)

CYRIL OF JERUSALEM

Cyril (c. 313–386) was bishop of Jerusalem during the Arian controversies of the fourth century. Though he seems hesitant in his writings to affirm the doctrine of the consubstantiality of Father and Son, he adhered to Nicene orthodoxy. His most well-known writings are the *Catecheses*. (See readings 34–35, 179, 230, 345–46, 357–58, 361.)

DIADOCHUS OF PHOTICE

Diadochus (c. 400–c. 486) was a bishop in Greece who attended the Council of Chalcedon of 451. Not much is known of his life.

His writings on asceticism and the spiritual life are included in the *Philokalia*, a collection of important texts from the Hesychast tradition of Eastern Orthodoxy. (See readings 97, 160, and 254.)

DIDYMUS THE BLIND

Didymus (c. 310 – c. 398) lost his sight at the age of four but nonetheless became remarkably learned in Scripture, grammar, logic, music, and mathematics. He held no ecclesial office but was a follower of Origen's writings, because of which he was condemned in the early medieval period. (See reading 231.)

DIONYSIUS OF ALEXANDRIA

Dionysius (c. 190 – 265) was bishop of Alexandria for seventeen years and a greater administrator than he was a theologian. Like Cyprian, his contemporary, he addressed Novatianism, faced persecution, and endured exile. His extant writings are mostly letters, but some exegetical fragments remain. (See reading 78.)

DOROTHEUS OF GAZA

Dorotheus (c. 505 – c. 565) was a monk and later abbot in Gaza. He practiced strict spiritual disciplines through an ascetic lifestyle and composed instructions for other monks. (See readings 211 and 341.)

EPHREM THE SYRIAN

Ephrem (c. 306 – c. 373) was a deacon in Nisbis (modern-day Turkey) and prolific writer of hymns, sermons, and commentaries, all in the Syriac language. His hymns are known as some of the most beautiful early Christian poetry. He died of the plague after ministering to its victims. (See readings 3, 196, 217, and 299.)

FULGENTIUS OF RUSPE

Fulgentius (468 – 533) was a monk and ultimately bishop in Ruspe of North Africa. He suffered persecution and was forced to flee numerous times under Arian political powers. In his writings he shows Augustine's influence, speaking against Arianism and Pelagianism. (See readings 96, 178, 185, and 216.)

GREGORY THE GREAT

Gregory (c. 540–604) was the first pope who was a monk prior to his appointment and was an industrious writer of letters, sermons, commentaries, and other ecclesial documents. He is still highly regarded in all church traditions—notably, John Calvin admired him for his refusal to adopt the title of "Universal Pope." (See readings 80, 84–85, 95, 191, 202, 205, 210, 291, 297, 316, and 332.)

GREGORY OF NAZIANZUS

Gregory (c. 325–389) was bishop of Constantinople and one of the three Cappadocian Fathers (with Basil the Great and Gregory of Nyssa), perhaps the most eminent theologians of the fourth century. He wrote extensively on the Trinity and fought the Arians throughout his career. He fused Hellenistic philosophy with his theological thinking. (See readings 6, 42, 108–9, 119, 136, and 313.)

GREGORY OF NYSSA

Gregory (c. 335–c. 385) was bishop of Nyssa, brother of Basil the Great, and with Basil and Gregory Nazianzus, one of the Cappadocian Fathers. Like them he was concerned with Trinitarian theology, and attended the famous Council of Constantinople in 381. Many of his exegetical and theological writings survive. (See readings 12–13, 60, 82, 89, 173, 182, 200–201, 248, 263, 270, and 363.)

GREGORY THAUMATURGUS

Gregory (c. 213–c. 270) was converted to Christianity under Origen and later made bishop of Neocaesarea, where he earned the name Thaumaturgas, or "Wonder-worker," for the miracles he performed. Tales recount of his healing powers and ability to move bodies of water and even mountains. (See readings 76–77.)

HILARY OF POITIERS

Hilary (c. 300–368) was born in, and later made bishop of, Poitiers in Gaul. He was passionately and actively anti-Arian and was highly influential on later Fathers, including Augustine. He wrote a substantial theological work on the Trinity and homilies on the Psalms. (See readings 183–84, 229, 281–82, 321, and 343.)

HIPPOLYTUS

Hippolytus (d. c. 236) was a priest in Rome and possibly the first antipope — a priest with a popularly supported claim in contention with a sitting pope. Details of his life have been mostly lost, likely because of his involvement in church disputes, but a number of theological works survive. (See readings 52, 232, 302, and 365.)

IGNATIUS OF ANTIOCH

Ignatius (c. 35 – c. 98) was bishop of Antioch, student of the apostle John, and one of the most prominent martyrs of his period. He wrote seven letters to churches on his way to Rome to be killed, in which he instructs churches on ecclesiology and the sacraments, as well as celebrates his own imminent martyrdom. (See readings 133, 151, 177, 249, and 310.)

IRENAEUS

Irenaeus (d. c. 202) was a bishop in Gaul and writer of the famous *Against Heresies*, a theological work written to combat Gnosticism. He emphasized Scripture, tradition, and the authority of bishops. His Scriptural citations have an important role in our understanding of the history of biblical canonization. (See readings 120, 125, 143, 167, 235, 283, and 330.)

ISIDORE OF SEVILLE

Isidore (c. 560 – 636) was bishop of Seville in Hispania for over three decades and considered one of the most learned men of his age. He wrote the *Etymologiae*, an encyclopedic collection of all useful knowledge, which maintained its relevance for over a millennium. (See readings 69 and 79.)

JOHN CASSIAN

John Cassian (c. 360 – 435) was a monk who, after learning from holy men in Bethlehem and Egypt, established monasteries back in his home of Gaul. He is known for his spiritual writings, especially his *Institutes*, in which he discusses the eight deadly sins and how to combat them. (See readings 128–30, 239–40, and 325–26.)

JOHN CHRYSOSTOM

John (c. 347–407) earned the name Chrysostom, or "Golden-mouth," for his beautiful speaking style as archbishop of Constantinople. He spoke out against clerical abuses, composed hundreds of artful homilies, and is considered among the most important Eastern Church Fathers. (See readings 1, 19–20, 24, 45, 48, 68, 92, 115–16, 121, 147–48, 155, 172, 175–76, 218–19, 226, 233–34, 261–62, and 351.)

JOHN OF DAMASCUS

John (c. 645–c. 754) was a Syrian monk and priest most famous for his defense of images in the iconoclasm controversy of the eighth century. A servant of a Muslim caliph in Damascus before moving to a monastery outside Jerusalem, he was a productive theologian and hymn writer. (See readings 156, 215, 247, and 319.)

JUSTIN MARTYR

Justin (c. 100–c. 165) was a Christian convert and thereafter apologist for the faith, mostly in Asia Minor and Rome. His Logos theology was a point of contact between Christianity and pagan philosophy. He was beheaded for not sacrificing to the gods of the Roman pantheon. (See readings 75, 113, and 212.)

LACTANTIUS

Lactantius (c. 250–c. 325) was a Christian apologist, advisor to Roman emperor Constantine, and tutor of his son Crispus. His most famous work is *The Divine Institutes*, and he is known for his beautiful writing style. (See reading 203.)

LEO THE GREAT

Leo (c. 395–461) was bishop of Rome and the most historically significant pope behind Gregory the Great. His *Tome* had enormous impact on the Council of Chalcedon in 451, and he is famous for his convincing Attila the Hun to turn back his invasion of Italy in 452. (See readings 2, 7, 29, 40, 47, 111, 168, 227, 265, 268, 271, 300, 318, 327, 349, and 356.)

THE LETTER TO DIOGNETUS

The Letter to Diognetus, also known as *The Epistle of Mathetes to Diognetus* (c. second century AD), is probably the earliest example of Christian apologetics, writings defending Christianity from its accusers. The Greek writer and recipient are not otherwise known. (See readings 308–9.)

MACARIUS

Macarius (fl. 312–334) was bishop of Jerusalem and opponent of Arianism. He accompanied Helena, the mother of Emperor Constantine, on her quest to discover the actual cross on which Christ was crucified. (See reading 307.)

MAXIMUS THE CONFESSOR

Maximus (c. 580–662) was a monk and theologian most known for his opposition to the popular Monothelite heresy. He was convicted of heresy, having his tongue and hand cut off to prevent him from speaking or writing his views. Soon after his death his theological position was affirmed, and he was made a saint. (See readings 72, 169, 220, and 344.)

MAXIMUS OF TURIN

Maximus (d. c. 415) was a bishop in northern Italy whose biography remains a mystery. He was, however, a prolific writer, and many of his treatises and homilies survive. (See readings 142, 237, and 279.)

MELITO OF SARDIS

Melito (d. c. 180) was the bishop of Sardis in Asia Minor and writer of homilies and theological works. Although little is known of his life, he is known for compiling the first authoritative Old Testament and naming it as such. (See readings 100, 244, 276, and 339.)

METHODIUS

Methodius (d. c. 311) was bishop of Olympus whose theology was strongly influenced by Platonism. He wrote numerous theological and philosophical works, particularly against various doctrines of Origen. He died a martyr under persecution in the early fourth century. (See readings 14 and 314.)

ORIGEN

Origen (c. 184 – c. 253) was a prolific Christian theologian and exegete, teaching mainly in Alexandria, whose reception throughout history has been mixed. He had a significant impact on Christian thinking just subsequent to his life, though his ideas were the center of multiple disputes, especially in the fourth and fifth centuries. (See readings 93, 139, 190, and 198.)

PATRICK

Patrick (c. 387 – c. 460) was a slave in Ireland before gaining his freedom and returning to Britain. He traveled back to Ireland as a missionary priest and converted thousands of Irish. Just two unquestionably genuine letters of his survive, besides other compositions of uncertain authorship. (See readings 71 and 98.)

PETER CHRYSOLOGUS

Peter Chrysologus (c. 380 – c. 450) was Bishop of Ravenna, Italy, from about 434 until his death. His sermons were so inspiring that he was given the title "Chrysologus" (meaning "Golden-worded") and was known as "The Doctor of Homilies." He spoke out against various heresies and was famous for clear and succinct teaching on a variety of Gospel subjects. (See readings 8, 27 – 28, 112, 186, 188 – 89, 241, 246, and 324.)

POLYCARP

Polycarp (69 – 155) was bishop of Smyrna, and with Ignatius and Clement, one of the chief Apostolic Fathers. He is famous for the account of his martyrdom, as told in the letter included in this volume. He was likely instructed in the faith by the apostle John. (The life of Polycarp is discussed in reading 273, from *The Martyrdom of Polycarp*; for his writings, see readings 41 and 192.)

PONTIUS OF CARTHAGE

Pontius (d. 260) was a deacon under Bishop Cyprian in what is now Tunisia and the author of *The Life and Passion of Cyprian*. He likely accompanied Cyprian in his exile and witnessed his execution. The work is considered the earliest Christian biography. (See readings 193–95.)

PSEUDO-CHRYSOSTOM

The Passover Homily quoted in this volume was once falsely attributed to John Chrysostom. Its true author is unknown and is thus attributed to Pseudo-Chrysostom. (See reading 338.)

SULPITIUS SEVERUS

Sulpitius Severus (c. 360–c. 425) was a Christian writer in Gaul best known for his *Chronicle*, a summary of sacred history, and his hagiography of Martin of Tours, of whom he was a disciple. He eschewed his wealth and high-standing in middle age and pursued a life of monasticism. (See reading 213.)

TATIAN

Tatian (c. 120–173) was an Assyrian Christian theologian and apologist and student of Justin Martyr. His major works are *Address to the Greeks*, an indictment of paganism and defense of Christianity, and the *Diatessaron*, which is a synthesis of the four Gospels. (See reading 11.)

TERTULLIAN

Tertullian (c. 160–c. 235) was a Christian priest in Carthage, North Africa, where he composed dozens of theological and polemical works. His Trinitarian theology was highly influential on later Western Christians, although he broke with orthodoxy for Montanism in his later life. (See readings 87, 117–18, 132, and 221.)

THEODORE OF MOPSUESTIA

Theodore (c. 350–428) was bishop of Mopsuestia in southern Asia Minor and notable practitioner of Antiochean hermeneutics, which is the forerunner of the modern historical-grammatical approach. He wrote against various heresies of his time, but was likely influenced by Pelagianism. (See reading 49.)

THEODORE THE STUDITE

Theodore (759–826) was a monk and abbot of the Stoudios monastery in Constantinople, and defended the veneration of icons. He was involved in various political and ecclesial controversies for which he was exiled multiple times. He is an important figure in Byzantine Christianity. (See readings 57 and 63.)

THEODORET OF CYRUS

Theodoret (c. 393–c. 457) was a theologian and bishop of Cyrus, Syria, and a follower of the Antiochean school. He oversaw a massive diocese, wrote many letters and works of exegesis and theology, and became involved in the Nestorian controversy of the fifth century. (See readings 228 and 292.)

THEOPHILUS OF ANTIOCH

Theophilus (d. c. 185) was a bishop of Antioch whom we know very little about. His *Apology to Autolycus* is his only extant work, which is a defense and explanation of Christianity, though other Fathers refer to writings that we no longer possess. (See readings 154 and 253.)

UNKNOWN AUTHORSHIP

Early Church Presbyter. (See reading 126.)
Second-Century Writer. (See readings 70 and 124.)
Fourth-Century Writer. (See readings 162–63.)
Sixth-Century African Writer. (See reading 364.)

VENANTIUS FORTUNATUS

Venantius (c. 530–c. 600) was a Christian poet and ultimately bishop of Poitiers, renowned for his eloquent poetry on both religious and secular topics. He was a friend of Gregory of Tours and a rich source for the history of the Merovingian dynasty. (See readings 258 – 59.)

VICTORINUS OF PETTAU

Victorinus (fl. 270 – d. c. 303) was a bishop of Syria and exegetical writer. Only his works on Genesis and Revelation remain, although Jerome reports that he wrote commentaries on various other books as well as treatises against heresies. (See reading 138.)

VINCENT OF LERINS

Vincent (d. c. 445) was a monk and ecclesial writer who was at one point charged with Semi-Pelagianism. He is better known for composing the *Commonitorium*, which aims to instruct the religious in discerning true doctrine from false. (See readings 295 – 96.)

ZENO OF VERONA

Zeno (c. 300 – c. 380) was a monk and bishop of Verona, Italy, and died either a confessor or martyr. He was not known as a writer until early in the sixteenth century when two Dominican monks discovered a collection of 105 of his sermons, most of which have been verified as authentic. (See readings 255 – 56.)

ACKNOWLEDGMENTS

We would like to heartily thank our editors, Madison Trammel and Robert Hudson, for their patience, insight, and guidance for the duration of this book project.

SCRIPTURE INDEX

Share Your Thoughts

With the Author: Your comments will be forwarded to the author when you send them to *zauthor@zondervan.com*.

With Zondervan: Submit your review of this book by writing to *zreview@zondervan.com*.

Free Online Resources at
www.zondervan.com

Daily Bible Verses and Devotions: Enrich your life with daily Bible verses or devotions that help you start every morning focused on God. Visit www.zondervan.com/newsletters.

Free Email Publications: Sign up for newsletters on Christian living, academic resources, church ministry, fiction, children's resources, and more. Visit www.zondervan.com/newsletters.

Zondervan Bible Search: Find and compare Bible passages in a variety of translations at www.zondervanbiblesearch.com.

Other Benefits: Register to receive online benefits like coupons and special offers, or to participate in research.